NOT IN OUR LIFETIMES

NOT IN OUR LIFETIMES

The
Future
of
Black
Politics

MICHAEL C. DAWSON

THE UNIVERSITY OF CHICAGO PRESS • CHICAGO AND LONDON

Michael C. Dawson is the John D. MacArthur Professor of Political Science and the College at the University of Chicago and the author of *Black Visions* and *Behind the Mule: Race, Class, and African American Politics*.

The University of Chicago Press, Chicago 60637
The University of Chicago Press, Ltd., London
© 2011 by The University of Chicago
All rights reserved. Published 2011.
Printed in the United States of America
20 19 18 17 16 15 14 13 12 11   1 2 3 4 5

ISBN-13: 978-0-226-13862-6 (cloth)
ISBN-10: 0-226-13862-3 (cloth)

Library of Congress Cataloging-in-Publication Data

Dawson, Michael C., 1951–
    Not in our lifetimes: the future of black politics / Michael C. Dawson.
        p. cm.
    Includes bibliographical references and index.
    ISBN-13: 978-0-226-13862-6 (cloth: alk. paper)
    ISBN-10: 0-226-13862-3 (cloth: alk. paper)   1. African Americans—Politics and government.   2. United States—Race relations—Political aspects.   3. United States—Race relations—Public opinion.   4. African Americans—Attitudes.   5. Hurricane Katrina, 2005—Social aspects.   I. Title.
    E185.615.D396 2011
    323.1196′073—dc22   2011014686

CONTENTS

PROLOGUE   vii

1   From Katrina to Obama   1

2   Katrina and the Nadir of Black Politics   21

3   The Obama Campaign and the Myth of a
    Post-Racial America   63

4   Black Political Economy and the Effects of Neoliberalism
    on Black Politics   92

5   The People United?   136

6   Conclusion: Toward New Black Visions   160

    Epilogue: Taking the Country Back   181

ACKNOWLEDGMENTS   187
NOTES   191
REFERENCES   203
INDEX   213

PROLOGUE

I am a barbarian, albeit an educated one. I have been aware of this status of mine for a very long time. But it was brought back to me with particular force recently during a class I was teaching, when I came across a passage by the late Harvard political scientist Samuel Huntington. "Becoming 'white' and 'Anglo-conformity,' " wrote Huntington approvingly, "were the ways in which immigrants, blacks and others made themselves Americans."[1]

I can play that game. It is nearly a requirement if one wants to become credentialed (not necessarily educated) in institutions of higher learning. I chose not to play a long time ago.

I'm also a materialist. Not in the sense often disparaged by contemporary political theorists, as someone who believes that all social and political consciousness emerges out of one's subject position, out of one's place in the multiple hierarchies of power. Nor am I a materialist in the sense that being "behind the veil" or, in the language of many Marxists and feminists, that occupying a certain standpoint necessarily implies a greater likelihood of having an enlightened (read: radical) political outlook.

I'm an old-fashioned barefoot materialist. I believe that being located at the bottom of the social order, especially at the bottom of more than one of the hierarchies, is to be unjustly condemned to a life of frequently crippling disadvantage. The existence of these power hierarchies calls the social order itself into question as a matter of simple justice. It follows that political movements, to be progressive, must center on the overcoming of injustice. Black and progressive movements begin in an account of the material realities that people face on the ground, in an understanding of how these realities were produced, and a keen grasp of how they are reproduced by the workings of power, both inside and outside disadvantaged communities. I believe in building movements to win justice for all—starting with justice for those at the bottom.

I contend that for democratic, progressive movements to thrive in the United States, a healthy black politics is indispensable. Black political movements historically have formed a leading edge, in many eras the leading edge of American democratic and progressive movements. Why this has been the case and, more important, what stands in the way of black politics regaining that dynamic status are questions that will be explored throughout the coming pages. For now it is enough to note that this status has been lost, that over roughly the last half century we have moved from an era of black insurgency in this country to what has been aptly characterized by Cornel West as a period of black nihilism. Misdirected anger and a throttling despair have taken over from a mobilization of forces that is correctly termed insurgent because the change sought by these forces was nothing less than transformative. Indeed, looking back at the demands levied by Malcolm X, Dr. King, and others, we can say without qualification that had these aims been even largely achieved, the political and social order we see around us would not exist. More to the point, we do well looking back on this period as an insurgency, not to romanticize the insurgents, but to better understand the counterinsurgency that it provoked and that is in many respects ongoing, even in the absence of effective challenge. Without a mobilized black politics, American democracy is even more vulnerable to attack from within by those such as the neoconservatives and neoliberals who have been openly suspicious of mass democratic movements for decades.

Therefore, in order to transform America into a just democracy, it is necessary to rebuild black politics—including its radical wing. This in turn means rebuilding black political organizations and the black public sphere. The latter is necessary to fulfill the two historic tasks of the black public sphere—first, as an arena for debate about black politics, justice, and which way forward; and second, as the platform from which interventions into local regional and national mainstream, predominantly white, political discourse are launched in an attempt to influence politics and policy. Understanding the necessity for transforming black politics is crucial for resurrecting the ongoing, but currently flagging, task of transforming American democracy into something it never has been—a just democracy. The revitalization of black politics is made more difficult by the increased salience of class divisions within black politics.

Black politics—African Americans' ability to mobilize, influence policy, demand accountability from government officials, and contribute and influence American political discourse, all in the service of black interests—is still extremely weak. This weakness undermines the quest for justice in two areas that have been central concerns of black political movements: the quest for racial justice and the quest for economic justice for all. The apparent recovery of black politics (signified by Obama's election and inauguration) from the low point it reached in the aftermath to the Katrina disaster is an illusion.

Dispelling this illusion is a critical and urgent task, one necessary if black politics is to be rebuilt. As meaningful as the election of Barack Obama may be from a number of important points of view, it is illusory to believe that it signifies the recovery of black politics. For many years now, the capacity of African Americans' ability to mobilize, influence policy, demand accountability from government officials, and contribute to and influence American political discourse—even exclusively in the service of black interests—has been extremely weak, and it remains so. This weakness undermines the quest for justice in regard to the two concerns just identified as central to black political movements—the quest for racial justice and the quest for economic justice for all.

Also illusory is the idea that we live in a post-racial America. One's life chances are still on average, especially for the poor, disadvantaged by being black. Market discrimination against blacks is still a reality, even for the well-off and well-educated. The black poor, if anything, find themselves in conditions of greater deprivation now than at any time in the recent past. Racial inequality remains a brute fact of life in this country, one aggravated, to be sure, by the intersection of race, class, and gender.

The interracial political unity that is supposed to herald a truly post-racial society also does not exist. Blacks and whites remain bitterly divided about the beliefs they hold about politics. Indeed, the continued chasm between black and white political opinion reflects the fragility of the illusion of national interracial political harmony. The spectacle of Obama's election and inauguration reinforces the illusion of the revitalization of black politics as well as the illusion that we live in a post-racial America. Yet racialized gender stereotypes are still all too capable of generating images in too many white Americans' minds of thuggish black males and black welfare queens.

One consequence of the downward spiral of life for many African Americans is a growing and already large difference in life chances between poor and affluent blacks—a divide that is beginning to be reflected in black politics. This growing class divide in black politics is in turn reflected in new divisions in black public opinion. The continued weaknesses in black politics makes it exceedingly difficult to address the material deprivations of poor black communities or the continued racial animus directed toward African Americans, black communities, and black politics, let alone address the even more monumental problems facing the overall progressive movement in the United States. The effectiveness of black politics must be regained by rebuilding black civil society and the black counterpublic, as well as reestablishing independent black political movements and organizations.

The terms "progressive," "black politics," and, in combination, "progressive black politics" will appear repeatedly in these pages, and to many the definitions to be associated with each might seem self-evident. As detailed in my book *Black Visions*, progressive black politics embraces a range of distinct ideological commitments. All but one of the black ideologies, black conservatism, however, have at least four features in common. First is a steadfast determination to gain black justice. African Americans have yet to achieve racial justice in the courts, in the streets, or in many other domains of American life. Second, whether black feminist, black nationalist, social democratic, or some further left variant, all forms of progressive black politics are deeply committed to black political empowerment. Third, all progressive black politics emphasize economic justice and equality, usually advocating a combination of individual and collective striving, as well as state-mandated economic redistribution. Fourth, no variant of progressive black politics includes either historical amnesia regarding the past and current status of African Americans, nor the neoliberal tendency to regard needy populations, such as those that appeared so starkly after Katrina, as disposable. Finally, most black progressives, not all, argue that American progressives must understand that American politics is fundamentally shaped by a racial order, which both substantially influences life outcomes based on race and conditions the kind of attention that is paid to that fact.

Rebuilding black politics will be contentious. While there remain broad areas of agreement, there are sharp disagreements on questions of gender and sexuality, on whom blacks should ally with, and, as always, on the correct strategy and tactics in the black quest for racial justice. These tensions deepen the necessity for African Americans to build multiple publics where the voices of those representing these disparate viewpoints can be heard. Only by democratically aggregating these diverse black publics into a democratic and diverse black public sphere, the black counterpublic, can effective and democratic black political movements be built.

Rebuilding black progressive movements also requires recovering the spirit and politics of the militant Martin Luther King Jr. of 1967–68— the King of *Where Do We Go from Here*. This King was anti-war and anti-imperialist, a severe critic of both the totalitarian impulses of Leninism and the savage denigration of poor people inherent to the brutal logics of unregulated capitalism. This was the King who explained in 1967, "Black Power, in its broad and positive meaning, is a call to black people to amass the political and economic strength to achieve their legitimate goals."[2] This was a King who was attempting to build both black power and a robust social democracy with teeth in the United States.

It was little more than a month before King was assassinated in Memphis that the National Advisory Commission on Civil Disorders, the Kerner Commission, released its report famously concluding, "Our nation is moving toward two societies, one black, one white—separate and unequal." Using the now-antiquated-sounding language of half a century ago, the commission concluded that the combination of white racism, poverty, housing segregation, and police brutality among similar factors were responsible for wave of urban black insurgencies that had marked the "long hot summers" of the previous few years. The year before, King had published *Where Do We Go from Here: Chaos or Community?*—a work largely ignored by contemporary politicians pontificating about what King would say about black people today. In this book King proclaims a politics far more racially and economically uncompromising and radical than what passes for "radical" among black leaders today. Among the book's many lessons still relevant for the black and progressive politics of our times is the need for blacks to fight both for black power and against the ravages of capitalism on behalf of all who are disadvantaged. Another lesson concerns method. The acute analysis of the deprivations due to class and racial oppression, the withering critique of imperialist military adventures, and the provocative policy positions all flowed from the methodical, careful examination of conditions in the United States as they actually were, not as we wished them to be. Blacks and all progressive movements must once again embrace Amilcar Cabral's difficult admonition. He stated in reference to the national liberation struggle of Guinea-Bissau that was being waged during the same era that to build successful political movements one must "tell no lies, claim no easy victories."

Today we must base our own political analysis and projects on the same rigorous attention to detail and concrete conditions. We must tell no lies. The country we live in, as we will see over the next several chapters, is one in which the smoldering racial resentment of too many whites has exploded in a fury of anger, much of it blatantly racist, aimed at the first black president of the United States. It is a country where commentators such as Patrick Buchanan can unashamedly call for white males to be restored to pride of place at the top of the nation's hierarchies of power and status. We live in a country where corporations such as Halliburton allied with massive financial institutions have replaced the robber barons of the turn of the last century and match their predecessors in the looting of public treasuries and shaping public policy to meet their collective interests. It is a country where, despite the fact that once again the official unemployment rate is in the double-digit range, poor Americans, and more generally working-class Americans, find it difficult to come together to protect their increasingly vulnerable interests. It is a country where successful progressive social movements are for all too many a memory of the past—a country where those who are most disadvantaged and their dwindling allies have great difficulty in imagining a better world.

Today we still need the pragmatic utopianism that Dr. King so brilliantly deployed in his long struggle to achieve justice for the disadvantaged in the United States and indeed for the disadvantaged of the world. His vision was utopian in the sense that he dared to dream of a better world, one not constrained by what was viewed as the "common sense" of the times—a vision that was willing to break the rules of society, economy, and polity, and if necessary destroy them, when those rules facilitated injustice. Dr. King's utopianism was pragmatic because the striving to achieve his vision of a good and just world would necessitate mass militant movement of African Americans and others who desired to live in a better society—the type of movements that from the 1950s through the first half of the 1970s achieved sweeping transformations of American institutions from college campuses to the military. We need not and should not copy the movements of earlier generations but, as they did, build movements based on our own twenty-first-century realities. What we can emulate from the movements of an earlier era is their uncompromising spirit and their realization that it takes the mobilization of entire communities to achieve the transformations needed to build a better society.

MY STUDENTS IN MY "BLACKS AND THE HISTORY OF THE U.S. Left" class asked what became of the cadres that "shook the pillars of heaven." The outcomes were diverse—many, probably most, went on to lead "normal" lives; others went into politics; some worked in and others exploited social service agencies; some went into academics; others into crime—sometimes in the name of revolution, sometimes not; and some continue—to the best of their ability—to fight the good fight (even if many of their former comrades no longer recognize it as the good fight). The implicit question, of course, was why did I enter the academy. There are the usual answers: I am fairly good at what I do; I had a couple of kids; I was burned out; the organizations I belonged to despite their non-white leadership had more than a little bit of embedded racism; and even then I had more than a few bourgeois tendencies of my own. But these answers are misleading. I had been in the workforce for several years before I returned to the academy. And although my family took a pay cut when I went back to school full-time, I was maximizing our long-term prospects by getting a degree. More to the point, though, by that time I had been out of the movement for all practical purposes for a few years. I wanted to know where things went wrong and what was to be done. In *Black Visions* I began to answer the question "Where did things go wrong?" This book is the first of my efforts to address the question "What is to be done?"

To answer that second question—"What is to be done?"—we must begin to directly address the racial myths that are central to political and social discourse within the United States, and this means dispelling the willful amnesia that we collectively cling to when it comes to matters of race. The centrality of political amnesia in our history in regard to America's racial myths is emphasized by Michael Rogin in his work on race and spectacle. Rogin draws on the French theorist Guy Debord, who notes a separation between images of reality and the underlying reality itself, such that an illusory and comforting unification is achieved on the level of the image only, regardless of the underlying state of reality. Progressive black politics has always sought to rip away the illusory racial myths that allow much too large a segment of America to comfort and congratulate itself about the degree of racial progress and unity that has been achieved. It is useful to think of the Obama presidential campaign as spectacle for two reasons. First, "spectacles," according to Debord, are a "means of unification." The Obama campaign played this role to significant degrees within the nation as the inauguration signified not only national triumph, but also national unity. Debord goes on to say, however, that a "spectacle" is also a "locus of illusion. . . . The unity it imposes is merely the official language of separation."[3] Even more fundamentally, as Lisa Wedeen argues, spectacles "help to foreclose possibilities for political thought and action, making it hard to imagine or enact a truly democratic politics."[4]

Hurricane Katrina, from this point of view, was not spectacle, but anti-spectacle: it exposed for all the world to see the reality of difference, of a discomforting non-unification, an abandonment of the most vulnerable members of society—and in the hysterical denial by important segments of the public and media that Katrina had anything to do with race, an implicit justification of that abandonment.[5] The notion of a post-racial politics, on the other hand, appears in these terms as spectacle, as being about doing away with the need for either black solidarity or, as important, black politics due to the achievement of racial equality for blacks. It is an aim of this book to critique the illusion of racial equality and unity and demonstrate how its modern incarnation is in part a consequence of a regressive neoliberal agenda.

The chapters of this book explore the questions and patterns that have been discussed in this prologue. Chapter 1 explores the implications of the substantial change in black public opinion that occurred between the aftermath to Katrina and the eve of the 2008 presidential election. This chapter also analyzes the implication of the continued black/white divide in public opinion. In chapters 2 and 3, I will examine the survey findings in more detail. Chapter 2 explores the enormous gaps separating black and white public opinion concerning the basic realities on display during the Katrina disaster, relating these differences to the workings of the public sphere and the issue of democratic inclusion. Chapter 3 examines whether it is correct to see the election of Obama as an actual muting of this interracial divergence, which bears on the question of what the black public is likely to accept as constituting substantive efforts to improve the state of black America. Here the point to be made is that the differences in black and white opinion about the Katrina disaster were neither merely technical nor superficial. This was not an argument about how to improve government performance and ensure better outcomes for citizens in the future. Nor, in the main, did it concern the details of what happened. At issue, rather, was who gets to define "reality." What were we all witnessing? Was it a tragic event in which a large number of citizens proved unexpectedly vulnerable to a freak event—which would explain, if not justify, the desultory government response? Or was this business as usual? That is to say, proof, once again, that some Americans count for more than others, and that skin color provides a brutally direct indication of who does count and who does not. In chapter 4 I explore in detail the hypothesis raised in chapter 1 that the Obama era is being marked by more class conflicts among African Americans. The state of black political economy in the early twentieth-first century is described as well as the implications of the new black political economy for a new black politics. In chapter 5 I tackle the difficult question of how the recent waves of immigrants have reshaped the racial terrain, and how this new reshaped racial order is reflected in public opinion. I conclude the chapter with a discussion of possibilities for and obstacles to forming multiracial political alliances. Drawing on Dr. King's writings from the last two years of his life, the conclusion asks what new black visions are needed for this century's black politics.

Just before Malcolm X was murdered in 1965, he spoke with SNCC workers in Selma, Alabama, about the doubts he had regarding their chances of success. He had no doubt that their struggle was just, but he suspected America would turn its back on them.

I don't want to make you do anything you wouldn't do. . . . I disagree with non-violence, but I respect the fact that you're on the front lines and you're down here suffering for a version of freedom larger than America's prepared to accept.[6]

Was Malcolm X correct? Do blacks continue to embrace a concept of freedom "larger than America is prepared to accept"? This book argues that we can only prove Malcolm X wrong by rebuilding vibrant black and progressive movements that once again demand an end to injustice.

Dr. King expressed the same worry toward the end of his life. He was quite explicit about what it would take to achieve his vision of a truly democratic America.

A nation that continues year after year to spend more money on military defense than on programs of social uplift is approaching spiritual death.

America, the richest and most powerful nation in the world, can well lead the way in this revolution of values. There is nothing to prevent us from paying adequate wages to schoolteachers, social workers, and other servants of the public to insure that we have the best available personnel in these positions which are charged with the responsibility of guiding our future generations. There is nothing but a lack of social vision to prevent us from paying an adequate wage to every American citizen whether he be a hospital worker, laundry worker, maid or day laborer. There is nothing except shortsightedness to prevent us from guaranteeing an annual minimum—and *livable*—income for every American family. There is nothing, except a tragic death wish, to prevent us from reordering our priorities, so that the pursuit of peace will take precedence over the pursuit of war. There is nothing to keep us from remolding a recalcitrant status quo with bruised hands until we have fashioned it into a brotherhood.[7]

This is the vision that black politics must reclaim and embrace.

Michael Dawson
Chicago, November 2010

1 FROM KATRINA TO OBAMA

From Katrina to Obama. The phrase barely captures the massive swing in political emotions among blacks during the period from the fall of 2005 to the fall of 2008. Three short years saw a substantial and rapid shift from despair to hope occurring among African Americans. Shortly after the aftermath to the Katrina disaster, barely 20 percent of blacks believed that racial equality for blacks would be achieved either in their lifetimes or at all in the United States. Three years later, slightly over half of blacks believed that black racial equality would soon be achieved.

Was this increase in hope indicative of an actual revitalization of black politics? Did the president's successful campaign reflect the rebuilding of independent black political organizations, movements, and the black public sphere? What does the change in black opinion—the reflection of the black public sphere—signify? Does it signify the rejuvenation of a progressive black politics? Or does it reflect a shift of opinion due to an extraordinary event, but one not associated with a transformation in the basic structural realities that shape black life in America?

I argue throughout this book that, despite the relative euphoria understandably generated by the election of the first black president, the election does not signal that there has been a resurgence in black political efficacy, an increased ability of the black public sphere to influence national discourse and policy, nor a fundamental lessening of the racial conflict generated by a hierarchical racial order that continues to disadvantage black Americans, and poor blacks in particular. Nor was the increase in black optimism marked by blacks abandoning political realism about the current status of African Americans in the political, social, and economic realms. What the election does signify is a new era where the racial and class terrain, particularly at their intersection, is more complex, therefore making the rebuilding of progressive black political movements more complicated.

I begin this chapter by describing in detail the shift in black public opinion and its roots, and contrast those changes in black public opinion with the public opinion of white Americans, starting with the depths of bitterness that typified black opinion in the aftermath to Katrina.

HURRICANE KATRINA AND ITS HORRIFIC AFTERMATH VIVIDLY highlighted the depths that black political failure had reached in the United States by the fall of 2005. The majority of whites throughout the nation saw neither the dire situation affecting the residents of New Orleans, above all the poor black residents making up the vast majority of those most seriously harmed by the storm, nor the failure of the government to respond in a timely and adequate manner as having anything to do with race. Prominent African American activists, academics, and celebrities as well as ordinary grassroots people heard their opinions denounced, ridiculed, and ultimately demonized when they begged to differ, drawing attention to the evident neglect and indifference on the part of government officials in the face of the highly disproportionate effect of the storm on black citizens. Blacks were ridiculed when they demanded justice for the victims of Katrina.

Blacks were also ridiculed for insisting that the lack of justice New Orleans black citizens received was not, as neoliberal pundits insisted, the result of (just) the technical ineptness of the Bush administration—an ineptness that, while unfortunate, had no meaningful racial component (for, after all, we live in a post-racial America). Conversely, blacks in very large numbers, both public figures and those in the black grassroots, furiously insisted that blacks in New Orleans were the victims of massive racial injustice—injustice perpetrated by the state, corporate leaders, and white civil society in the Gulf. Blacks grimly marveled at what they viewed as massive white delusion as the great majority of whites in poll after poll stated that the Katrina disaster was not about race. Finally in the end, blacks were ridiculed for insisting on their democratic right to individually and collectively state their opinion, critique the state, and disagree with their fellow white citizens, even if the latter represented a (shrinking) majority.

Table 1: Black Public Opinion in the Fall of 2005

Believe blacks unlikely to soon achieve racial equality?	82%
Believe their fate is linked to that of the race?	73%
Should the U.S. apologize for slavery?	80%
Should form a black political party?	34%
Blacks form a nation within a nation?	39%

Not only did African Americans find themselves unable to contribute effectively to the public debate around Katrina's aftermath, but an organized black political response to the outrage proved sorely lacking. This is in stark contrast to the impressive marches mounted just a few months later by a coalition of immigrant rights organizations in support of undocumented workers and immigration reform. Even as the demographic base of African American political power in New Orleans itself disintegrated, with hundreds of thousands of now homeless blacks being displaced across the nation, black political leadership on the national level was caught largely without answers to the dilemmas exposed by the Katrina disaster.

That the political lessons of Katrina and its aftermath were not lost on African Americans is shown by table 1, registering, as of October 2005, a marked pessimism concerning the racial dynamics in the country.[1] More than 80 percent of blacks surveyed believed that racial equality in the United States would never be achieved or would not be achieved in their lifetimes. An almost equal number believed that African Americans were owed an official national apology for slavery, and nearly two-thirds voiced support for reparations.[2] Nearly half of the respondents viewed themselves as the Other in respect to their "fellow" Americans, with a substantial minority convinced that African Americans comprise a separate nation within the United States, as opposed to an ethnic group like Irish, Italian, or Polish Americans. A similar proportion supported the formation of a black political party, having evidently given up on the idea that their interests could be represented in a party shared with whites. In a measure that has held relatively constant since the Reagan era of the 1980s, nearly three-quarters of African Americans believed that their fate is linked to that of the race as a whole. In contrast, that is, to what might be regarded as a founding article of the American faith, a large majority of African Americans stood convinced as a group that black fortunes are not decided on the basis of individual merit.

Table 2: Approve Military Action in Iraq?

Approve War?	2003	2004	2005
Blacks	44%	45%	39%
Whites	75%	65%	66%

Collectively, these results reflect substantial black ambivalence about African Americans' connection to the country in which they reside as citizens. Contemporary political institutions are seen as at least partly failing blacks, and American democracy remains a potential unfulfilled. In 1963 Martin Luther King Jr. accused the United States of having bounced the check of democratic promise that had been issued to African Americans. That check, most blacks clearly felt in 2005, was still bouncing.

Another source of African American political anger in 2005 was the war in Iraq. A majority of African Americans opposed the war from the beginning (the 2003 data collection was begun the week the United States went to war in Iraq). By the time of Katrina's aftermath, support had declined to under 40 percent, as table 2 indicates. Given how strongly President Bush was associated with the war, it is no surprise that black disenchantment with the war tracks decline in his support among African Americans.

Table 2, however, tells another story as well. The gap between blacks and whites on support for the Iraq war is very large—nearly 30 percent for two of the three years, and still a very healthy 20 percent in the other year. This gap was exacerbated by a similar gap in the belief on whether anti-war protest was unpatriotic. A very large majority of African Americans believed that it was reasonable for those who opposed the war to engage in protest activities. A majority of whites believed anti-war protest was unpatriotic. Blacks and whites not only strongly disagreed on whether military action in Iraq was justified but, in some ways more fundamentally, differed on whether anti-war protest was not only illegitimate, but unpatriotic. The very large gaps between blacks and whites on questions of evaluations of war and peace, political leaders (as detailed in the next chapter), and the Katrina disaster left blacks politically isolated and bitterly disillusioned about the state of affairs in the nation.

Also consistent with blacks' view of a flawed democracy is that blacks overwhelmingly believed that the 2000 election featured massive suppression of black vote. Nearly 90 percent of African Americans believed that reports of voter suppression in Florida signaled a very important problem. However, nearly 60 percent of white Americans believed that the reports of suppression represented a not very important problem, including 37 percent who believed that the reports of voter suppression were an outright "fabrication of the Democratic Party." Blacks believed that at least in part the 2000 presidential election was rigged, and the 2000 elections provided more proof that American democracy was a myth—that American democracy was fundamentally deformed. In 2005 mainstream blacks' and whites' understandings of the status and nature of American democracy were incommensurable with each other, as was the public opinion produced by black and white political discourse in Katrina's aftermath.

White and black opinion was incommensurable because each is a product of a different worldview—the interpretive patterns by which we make sense of social and political reality. These interpretive patterns in turn are the product of what Jürgen Habermas calls the "lifeworld." According to Habermas, the lifeworld "offers a storehouse of unquestioned cultural givens from which those participating in communication *draw agreed-upon patterns of interpretations for use in their interpretive efforts.*"[3] It is the lack of "agreed-upon patterns of interpretations" that is so prominently displayed in the black/white cleavage in public opinion. The public opinion responses demonstrate not merely a difference of opinion between very large percentages of blacks and whites, but completely different patterns of assigning meaning to the events that followed, as well as different normative evaluations of those events.

The Katrina disaster is the most vivid recent event highlighting the continued existence of a racialized social structure in the United States, producing the racialized worldviews displayed in Katrina's aftermath and the persistently negative effects on the life chances of African Americans—particularly those of poor blacks. These different worldviews are just one product of the American racial order. The racial order structures civil society in the United States and fragments it along racial lines, producing racialized publics and undermining the democratic potential that many theorists of civil society claim is one of its central attributes. This order, as Cathy Cohen argues, produces systematic disadvantage in the distribution of life chances, and the social disadvantage can directly lead to political disadvantage as well.[4] The racial order in the United States structures American society, politics, political institutions, and the state. Yet even in the immediate aftermath of Katrina, the majority of whites had worldviews rejecting the belief that blacks remain substantially disadvantaged by race within American society.

The mainstream white worldview has as central elements the belief that racial justice has been achieved; that blacks engage in endless special pleading about imagined slights or ancient events irrelevant to contemporary America; and that a critical task for the nation is the conservation of a righteous social order or, for some liberals, to instead rely on incremental change to correct some "anomalies" in the functioning of American democracy. Michael Rogin argues, and I agree, that this worldview can only be sustained through a conscious act of political amnesia.[5]

Another central element of mainstream white discourse is the demonization of blacks who challenged this worldview. Historically, the mainstream black worldview had as central elements a realist assessment of contemporary racial subordination, deep memories of past injustices, and the conviction that in the United States there exists neither racial justice nor true democracy. The corollary to that set of elements was the view common in African American discourse that the claim that America was already a just democracy was a dangerous illusion. To borrow the title of the book by the late philosopher Richard Rorty, for blacks, "achieving our country" would only come about by the radical transformation of American society, the economy, and the polity.

One of the reasons that American democracy has remained deformed is because of liberal and progressive complicity in whitewashing American history. Many commentators, like Rorty, truly desired to see a just democracy established in America. They could not and cannot face the truth that American democracy is unachievable until racial subordination and exclusion are eliminated from state practices and civil society. They refuse to face this truth and prefer to live with comfortable whitewashed lies about everything from the history of American progressive movements to the current status of blacks in the United States.[6] The failures of progressive movements are due to their inability to escape these comfortable lies. Instead, progressives effectively reinforce neoliberal insistence that discussions of race, like discussions of political regulation of the economy, have no place in modern

America. Racial conflict, much like politics, is messy and cannot be reduced to the sanitized mathematical models preferred by the neoliberal technocrats running the country's economic, governmental, and increasingly academic institutions. Messy social movements are replaced by organizations that play by the "rules," thus reducing movements insisting on social justice to largely ineffective organizations that lobby on "behalf" of the disadvantaged. Liberals and conservatives both reject the prospect of fundamental transformation of American society and politics—continuing to embrace an outlook that remains raceless through exclusion—one in which both the right and left demand that blacks submit and subordinate their interests for some whitewashed greater "good."

Real democracy requires facing the truth. In the United States, one truth is that full democracy will not be established unless the racial order is dismantled, not just in order to achieve racial justice, but American democracy itself. Historically, black visions constituted one of the most robust, egalitarian, and expansive of American democratic visions. In the first several years of the twenty-first century, African Americans became increasingly despondent about the potential for achieving racial justice in the nation as they saw their views on the country's central issues—such as the 2000 presidential election, the Iraq War, the legitimacy of anti-war protest, and their evaluation of the Katrina disaster—overwhelmingly rejected, ridiculed, and demonized by white Americans.

Black opinion in 2005 reveals another facet, one that suggested a potential for the revitalization of black politics. A substantial segment of the black population seemed available for political mobilization by organizations centered on issues of racial justice for blacks. Over a third thought it was necessary to form a black political party. On the other hand, black grassroots views on reparations and an apology for slavery (as well as for Jim Crow and to the survivors of the anti-black pogroms conducted against the black communities of Tulsa and Rosewood early in the twentieth century) were considerably more radical than either the great majority of black leadership or the remaining black civil rights organizations. For a variety of reasons, all of which highlighted the weaknesses present in black politics, this opportunity was squandered. These weaknesses included failures in black leadership—due in no small part to an ever-increasing fraction of black leaders' embrace of neoliberal ideology; the deinstitutionalization of black civil society; and the demobilization of mass black politics, particularly its nationalist, leftist, and feminist wings. Structural changes—such as the erosion of the economic fortunes of the black poor, working, and lower-middle classes, due both to shifts in the American political economy and government policies, as well as mass incarceration and the disinvestment in poor black communities—also contributed to growing weaknesses in black politics.

During this period there were a few examples of relatively successful black political mobilization. Racial violence emanating from both the state and white civil society remains a fact of life for all too many black communities. For example, during late November 2006, anti-black hostility erupted in Jena, Louisiana, leading to the hanging of three nooses at the local high school. Justice Department officials stated that the incident had "all the hallmarks of a hate crime." A few days later a white youth was assaulted, and six black youths were charged with what their supporters claim were very excessive charges. The case of the Jena Six, as it became known, sparked strong mobilization within the black community, combining traditional methods of mobilizing with the use of new information technologies and new media outlets. It is possible that this combined mode of organizing marks an advance that will be useful in the coming years.

Nevertheless, the period following the Katrina disaster can be characterized as one of black deinstitutionalization. Between 2005 and 2008, the percentage of blacks belonging to organizations that worked on black issues declined from 20 to 16 percent, while declining the previous decade by 3 percent. The anemic political response to Katrina by black America can be attributed, in part, to this weakening of the institutional base of black politics. One may legitimately question whether these inadequacies in New Orleans prior to Katrina provided a measure of the indifference toward black America felt by mainstream society. Surely it is the case that they signal the relative absence of what could have been a mitigating factor were the institutions of an independent black civil society sufficiently robust to step in and either meet citizens' needs or effectively demand an end to the neglect.

But the storm and its aftermath, while posing an extreme example of the weakened institutional base of black politics, are hardly an isolated example. I will describe in the pages that follow a more general review of the bleak state of contemporary black America and what it means for the future of black politics. Here it suffices to note that racial violence, perpetrated both by agents of the state and by members of white civil society, remains a reality in an appalling number of black communities.

The deinstitutionalization is particularly unfortunate given that African Americans faced several severe challenges during this period that could have potentially been addressed by black movements with a stronger institutional base. An example of an incident that in the past would have generated a strong movement against police brutality is the case of Oakland's Oscar Grant, twenty-two years old, who was killed on New Year's Day, 2009, by Bay Area Rapid Transit Police while unarmed and being restrained. Racial violence from the state often goes unreported by the media unless a death is involved. Police misconduct aimed toward blacks was a constant part of the black community lived experience from Tenaha, Texas (where the police would target vehicles with blacks and Latinos in them for extortion), to Pennsylvania, where blacks in both Erie and Philadelphia were the victims of high-profile cases of racially based police misconduct. State violence against blacks is normative, to be expected, and usually approved of by mainstream society, unless death is involved and/or video is posted online, as in Grant's case. While there were demonstrations at the time of Grant's killing, generally the type of institutional presence needed to wage long campaigns against either police brutality or, relatedly, the mass incarceration of blacks was not present in this era's African American communities.

Massive levels of incarceration have racked the black community, wrecking lives while simultaneously undermining black political power. Politically, the high levels of incarceration not only have depressed the voting power of black communities, but artificially and unjustly inflated the rural areas that house the nation's prisons since the prison populations are counted as part of the areas where the prisons are located. Black political power was being undermined in other ways as well. As late as 2009, after the election of President Obama, the *New York Times* found it necessary to run an editorial lambasting conservative legislators in Florida for continuing to engage in voter suppression aimed largely, if not exclusively, at black voters. The Bush years also saw a steep decline in the economic fortunes of African Americans, and by the end of 2010 black unemployment had reached catastrophic

Table 3: Black Public Opinion in the Fall of 2008

Believe blacks unlikely to soon achieve racial equality?	47%
Believe their fate is linked to that of the race?	69%
Should the U.S. apologize for slavery?	74%
Should form a black political party?	8%
Blacks form a nation within a nation?	47%

levels nationally while many blacks were embroiled with devastating sub-prime loans. The combination of the severe problems facing African Americans and the lack of an effective political response led to high levels of black disillusionment with the United States.

Yet a mere three years after Katrina, black America was in a state of relative euphoria. The impossible was imminent—a black man was about to be elected president of the United States. Not only did President Obama's successful campaign transform beliefs of many around the world about what they thought was possible in America, but it also significantly changed how many African Americans viewed the racial dynamics of the nation. As can be seen in table 3, there was a dramatic shift in African American opinion in some key areas.

Less than half of African Americans remained pessimistic about the long-term prospects for racial equality only three years after the Katrina disaster. The support for an independent black political party had evaporated (although in 2008 many blacks answered with a "let's wait and see" response). Support for a government apology for slavery and the belief that one's fate is linked to that of the race, while still substantial, noticeably declined. The only anomaly is that the belief that blacks form a nation within a nation increased, albeit in the context of greatly increased optimism about the future of the race in America. It is indeed the case that there was still nearly 50 percent of the black nation that had an intensely negative view of the future. Nearly 100 percent of African Americans (98 percent) continued to believe that racism was still a problem, with 71 percent believing it was still a major problem. African Americans clearly felt that the imminent election of President Obama would not herald the advent of a post-racial society, but overall were dramatically more optimistic about the future. Black opinion while hopeful remained grounded in a sophisticated understanding of the

Table 4: Black Pessimism on the Likelihood of Achieving Racial Equality

	1993–94	2000	2003	2004	2005	2008
Unlikely to achieve soon black racial equality	65%	73%	71%	82%	82%	47%

Table 5: Black Warmth toward President

	1993–94 Clinton	2000 Clinton	2001 Bush	2003 Bush	2004 Bush	2005 Bush	2008 Obama
Warmth (0 = cold, 100 = warm)	67°	80°	40°	36°	23°	21°	89°

continuing lack of racial justice for African Americans, even while many blacks now had some hope for the future.

Black pessimism about the prospects for racial justice has been growing steadily since the early 1990s. The Simi Valley verdict in 1992 that acquitted the officers who had brutally beaten Rodney King marked a turning point in black opinion. Throughout the early 1990s, the black poor had an understandably jaundiced view of their prospects in America. Lawrence Bobo's research, however, demonstrated that public opinion among more affluent African Americans substantially shifted toward pessimism after the verdict.[7] A year later a survey conducted by Ronald Brown and myself confirmed that the effect Bobo found in Los Angeles had occurred nationally and had persisted. As can be seen in table 4, a full 65 percent of African Americans at the time believed that racial equality would not be gained for blacks in their lifetimes if at all. Yet as pessimistic as that view was, it was exceeded during the first half decade of the twenty-first century as black pessimism first climbed to more than 70 percent, and then to more than 80 percent, as what was perceived in the black community as the crimes of the Bush administration led to increased black disillusionment about America.

Increasing black disillusionment with the politics of the years leading up to Katrina can also be seen in table 5. President Clinton's standing among blacks increased over the two terms of his administration. President Bush's rating among blacks started low and then took a nosedive, reaching lows comparable to those Nixon received during the Watergate scandal. Note that black pessimism on the prospects of achieving racial equality rose as black disgust with President Bush grew.

Barack Obama's run for the presidency provided a large dose of hope for many African American activists, theorists, and citizens who suffered in the bleak landscape that characterized black politics after Katrina. Obama was the first black candidate for president with reasonable possibilities for winning both the Democratic nomination and the general election. Yet Obama's candidacy and rise to national prominence also produced significant concerns and complications for some observers and practitioners of black politics. President Obama was and remains more conservative and mainstream, and much less interested in making quasi–black nationalist appeals to African Americans than previous generations of black politicians. As the first black politician with a national stage who did not emerge out of the civil rights or earlier generations of race leaders, then-candidate Obama represented a new wave of more "cosmopolitan" black politicians who have technocratic credentials and statewide or higher aspirations, thus making them both more attractive to, and more interested in, winning the support of non-black citizens. Both the hope and concerns generated by Obama's rise to prominence were indicative of a number of formidable challenges facing those concerned with winning social justice for African Americans and the disadvantaged of American society.

First, blacks found themselves increasingly isolated from the rest of the polity after Katrina as black opinion was at odds with white opinion on questions such as support for the war in Iraq, evaluations of the aftermath of the Katrina disaster, and evaluations of major political leaders. The bitter divides in public opinion that marked the aftermath to Katrina, the racialized and at times racist 2008 presidential campaign, and wildly different material conditions between large segments of both races (more on that in chapter 4) have all served to maintain the large gap between black and white public opinion. Table 6 provides evidence of the continued chasm between black and white public opinion.

A wide gulf remained evident between black and white opinion in 2008, even with the black shift toward more optimism on the prospects of black racial equality. Nearly 50 percent of white Americans (49 percent) believed that blacks had already achieved racial equality—a sentiment with which only 11 percent of African Americans agreed. Given the large differences on

Table 6: The Black/White Divide in Public Opinion in 2008

	Blacks	Whites	Difference
Believe blacks unlikely to soon achieve racial equality?	47%	21%	26%
Discrimination still a major problem?	71%	32%	39%
Should the U.S. apologize for slavery?	74%	23%	51%
Should the U.S. apologize for Japanese American internment during WWII?	67%	33%	34%
Should felons be allowed to vote after serving their time?	72%	46%	26%
In post-9/11 world, profiling keeps nation safe?	30%	46%	16%
Mean warmth toward candidate Obama (0 = cold, 100 = hot)	89°	51°	38°

the perceptions of racial equality, it is not surprising to find a very large difference between blacks and whites as well on the perception of whether racial discrimination remains a serious problem. Large differences remained in beliefs about the whether the U.S. government should apologize to blacks and Japanese Americans, respectively, for slavery and the World War II internment camps. Similarly, large gaps appeared on questions concerning whether felons who have served their time should be allowed to vote and the suitability of profiling as a security policy. A very large gap persisted in how warm blacks and whites felt toward then-candidate Obama. Blacks, even in a period of growing hope, remained isolated on the margins of "American" public opinion. Black opinion remained incommensurable with white opinion even in the late fall of 2008. Blacks and whites still possessed radically different views of the world they jointly inhabited.

Second, African Americans still remained substantially more pessimistic about the state of race relations than any other racial or ethnic group. This pessimism has a real possibility of leading to further erosion in black political participation, particularly after the euphoria of the 2008 campaign dissipates. Third, growing class, generational, and gender differences threatened to undermine a long tradition of black political solidarity (and continue to threaten, as we will see in chapter 4). Fourth, as the Katrina disaster demonstrated, African Americans were largely unable to inject their viewpoints on a sustained basis on matters that the great majority of blacks saw as critical. Consequently, African Americans had been largely ineffective in affecting policy during crises whether domestic (e.g., Katrina) or international (e.g., Darfur, AIDS in Africa, or the war in Iraq). These challenges underlay the despair with which many practitioners viewed the state of black politics in the United States. The magnitude of these challenges bedeviled black activists and leaders. The nadir of despair in black politics was reached during the aftermath to Hurricane Katrina. Thus, for some, Obama's candidacy represented a timely and much-needed reed of hope to be grasped with all one's strength.

It was not only the prospect of having a viable black candidate for president that generated substantial excitement and hope within black and many other communities. Barack Obama displayed during the campaign an exceptional combination of charisma, programmatic vision, and political savvy that distinguishes him from the great majority of politicians. President Obama and his associates were able to translate these strengths into a strong base for his run. Politically and stylistically, President Obama represents a relatively new trend in African American politics. Black politicians such as Harold Ford Jr. (Tennessee), Cory Booker (New Jersey), and Michael Steele (Maryland) had all been associated, along with Obama, with what some conservative pundits have called "the new black realism." The president attracted many white liberals and middle-class blacks with his charisma, intelligence, and sense that he is a politically safe African American who makes them feel, if not necessarily satisfied about, at least hopeful for the future of race relations in the United States and black economic success.

Obama's candidacy and now his presidency, however, did not and does not solve the quandary of how to inject a substantive discussion of race into American politics without the discussion degrading into the usual race baiting. Many campaign professionals from both parties believe that any discussion of race poisons their candidate's chances. Nor has the Obama campaign or presidency so far sparked increased attention on questions of economic disadvantage. Not even the devastating combination of Hurricane Katrina and the Bush administration's malign and negligent response have provided fodder for Democratic presidential candidates during the last electoral cycle.

Obama's campaign generated further conundrums for black activists and theorists. Barack Obama poses several challenges to traditional conceptualizations of black politics. As noted earlier, Obama is more conservative on many issues than mainstream black politicians (as well as grassroots African Americans) have tended to be. Many African Americans were suspicious of his close ties with the conservative Democratic Leadership Council (DLC), including Obama's embrace of Senator Joseph Lieberman (widely viewed with particular suspicion by anti-war Democrats). Many left-leaning black pundits believed that the DLC actively promoted the president's career as a way to further neutralize the generally progressive influence of African Americans within the Democratic Party. At the grassroots level, blacks still broadly and strongly embrace the twin foci of the Civil Rights and Black Power movements—racial empowerment and the achievement of economic equality through both personal striving and state-mandated economic redistribution. Obama did not feature either the racial empowerment or economic redistribution agendas as central components of his campaign.

It is true, for example, that both candidate and President Obama emphasized commonalities among all races of Americans and not the differences. At one level, of course, this is laudable—progressives have been trying to build interracial unity in this country for well over a century. The question remains whether such unity can be soundly built by ignoring the particularly stark political differences between black and white Americans. As we have seen, over the past few years very large majorities of blacks and whites have disagreed on a wide range of issues. The Obama campaign, like its competitors for the Democratic nomination, showed little inclination in trying to build progressive unity within the electorate through recognition of long-standing racial divisions and trying to address the roots of those divisions. In any case, it is not clear to what degree it is either possible or desirable for black progressives to try to build on the president's success in forging a broad coalition. The grounds upon which President Obama built his coalition are more conservative than what progressives should accept and paper over political differences that would undermine the grounds for long-term success in coalition building. One of the central themes of this book is to consider the question of the grounds on which coalitions can be built that will address the hard questions facing black America, such as the economic devastation of poor and working-class blacks, the crisis of incarceration, and the lack of black ability to effectively intervene in democratic debates about how to address the nation's various crises.

It would behoove progressive African Americans, however, to recollect the lessons learned from Jesse Jackson's presidential campaigns. Concentrating on a single candidate, no matter how attractive or charismatic, is not the best way to build a progressive movement. The Rainbow Coalition that supported Jackson's candidacies in 1984 and 1988 had great potential for mobilizing a wide range of progressive forces around both local and national issues. Some chapters organized around an ambitious agenda of local issues. The Rainbow Coalition was dismantled, however, when it no longer served the campaign's purpose. The lesson to be learned is that it is possible to generate significant mobilization around the campaigns of exceptional candidates, but without the independent institutionalization of the movement, it cannot become the basis for a progressive movement that has the power to last beyond the electoral cycle. Further, an independent movement is necessary for the inevitable times when one must criticize a candidate's or officeholder's policy positions. Finally, progressive blacks must strive to prevent discourse about race and politics in the United States from being reduced to merely a discussion of how "since a black man was elected president, isn't it nice that we now live in a post-racial society." Electing what at the time seemed to many to be a moderately progressive (at least in terms of domestic policy) black president was certainly a historic symbolic victory. The examples of Justice Clarence Thomas and Secretaries Condoleezza Rice and Colin Powell, however, should be sufficient to remind us that symbolic placement in positions of power are no guarantee of policies that are either supported by, or beneficial to, the black and progressive communities. Building an independent black progressive movement is critical if the massive problems that confront black communities are to be addressed.

The scale of the problems confronting those dedicated to social, economic, and political justice for blacks remains truly immense. In addition to the problems I alluded to above, the "state of black America" in some domains is still distinctly bleak and distinctly different from the experience of the great majority of white Americans. It is this difference in material conditions that forms a key foundation for the production of such radically different black and white worldviews. Blacks as a group still remain economically disadvantaged as compared, in particular, to whites in the United States. Along with Native Americans, African Americans as a group remain at the bottom of the American economic order. In 2007 median black income was only 59 percent that of white Americans.[8] At the bottom of the income distribution, the racial disparities are even greater. Black poverty rates run twice that of whites. As has been the case for several decades, black wealth is a minuscule fraction of that of whites. Median net worth of blacks is $5,446, while for whites it is $87,056—which works out to a wealth ratio greater than 15 to 1. The black unemployment rate had risen to over 13 percent by March 2009—one and a half times the white unemployment rate.[9] The housing crisis has been magnified in black communities due to a combination of factors, including the concentration of blacks in segregated areas, blacks being at the lower end of the economic distribution, and discriminatory loan practices. Sixty-four percent of African Americans remain confined to segregated neighborhoods. Residing in segregated neighborhoods, as the authors of the "Racial Equity Status Report" make clear, adversely affects wealth generation, job opportunities, and other economic opportunities for the residents of these neighborhoods. Yet worse, 75 percent of Americans who live in the worst concentrations of poverty are black or Latino. Blacks represent only 13 percent of the population, but held 50 percent of the high-cost mortgages that have been so burdensome during the financial crisis. On the other hand, one-third of blacks seeking conventional home loans were denied, as compared to only 15 percent of white applicants. Some of the adverse black economic statistics reported above may be significantly underestimated. It has been determined, for example, that because of the high incarceration rates of black youth, the wage gap between young black and white men is much larger than reported.[10]

The extraordinary rate of incarceration of African Americans represents another monumental crisis facing political activists and the black community. In 2007, 1 out of 100 Americans was incarcerated—an extremely high proportion of the population behind bars by world standards.[11] The rate was much worse for African Americans. For example, 1 in 9 black men between the ages of 20 and 34 were in jail or prison; 1 out of 15 black male adults were behind bars, as were 1 out of 100 black women (as compared to 1 out of 335 white women). These extreme rates of incarceration burden individual states as well as the nation as a whole. One out of every 9 state employees work in the prison system. In 2006 California alone spent $500 million on overtime for prison workers! Nationwide the states spent $44 billion on the prison system—a 313 percent increase from just twenty years earlier.

The black community is also facing multiple severe health crises. Black children are at greater risk of death by both "natural" and unnatural causes. Blacks have a 600 percent greater chance than whites of dying from ho-micide and an 800 percent greater risk of mortality due to "chronic lower respiratory disease." One-third of Latinos and 40 percent of black adults did not have health insurance in 2007 (as opposed to 14 percent for whites). According to the 2006 report "Race, Race-Based Discrimination, and Health Outcomes among African Americans," black mortality rates were the same as white rates thirty years earlier. Black/white health disparities persist even after controlling for social economic factors, and discrimina-tion has been shown to have a substantial and direct effect on black health outcomes.[12] Blacks have the highest rates of heart disease, diabetes, strokes, and hypertension. Even after socioeconomic status, age, and insurance sta-tus are controlled for, a major study found that doctors are less aggressive, give fewer referrals, and generally provide poorer care to African American patients.[13] As a result, blacks suffer nearly 70,000 more deaths per year relative to whites from disease, and only half of the increased mortality can be explained due to class, educational, and other social differences.[14] Environmental effects also contribute to racial disparities in health. Places where blacks tend to live are unhealthier and cause higher rates of respira-tory disease rates due to higher levels of pollution.[15] Specifically, "blacks live disproportionately in cities with higher industrial air pollution. . . . [W]ithin any given metropolitan area, Latinos as well as blacks tend to live on 'the wrong side of the environmental tracks.' "[16] Finally, blacks continue to be ravaged by HIV/AIDS.[17] Fifty percent of those diagnosed with HIV/AIDS in 2005 were black. The rate of diagnoses for black adults and adolescents was ten times that for whites in 2005. According to a CDC report, since the beginning of the epidemic, blacks "have accounted for [42 percent] of the estimated cases diagnosed in the 50 states and the District of Columbia." More than 200,000 blacks are estimated to have died from AIDS since the beginning of the epidemic through 2005. Despite representing 13 percent of the population, blacks in 2005 represented 49 percent of estimated new cases. Of the nearly 20,000 people under age of twenty-five diagnosed with HIV/AIDS in 2001–4, 61 percent were black.

As the grim black HIV/AIDS statistics attest, the crises facing the black community do not equally impact all segments of the community. Class, gender, and sexuality all affect how different populations within the black community experience the various crises that blacks are struggling to overcome. As Cathy Cohen has theorized and demonstrated, some groups of blacks suffer secondary marginalization from dominant groups within the black community. Historically, the black middle class has often tried to marginalize and isolate the black poor. Cohen's research shows that at the beginning of the AIDS crisis, black organizations and leaders marginalized the black gay and lesbian communities as well as intravenous drug users.

This brief recounting of the crises facing the black community is meant to set the context for the discussion of the future of black politics. Jointly, the Katrina disaster and Obama's successful quest for the presidency had one salutary effect on black politics and the politics of race more generally. Together, they put race back on the nation's political agenda. During the Clinton years and the first few months of the Bush administration, a robust and sometimes bitter discourse on race was building in the nation. Even local television stations and major newspapers in cities such as Boston that had relatively small black populations were beginning to cover issues such as reparations for African Americans. However, 9/11 completely suppressed discourse about racial divisions in the nation. Even parts of the left seemed to forget that not only did racial divisions remain fundamental to understanding oppression and resistance in the United States, but that the strongest source of anti-war sentiment could be found within the black community.[18] The spectacle of racial inequality displayed during the Katrina disaster, as well as the hysterical denial by important segments of the media that Katrina had anything to do with race, combined with the spectacle of the first successful presidential campaign by an African American, all served to once again bring the peculiarities and contradictions of race in America back into the nation's consciousness.

The central task of this book is to reflect on the impact that two factors have on the future of black politics. The first factor is the multiple political transformations of black expectations, beliefs, and dreams that occurred during the period that spanned from the aftermath of Hurricane Katrina through the early days of the Obama administration. The second factor is the grim sets of crises that continue to confront African Americans. One question that follows from this reflection is whether the observed change in black public opinion and Barack Obama's election both foreshadow a newly reemerging politics of class within black politics. Another question this book will begin to answer is what new modes of organizing and political action are likely to be successful in this era. The final questions are first: Where do we go from here? What are the key goals and tasks confronting the theoreticians and practitioners of black politics? And what are the new black visions that have the best chance of revitalizing energetic, independent black political movements?

The journey begins in the next chapter with a deeper analysis of the implications of the aftermath to the Katrina disaster for black politics.

2 KATRINA AND THE NADIR OF BLACK POLITICS

I've got the political blues, Hurricane Katrina broke the levee today.
I've got the political blues, the African Americans and the poor folks are floating home.[1]

Katrina lays bare what many people in the United States do not want to see: large numbers of poor black and brown people struggling to make ends meet, benefiting very little from a social system that makes it difficult to obtain health insurance, child care, social assistance, cars, savings, and minimum-wage jobs, if lucky, and instead offers to black and brown youth bad schools, poor public services, and no future, except a possible stint in the penitentiary.
Henry Giroux[2]

Reportedly, people in New Orleans "wonder[ed] if some leaders have stopped thinking of their home as an American city at all."[3] The aftermath of Katrina highlighted the limitations of civil society—especially in the face of severe societal trauma and abandonment by the state of its obligations to its citizens—and starkly illuminated many of the central concerns of this book. The central questions I address in this chapter are (1) how a hierarchical racial order affects in practice the workings of civil society and its associated public spheres and counterpublics; (2) how the racialized nature of mainstream publics led to the demonization of black Katrina residents and their defenders; (3) how the demonization within, and the exclusion of, black opinion from mainstream publics demonstrated the anti-democratic workings of American publics; and (4) how black politics, in turn, failed in this racialized environment and reached its nadir, unable to overcome the demonization of the black citizens of New Orleans in order to effectively and democratically intervene in the national debate on how to respond to the disaster and aid its victims.

The Katrina disaster highlighted once again the racialization of American public opinion, one consequence of which is the huge gulf between blacks and whites in how to conceptualize, analyze, and interpret the aftermath of the storm. In a survey of a random sample of Americans designed by Melissa Harris-Lacewell, Cathy J. Cohen, and myself, we asked whether racial considerations played any role in the government's response to the crisis that followed Hurricane Katrina:[4]

> Most of the people stranded in New Orleans following the hurricane were African American. Do you think the government's response to the situation would have been faster if most of the victims had been white, or don't you think it would have made any difference?

The percentage reporting that the government response would have been faster if victims were white were as follows:

Blacks 84%
Whites 20%

This large gap between black and white opinion also appeared in responses to the question of what was more important, fully restoring the city and returning those displaced by the storm to their homes or taking into account fiscal responsibility:

1. The federal government should spend whatever is necessary to rebuild the city and to restore these Americans to their homes.
   Or
2. Although this is a great tragedy, the federal government must not commit too many funds to rebuilding until we know how we will pay for it.

The percentage stating that the government should spend whatever is necessary to restore people's living conditions was

Blacks 79%
Whites 33%

These gaps represented a huge difference of opinion in how blacks and whites evaluate the import of Katrina, and to label them "huge," in the context of American public opinion and politics, is not hyperbole. The gender gap, for example, which is regarded as quite significant and has on occasion proven to be extremely consequential, is usually in the 5–10 percentage point range. Nor is the racial gap unique to issues surrounding Katrina. The divide between black and white support for the invasion of Iraq in March 2003 dwarfed the difference between Democrats and Republicans, men and women, young and old, and even self-identified liberals and conservatives.[5] Only in the chasm between black and white opinion do we see a difference this consistent across an entire range of issues.

Another fundamental disagreement between blacks and whites evident in our survey results was over the relationship between the hurricane and social problems in the United States. We also posed the following question (replicating a question from a Pew Center survey):

> In your view did this disaster show that racial inequality remains a major problem in this country, or don't you think this was a particularly important lesson of the disaster?

The percentage stating that the disaster showed that racial inequality remains a major problem was

Blacks 90%
Whites 38%

These fundamental black/white disagreements on the relationship between racial inequality and the response to Katrina reflect a deep division between the great majorities of blacks and whites in their respective understanding of how much progress has been achieved in securing racial equality for African Americans. As we saw in the last chapter, these positions have hardened over the past decade (until the advent of Barack Obama's campaign for president), with blacks becoming more pessimistic, while whites increasingly believe that racial equality has been achieved.

The large gap between white and black opinion on how to rebuild New Orleans also exists among New Orleanians themselves, whether currently residing in the city or dispersed. On the sensitive question of whether it is important to preserve the pre-hurricane "racial mix" in New Orleans, a very large majority of blacks, 63 percent, believed it was important or extremely important, as opposed to only 25 percent of whites.[6] This result is not surprising. Given that political power—including influence over the process of rebuilding the city, as well as developments in many other areas—is tied to the "racial mix" through the electoral process, the racial difference in the importance of preserving the "racial mix" becomes understandable. The "old" racial mix, as we shall see, was one in which blacks formed a strong majority, able, when unified, to dictate electoral politics in the city. But this difference also tells us that perceptions of individual interests are still viewed as linked to perceptions of racial group interests.[7] The perception of fairness is also shaped by one's race. While 70 percent of the respondents believed that New Orleans can be "restored," they believed it would only happen if the process involved "regular" people.[8] One-half of respondents, however, expected that the plan to rebuild would be unfair—and blacks were more likely to have this expectation than whites. Indeed, as we shall see, "fairness" has not necessarily figured as a central value for many of the developers critically involved in formulating plans for rebuilding New Orleans.

A year after Hurricane Katrina devastated the Gulf Coast, many African Americans believed the nation to have become mired in a state of willful forgetfulness. Promises for aid and recovery had been forgotten and broken; elections had been structured with the apparent aim of undermining black political power; black victims had been demonized; and through it all, as a war dragged on and other more manageable domestic political conflicts pushed Katrina out of everyday national political discourse, a deafening silence seemed to descend on issues related to New Orleans. For many African Americans, the perception of national neglect and malicious manipulation by local elites to rebuild New Orleans as a smaller, richer, whiter city reinforced their pessimism about the likelihood of achieving racial justice in the United States. To many blacks, it seemed that New Orleans had been abandoned and its black residents left to shift for themselves against powerful forces—reminiscent of the way their ancestors had been abandoned by the national government to face murderous, vengeful white supremacists and terrorists after the fall of the Reconstruction governments that had attempted to build a democratic South after the Civil War.

Perhaps because of this historical resonance, Katrina became a strong presence in the political and artistic discourses of African Americans. The most prominent example during the year following the hurricane was Spike Lee's powerful miniseries for HBO, *When the Levees Broke*. But Lee had plenty of artistic company in trying to keep the tragedy of Katrina alive for the nation as a whole, but particularly for black people. Jazz groups such as the World Saxophone Quartet and rap performers such as Public Enemy and Paris dedicated entire CDs to the political status of black America in the wake of Katrina. Even rappers like Ice Cube and Lil Wayne—known perhaps for their edginess, but not particularly for political statements—released songs expressing deep anger about the events that occurred in New Orleans.

Kanye West, a star rapper from a middle-class background—considered safe enough at the time by NBC to be included in a live benefit broadcast in the days following storm—departed from scripted remarks to issue the following statement:

> I hate the way they portray us in the media. You see a black family, it says, "They're looting." You see a white family, it says, "They're looking for food." And, you know, it's been five days [waiting for federal help] because most of the people are black. And even for me to complain about it, I would be a hypocrite because I've tried to turn away from the TV because it's too hard to watch. . . . We already realize a lot of people that could help are at war right now, fighting another war—and they've given them permission to go down and shoot us! . . . George Bush doesn't care about Black people.[9]

These remarks—not surprisingly given the fame of the rapper, the notoriety of the genre, and the context of the hurricane—caused a publicity stir for a brief period of time. Rappers, often considered by opinion makers to be the face of uncontrolled and dangerous black popular culture, are looked upon by large segments of white America with great suspicion (although not its youth). For West to directly attack the president and accuse him of not caring about black folks both crossed a line in the minds of many whites and simultaneously confirmed the deeply held suspicion that even "safe" blacks were neither safe nor reasonable. My colleagues and I also put West's remarks on the 2005 survey, asking whether they were unjustified, and the percentage who said they not justified were

Blacks 9%
Whites 56%[10]

That the majority of whites believed that West's remarks were unjustified provides the first evidence of what we shall see is a white pattern of rejection of mainstream African American opinion and its labeling as "unjust," "ridiculous," or otherwise outside of the boundaries of acceptable speech. This rejection of black mainstream viewpoints has consequences that will be explored in detail throughout the remainder of this chapter. First, during racialized political and social discourse in the United States, more often than not African Americans' views are viewed as illegitimate, thus not even meriting serious debate. In effect, the black public's consensus viewpoints are not allowed to be represented and debated in what Jean Cohen (1999) calls the "public of publics"—the public sphere that in democratic societies is supposed to allow all the partial publics and counterpublics to come together to democratically, critically, and respectfully consider and debate each other's views. Second, as I also show later in this chapter, not only is the speech labeled illegitimate, but black speakers, whether they represent grassroots black opinion or are part of academic and activist discourse, are also labeled illegitimate. Drawing on the work of Michael Rogin, I use the term "demonization" to designate this process of systematically labeling the speaker illegitimate and the speaker's speech unwarranted, thus excluding both from the "public of publics." The demonization of black speech and of African Americans themselves in the wake of Katrina appears in many of the empirical examples I discuss later in this section. Not only is there an enormous gap between the black and white mainstreams in how to evaluate the events that occurred after Katrina, but the "public of publics," which theorists have argued is the site where democratic non-exclusionary discourse in pluralist societies resides, is actually the arena in which much of the work to demonize and exclude African Americans and African American opinion takes place.

While the size of the gap between the respective mainstreams of black and white perceptions is stunning in its own right, we should also differentiate between the nature of the gaps that exist for each of the questions. For example, on the one hand, the interracial gap on the policy question about the relative importance of restoration of the city versus fiscal responsibility could be the result of citizens who share the same worldview. The majority of blacks and whites could easily disagree on the restoration versus fiscal responsibility question due to partisan differences, differences in perceptions of the technical ramifications of the policy alternatives, or the "simple" calculation of self-interest. The question about Kanye West, however, as well as the questions about the status of racial equality and race as a reason for the slow federal response questions reflect different views about how the world is ordered and about what the real status is of racial groups within society; in other words, worldviews that are fundamentally incommensurable with each other across racial groups. Whites viewing the aftermath to Katrina see a relatively uncomplicated landscape dominated by inept government and blacks behaving badly (both in New Orleans and, in examples such as Kanye West, outside the city). Blacks viewing the aftermath to Katrina, much like the 1968 Kerner Committee Report, see two countries, black and white, separate and unequal. The racial gap on most of the questions is a result of large majorities of blacks and whites possessing fundamentally different worldviews on how race structures social, economic, and political outcomes in the United States.

What explains these incommensurable worldviews? I use the remainder of this chapter to answer that question, using the lens of Hurricane Katrina and its aftermath to focus on the source and nature of racial divisions not only in American public opinion, but more fundamentally in civil society theoretically and concretely in the United States. I present the answer in two parts. First, I offer a quick review of the events of the hurricane itself and analyze several aspects of what happened "on the ground" afterward, building a picture of the actual state of post-Katrina dynamics and the views of events formed by various factions, as represented especially in the media. Then I re-

visit this empirical material from a theoretical perspective, exploring specifically how the American racial order produces racialized and mostly separate
understandings of American society, which are reflections of a fragmented
civil society and a racially exclusionary public sphere.

We Need Help
People are dying . . .
They don't have homes . . .
They don't have jobs . . .
The city of New Orleans will never be the same.[11]

Hell No We Ain't All Right[12]

Even before Hurricane Katrina ravaged the Gulf Coast, the population of
New Orleans was one of the poorest in the nation. In the Lower Ninth Ward,
a majority-black neighborhood that would be one of the areas most devastated by the hurricane, 36 percent of the 20,000 inhabitants lived below
the poverty line—twice the state average.[13] In the year preceding Katrina,
61 percent of New Orleans households were earning less than $20,000 a
year,[14] and of those evacuated to shelters during the storm, nearly half had
pre-hurricane incomes of less than $15,000 per year.[15] One poverty-caused
factor that would prove to be of particular importance during the storm was
a lack of access to transportation. New Orleans ranked fourth worst out of
297 metropolitan areas in the "proportion of households lacking access to
cars"[16]—with the three metropolitan areas faring worse all located in greater
New York, where extensive public transportation is available. Of 140 metropolitan areas in the United States, New Orleans has the ninth worst public
transportation system. The lack of access to private vehicles was particularly
marked for black residents of New Orleans, who were more than five times
more likely than non-Latino whites to lack access to automobiles (27 vs.
5 percent). Even when compared to other blacks in the United States, black
residents of New Orleans were worse off—with "only" 19 percent of blacks
nationwide without access to private transportation. In the end, it was estimated that there were approximately 130,000 residents of New Orleans
who needed transportation out of the city.

Given the advance warning of the storm and the known potential for disaster specifically in New Orleans, including the lack of private transportation, one might have expected local officials to have done a better job arranging for the public evacuation of the city's most vulnerable population. In fact, the story as regards preparation and planning in the days leading up to landfall of the hurricane mirrors the wider narrative of neglect and public nonfeasance. Instead of blaming resource-poor citizens for their inability to escape the storm and its aftermath, attention should be focused on the government's (local, state, and federal) chronic failure to provide for the safety of its most vulnerable citizens—this time with devastating results. It has not escaped notice by many who suffered the most that protecting New Orleans from natural disaster has become a low priority in recent years. A year after Katrina, one respondent to a survey remained bitter, exclaiming, "Send our troops home!! How can you build a wall across the border, but a levee can't protect the city?"[17] The fact that 80 percent of the budget requested in advance of the hurricane to make the New Orleans flood control system safe was cut, with many of the funds diverted to help pay for the war in Iraq, was to prove an especially deadly decision. Further exacerbating the impact of the hurricane on the city's impoverished residents was the lack of planning for providing needed resources for those who remained in the city to ride out the storm—the Superdome was provisioned with food for only 15,000 people for three days.

The destruction wrought by Hurricane Katrina and the continuing disaster of the aftermath had life-threatening health consequences for blacks, the poor, and the elderly—and particularly for individuals falling into all three categories. The dire situation may best be summarized perhaps in reference to the one public hospital responsible for providing health services not only for poor black communities but the medically indigent of all colors, which was located in an area vulnerable to flooding and early in the aftermath was no longer able to function. Another telling narrative appeared in the April 13, 2006, *New England Journal of Medicine*, quoting Fred Lopez, vice chair for education at Louisiana State University (LSU) School of Medicine: "The desperate week we spent inside Charity [Hospital] after Katrina is the one that everybody saw on CNN, but that was the easiest week of the last six months [since the storm]." The report goes on: "Many believe that mortality has also increased substantially, although specifics are difficult to obtain. . . . As a crude indicator, there were 25 percent more death notices in the *Times-Picayune* in January 2006 than there were in January 2005."[18] And as we know from the work of social analysts at the New Vision Institute, the elderly were disproportionately more likely to die, and the black elderly especially so, as a result of the storm.[19]

In the face of these data, many argued that the storm had no disparate racial impact, or, if it did, whites were the ones disadvantaged. Based on bad statistical analysis and unfounded anecdotes, one *New York Times* online commentator, John Biguenet, ventured that "white Orleanians died in proportionately higher numbers." Not surprisingly, someone capable of that conclusion was also able to observe, based on no credible evidence, that "another misconception that has persisted is the notion that many who died in the Lower Ninth Ward were stranded there because they had no means of transportation with which to evacuate."[20] Biguenet's impressions differ substantially from readily available empirical evidence on both who died and the extent to which the black poor in particular lacked access to private transportation. Yet the discrepancy highlights one of the central themes of this chapter: Americans of all races and classes feel that they know what happened in New Orleans, and only a few are aware of the way ideological presuppositions have shaped their interpretation of the "facts."

If dubious priorities and government mismanagement had already contributed to making a dire situation worse, neglect appeared in yet another form. New Mexico Governor Bill Richardson offered much-needed help from the New Mexico Guard, which ended up being delayed for critical days due to federal red tape. Worse, there were reports from observers such as Lance Hill, executive director of the Southern Institute for Education and Research at Tulane University, that government agencies actively stopped aid from reaching the beleaguered residents of New Orleans. As Hill described the scene:

> There was widespread—and ill-founded—fear in the white community that black people at the Superdome and convention center would simply take relief supplies and return to the areas of the city that never flooded. . . . On Friday, September 2nd my wife and I packed up my car with all the supplies we could

gather and began the first of four runs into the convention center, where I en-
countered no danger, only grateful and orderly people desperate for food and
water. On my fourth run I was met by a contingent of the New Orleans and
State Police who ordered me not to distribute the water I had brought. A line of
white state policeman with automatic weapons faced off against the crowd who
were shouting to let me unload my supplies. It was an explosive situation and
the police quickly relented but told me not to return. . . . Red Cross officials are
on record saying they had relief supplies in New Orleans but were ordered not
to distribute them. American Red Cross president Marsh "Marty" Evans went
on national television and said that the Louisiana Department of Homeland
Security had ordered the Red Cross not to provide relief supplies to refugees
inside the city, arguing that the presence of the Red Cross "would keep people
from evacuating and encourage others to come to the city." The same story was
provided by other Red Cross officials and even the Red Cross website carried a
FAQ repeating that authorities had prevented them from providing relief supplies to the storm victims at the convention center.[21]

Other eyewitness accounts, as well as any number of rumors, told of government agencies stopping aid to those who needed it most. And reporters
provided damning evidence of armed suburban police from Gretna (located
in Jefferson Parish, one of the parishes won by former KKK leader David
Duke in his campaign for governor) using the threat of armed force to block
black citizens of New Orleans from crossing a bridge leading out of the city
to safety.

The story related by Hill and the action of police blocking the bridge
to safety were just two of many cited cases in which race and class figured
prominently in how victims of Katrina were treated. It is also the case that
some victims of the storm were deemed more "worthy" of succor than others. Michael Eric Dyson tells how the evacuation of the desperate population at the Superdome was halted to allow the evacuation of seven hundred
guests and workers at the nearby Hyatt, who were in much better shape,
health-wise, psychologically, and in terms of resources than the Superdome
evacuees. More generally, the argument has been made that the reason
FEMA, the Bush administration, and federal agencies as a whole were much
more hands-on and effective after the 2004 Charley and Frances hurricanes

was because the victims were white and residents of a state judged more politically important than Louisiana.[22]

Given the desperate circumstances of the evacuees, it was predictable that Texas officials would be worried about the impact of the influx of desperately poor people on the already-strapped state resources devoted to what remains of the social safety net, in addition to whatever political worries that the new residents might engender. Unfortunately, since one aspect of the demonization of blacks is the stereotype linking poor blacks to crime, it could also be predicted that the new residents would be blamed for a rise in the crime rate of cities such as Houston.[23] The sentiment that one Houston businesswoman expressed, "It's time for them to go home," mirrored the private sentiment of many Texas civic leaders, according to the *Los Angeles Times*.[24] Sadly, many black exiles from New Orleans believed with some justification that they were not welcome at home either.

This attitude toward poor black citizens is what Henry Giroux, writing in the *Toronto Star*, labels the "politics of disposability." Speaking of the Bush administration's "pathological disdain for social values and public life, and its celebration of an unbridled individualism and acquisitiveness," he captures this mind-set in the following quotation:

> Katrina revealed with startling and disturbing clarity who these unwanted are: African-Americans who occupy the poorest sections of New Orleans, those ghettoized frontier zones created by racism coupled with economic inequality. Cut off of any long-term goals and a decent vision of the future, these are the populations . . . who have been rendered redundant and disposable in the age of neoliberal global capitalism.[25]

One of the most dramatic results of the post-Katrina catastrophe was the dispersal of hundreds of thousands of New Orleans residents, mostly black, not only out of the city, but by and large out of the state of Louisiana, resulting in what some have labeled the Katrina Diaspora. As Spike Lee documented in his film *When the Levees Broke*, in the days following the storm many evacuees from New Orleans did not know where they were being sent, as they were separated from their families and not allowed to bury their loved ones. Some ended up in places as remote as Utah, a state with

Table 7: FEMA Dispersal Report

Metro Area	No. of Applicants
1. New Orleans–Metairie-Kenner, LA	394,359
2. Houston-Baytown–Sugar Land, TX	314,045
3. Baton Rouge, LA	177,286
4. Beaumont–Port Arthur, TX	132,741
5. Gulfport-Biloxi, MS	92,800
6. Mobile, AL	84,481
7. Jackson, MS	82,919
8. Lake Charles, LA	75,693
9. Houma–Bayou Cane–Thibodaux, LA	67,290
10. Pascagoula, MS	59,101

Source: FEMA. Graphics reporting by Tom Reinken, in Bustillo 2006.

scant experience of any black presence at all. Others found themselves in places like Chicago, a historic recipient of large numbers of black southern exiles. Most citizens from New Orleans remained in the South and most of those in Texas. There is great uncertainty involved in estimating where people ended up, but one measure of the dispersal nearly a year after Katrina is given in table 7, which is based on the location of applicants for disaster relief made to FEMA.[26]

The FEMA numbers indicate the enormity of the demographic displacement in the aftermath of the storm, but they do not give us a sense of the racial breakdown. Available estimates on this latter count, however, suggest a city radically transformed along lines of race and class. Brown University sociologist John Logan estimated that of those eligible to vote in the May 2006 election who were scattered outside the state, 102,000 were African Americans, as opposed to 48,000 whites.[27] Logan's estimates of New Orleanians dispersed inside the state, on the other hand, include only 31,000 African Americans as opposed to 92,000 whites. He has characterized the in-city electorate post-storm as distinctly white and middle class—a complete reversal of the city's pre-storm electoral demographics. The Louisiana Recovery Authority Support Foundation (LRASF) estimated that the parish had only 39 percent of its population in October 2006, as compared to 2000 U.S. census data. A population that had amounted to nearly half a million in 2000 (484,674) had been more than halved, to less than a quarter of a million (187,525). The black population declined even more precipitously. Sixty-seven percent of the population in 2000 was black, according to the U.S. census. By October 2006 the black population had declined by nearly 250,000 residents (239,030). The result is that New Orleans was no longer a majority-black city, with African Americans now comprising only 46 percent of the Orleans Parish population.

Perhaps more telling are figures pertaining to the welfare of these dispersed citizens. A study by the Texas Health and Human Services Commission, which estimated that over a quarter million evacuees (down from an estimated high of 400,000) were still residing in Texas as of August 2006. The study found that these remaining evacuees were financially devastated by Katrina and its aftermath: "Of adults, 59% were unemployed, and 54% were still receiving housing subsidies. Eighty-one percent were African American."[28] Another survey of evacuees in Houston shelters immediately after the hurricane found similar results. These were the poorest of the poor, those most at risk both before and after the storm. Not surprisingly, the largest segment of this population came from the Superdome, rooftops, and the Convention Center.[29] The devastating economic impact of the storm's aftermath on this population, given their location at the intersection of the bottom of both the racial and economic orders, is not surprising. While 60 percent were employed before the hurricane, only 20 percent had jobs post-Katrina. As noted above, about half of the population had incomes of less than $15,000 per year prior to the hurricane; this percentage grew to 74 percent a year after the hurricane struck. Nor was the devastation just economic: 30 percent of respondents reported a decline in their health, at the same time that the percentage of those surveyed with no health insurance rose from 29 to 46 percent. Even though the evacuees reported both increased alienation and the breakdown of their accustomed social networks, more than two-thirds reported that they were likely to stay in Houston, which can be best understood as a further indication of their strained circumstances.

Perhaps the broadest picture of the devastation to Louisiana a year later is found in the results from the LRASF survey cited above. Of all members of the Katrina Diaspora, 57 percent stated they were likely or somewhat likely to return—although those who ended up still within Louisiana, a group that is disproportionately white, stated they were much more likely to return when compared to those dispersed outside the state. Figure 1, extracted from the

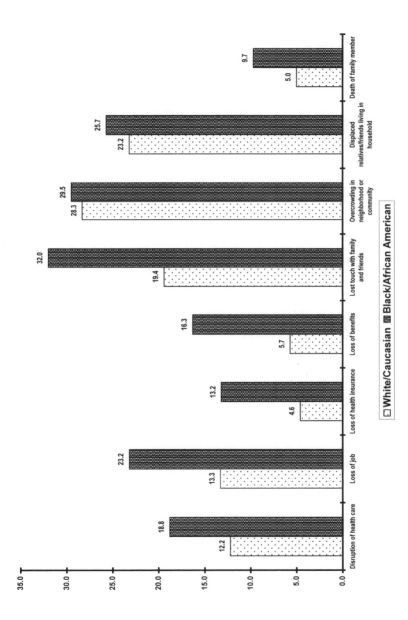

FIGURE 1: Effects of the aftermath of Katrina by race.

Source: Louisiana Recovery Authority Support Foundation, 2006 South Louisiana Recovery Survey: Citizen and Civic Leader Research Summary of Findings, http://lra.louisiana.gov/assets/junemeeting/2006RecoveryResearchFinal061506.pdf (accessed October 22, 2006).

LRASF report, clearly shows how blacks were particularly disadvantaged by the hurricane and its aftermath.

The report makes clear that blacks were systematically disadvantaged across the board, but three areas in which blacks were particularly disadvantaged stand out. These involve the threat to personal health, exposure to economic hardship, and the tear in the fabric of civil society, all of which showed heightened levels of racial disparities. The largest gap registered in figure 1 lies right at the heart of civil society, by which I mean here the larger community in which all individuals are embedded, consisting of family, friends, community associations, infrastructure, and quite generally the wherewithal with which one prospers, or does not, in going about the business of life, and political life in particular. While a significant 19 percent of white citizens reported losing touch with their family and friends, nearly one-third of African Americans reported such a loss. Similarly, there were 8–10 percentage-point differences in the numbers of African Americans, as opposed to whites, reporting that they had lost their health insurance, benefits, and—tellingly—their jobs. Blacks were on average nearly twice as likely to report having had a family member die due to the storm and its aftermath.

As noted above, the majority of those dispersed by the storm and its aftermath, when asked, indicated a desire to return home to New Orleans. Many of these evacuees, however, have reluctantly made the decision to remain in the locales to which they were sent, given the high price of housing, the lack of services in the predominantly black and poor neighborhoods, the lack of jobs back in New Orleans, and the destruction of the social networks and institutions that were the foundation of black civil society. Some former New Orleans residents found their new locales much more fiscally and socially viable than New Orleans—one of the poorest American cities before Katrina.[30] The obstacles that African Americans faced in returning further contributed to the devastation of civil life in black New Orleans. The assault on black civil society in turn further weakened the black public sphere, thus making it harder for African Americans to influence the debate about rebuilding New Orleans in a manner that would facilitate revitalization of black communities, black civil society, and local black public spheres. Be that as it may, many citizens of the city were determined to make their way back home to the Crescent City. Ironically, many of their own civic leaders and more affluent fellow citizens did not want them either. I discuss this grim turn of events in the next section.

I was born in a boot at the bottom of the map
New Orleans baby
now the White House hating
trying to wash us away like we not on the map
wait have you heard the latest
they saying you gotta have paper if you tryin' to come back.[31]

The widespread perception that it was necessary to "have paper"—money or resources—if you wanted to return home was easily confirmed in both public pronouncements by various civic leaders and policies governing which neighborhoods would receive the material assistance necessary to rebuild. The formidable obstacles the disadvantaged face in returning have been made even more difficult, according to Oxfam America, by the way disaster assistance was being funneled by the federal and state governments away from those who needed it most to the affluent and to corporate interests:

> Common sense would also suggest that those who face the most difficulty rebuilding would receive the most government support. The exact opposite is true. Federal disaster assistance favors people who have economic assets at risk—that is, the affluent. . . . Poorer residents, whose homes may cost less to repair or rebuild and now have fewer alternative resources on which to draw, also have a harder time meeting program eligibility requirements based on income level and credit history.

They conclude, "Access to opportunity remains unequal—and unfair." And this was true not just in New Orleans. In Biloxi, Mississippi, "government officials acted first to save the city's battered casinos by convincing state lawmakers to allow gaming on land. Not ensuring that the low-income residents of East Biloxi shared in the economic benefits, however, has made them victims of an enormous land squeeze, forcing them out of their neighborhoods and homes."[32]

But more is at stake here than the chronic reality that vulnerable populations fare badly in situations in which resources are required. It was also widely perceived that the necessity of having resources as a precondition to being able to return to the city was part of at least the hope, if not the design, of some civic leaders in New Orleans that the poor black population would dramatically shrink as a result of the Katrina disaster. This perception was confirmed in the public statements of an influential segment of the white elite of New Orleans. As the *Los Angeles Times* noted in its coverage of the mayoral election in the spring of 2006:

> Some candidates have talked about shrinking the city's footprint, or reducing the areas within the city where homes can be built. They argue the city can never justify nor afford to operate as though it still had its pre-Katrina population. That suggestion also has taken on racial overtones. "Smaller footprint is code for race," Stonecipher [a local polling expert] said. "It means evacuees don't get to come back and rebuild and live here anymore."[33]

Indeed, some white elites were explicit about the racial and class mix of the city needing to be changed. This was the view, for example, of Mayor Ray Nagin's former chairman of the New Orleans Regional Transit Authority, James Reiss, according to the *Wall Street Journal* in a piece shortly after the hurricane struck:

> The new city must be something very different, Mr. Reiss says, with better services and fewer poor people. "Those who want to see this city rebuilt want to see it done in a completely different way: demographically, geographically and politically," he says. "I'm not just speaking for myself here. The way we've been living is not going to happen again, or we're out."[34]

According to the *New York Times*, the housing projects are "essentially closed and many poorer neighborhoods are still devastated." The article continues, "Tens of thousands in the African-American working-class backbone remain unable to return." Again, whether by design or due to the "contingencies" of the situation, we find the conclusion that the city will be smaller, richer, whiter, and that neighborhoods like the Lower Ninth Ward are "unlikely to be rebuilt anytime soon, if at all."[35]

Demands for low-income housing and the rehabilitation and restoration of public housing emerging from the black counterpublic in New Orleans and beyond have gone ignored by developers and government officials alike. Some planners argued that the Lower Ninth Ward, in particular, could be rebuilt without demolition in a "cost-effective way."[36] And it was in the face of impassioned public testimony from the black community that federal officials decided to demolish public housing, offering no justification for their decision. Public housing was to be replaced with "less dense, modern housing," it was said, that would include far fewer units for the low-income residents who had previously lived in the neighborhood. As one Loyola University legal adviser stated at a hearing on the demolition where federal officials refused to respond to their questions, "This is a government-sanctioned diaspora of New Orleans's poorest African American citizens. . . . They are destroying perfectly habitable apartments when they are more rare than any time since the Civil War."[37]

It is of note that white elite opinion makers, when they do offer justification for the decisions being made in New Orleans, use the language of "rationality," as, for example, in the decision to demolish housing stock in the Lower Ninth Ward. This same language is invoked elsewhere to further attack black interests and make black subordination more severe. Newspapers' editorial voices joined business interests in a call to dramatically reshape the city in such a way that "the unwanted element" does not return. Another example of the drive to reestablish a greater degree of black subordination was found in an October 17, 2005, editorial in the *Baton Rouge Advocate*. Putting the matter in the starkest terms, the paper stated, "It is time to think rationally, not politically: New Orleans and Louisiana would be better off if the state does not rebuild Southern University in New Orleans." The editorial continued by saying, "Its existence has always been more about racial politics than education policy." The suggestion was that the students of this historically black university could "attend community colleges." This is yet another example of elite opinion calling for a policy change that would severely disadvantage African Americans, using the language of rationality.

In the rebuilding of New Orleans, the veneer of "rationality" was also used to further exclude black opinion from the policy formation process, undermine democratic processes, and implement policies that would ensure that a devastated black civil society could not be rebuilt. By ensuring that black civil society could not be rebuilt, it was also ensured that a governing majority of poor, working-class, and middle-class blacks could not be reforged. An alliance of elite white opinion makers, developers, and government officials was able to seriously damage, and perhaps end, democratic black power in New Orleans.

The political implications of the racial and class transformations of New Orleans are immense, both for the city itself and the locales that received the dispersed population. New Orleans, a liberal and Democratic bastion in the solid Republican South, will, at the least, be much less so in the future, jeopardizing the ability of white Louisiana Democrats to win statewide elections. More fundamentally for many, the black population, and poor New Orleanians more generally, will have an even harder time having their voices heard and interests represented in the smaller, richer, whiter city that is likely to be the result of rebuilding plans. On the other hand, many politicos in states like Texas are worried that the demographics swing in the liberal direction that was already occurring (due in part to the growth of the Latino population) will be accelerated by the infusion, perhaps permanently, of black Democrats into cities such as Houston. To many observers, including New Orleans's mayor, these dynamics of race and class were a central theme in the mayoral election that was held in the spring of 2006. Speaking to the National Association of Black Journalists, Mayor Nagin argued that Katrina "exposed the soft underbelly of America as it relates to dealing with race and class." He continued, "And I, to this day, believe that if that would have happened in Orange County, California, if that would had have happened in South Beach, Miami, it would have been a different response."[38]

This line of argument represented a drastic change of profile and rhetorical strategy for Nagin. His previous profile had been similar to that of other new wave black politicians such as Harold Ford, Cory Booker, and Barack

Obama, who not only downplayed their racial heritage, but also emphasized their technocratic and moderate-to-conservative politics in attempting to appeal to affluent voters across racial lines. Nagin was elected with the support of white elites due to his moderate politics and outstanding corporate credentials. This strategy became untenable after the hurricane with the demographic changes in the city that I have already discussed. More abstractly, but also more fundamentally, the hurricane destabilized the racial order in New Orleans. This destabilization due to the dispersal of the black population and the consequent savaging of black civil society provided an opportunity for a more oppressive regime to be put in place, for black political power to be dismantled, and for the black counterpublic to be silenced. This last point is of particular importance. Much public sphere theory conceptualizes political influence as flowing from public sphere to the policy formation process—from the public to the state.[39] But for subordinate counterpublics, publics that must fight to have their voices heard and considered, the causal arrow is at least partially reversed. In a pluralistic democratic society, the ability for the counterpublic views to be heard and be influential in the larger "public of publics" and have an impact on the state, the subordinate population must wield sufficient political power that their views would be heard and considered. That political power could come from three sources: (1) local mass mobilization from within black civil society; (2) local political power exercised through the electoral system; and (3) substantial political pressure from outside of New Orleans—most likely, as is usually the case for subordinate populations, from their compatriots nationally. In this era of the triumph of neoliberal sensibilities even within black politics, local or national black political mobilization is rare, and the limited leverage provided by black electoral power has had to serve as the main, if not ideal, protector of local black interests. Katrina provided an opportunity to severely curtail both black electoral power and particularly poor African Americans' ability to mobilize politically.

The same conservative white elites who had supported Nagin for mayor in the past now decided that they no longer needed a technocratic African American to front for them. While Nagin had served as a major functionary within the dominant public sphere, he suddenly found himself immersed in a hostile environment where he faced former white members of his inner circle as well as former political allies. In such an electoral environment, New Orleans University political scientist Susan Howell explained, racial identification becomes an important component of voters' decision-making calculus.[40] Thus, Nagin switched in the primary from his normal technocratic appeals to more explicitly racial appeals.

It was not only at the level of individual vote choice, however, that race played a major role in the post-Katrina mayoral election. As the *Los Angeles Times* reported, "Race has also been at the center of complaints over election logistics."[41] The changed demographics not only affected Nagin's campaign, but also who would have the right to vote. As we saw earlier, Brown sociologist Logan has characterized the city's new electorate as being distinctly more white and middle class. The pleas of organizations such as the NAACP and many others fell on deaf ears as both state officials and federal judges refused to either revise the rules, by setting up out-of-state polling places, for example, or delaying the election until either more residents could return and/or more inclusive election rules could be crafted, finding the rules adequate to ensure a "fair" election. Civil rights and community groups fought unsuccessfully to block the election on grounds that it was racially unfair.

Black and other progressive groups reacted by focusing on the election itself. Progressive community-building organizations such as the Association of Community Organizations for Reform Now (ACORN) mobilized to bring buses of dispersed New Orleans residents back into the city in order to vote—some for the first time.[42] Many groups aided dispersed residents in filling out and sending in absentee ballots. Progressives in the black community worked within Nagin's campaign crafting a public message and agenda more suitable for winning over and mobilizing grassroots blacks. The result was that Nagin was able to win the general election and remain mayor.

The general election campaign, however, highlighted the tensions that remain in black politics in New Orleans. The on-the-ground organizing in the black community remained relatively weak. We know from the work of scholars such as Sudhir Venkatesh how very poor urban communities lack many of the resources necessary for sustained political mobilization and influence.[43] New Orleans, already one of the very poorest of black urban communities, was even more devastated after the disaster—the black civil society of New Orleans was nearly demolished. Since Nagin once more actively appealed to his elite business base in the general election, Nagin's "new" constituency's ability to hold him accountable is problematic given the weakness of black civil society, the lack of local political mobilization, and relatively weakened electoral leverage. Further, Nagin had never functioned as a voice for the black counterpublic—his constituency had been local and national corporate interests.

The stakes were huge. Much of the discussion on how to rebuild the city had been delayed until the new administration was in place. A strong local government that represented the interests of disadvantaged blacks could stand as a strong bulwark against, for example, federal authorities who wanted to demolish low-income public housing or racist local white interests that wanted to dismantle an institution central to the city's and region's black communities (Southern University). A strong local government could (and in this case, the Nagin administration temporarily did) partner with progressive forces such as unions, which could focus resources on New Orleans that aided the poor instead of using resources to further disadvantage poor communities, as many developers and local elites were attempting.

A democratic initiative that countered this trend of corporate-centered redevelopment worsening residents' prospects in the region was a massive investment planned by the AFL-CIO. The unions partnered with local residents, local charities, local government, and Tulane University's Department of Architecture with planning assistance from a faculty-student team from MIT led by Phillip Thompson. Over several years the AFL-CIO planned to invest over $1 billion in neighborhood restoration as well as economic development. The first neighborhood to be targeted was Tremé—a predominantly black working-class community that was somewhat less damaged by the storm than similar neighborhoods.[44] Not only was the labor federation going to invest over a quarter of a billion dollars in low-cost housing; the jobs that were to be provided both in construction and in the large-scale economic development projects (a hospital and hotel) would be unionized, resulting in higher wages than often found in a South dominated by anti-union right-to-work laws. An important component of the planning process, as Thompson stated, was to ensure that the plan "emphasize[d] the critical importance of full participation, especially by poor residents who are a majority in most devastated neighborhoods, in the rebuilding process."[45]

Not surprisingly, given the sentiments presented above, the plan met resistance from some local elites fearing there would be too much affordable
housing. Pres Kabacoff, a local developer, argued, "You can overload the
city with affordable housing," and went on to say, "It's important we don't
end up with concentratedly poor neighborhoods."[46] Throughout the region,
but particularly in New Orleans, conflict over the race and class makeup
of restored communities threatened to engulf each major development
project.

A strong black counterpublic could mobilize black and other citizens
to demand that the AFL-CIO initiatives would be the template by which
the great majority of restoration projects would be governed. Conversely, a
strong local government that represented the interests of the black counterpublic could also demand and facilitate the black counterpublic's voice
being heard and considered. All of these functions are severely jeopardized
in the current environment, given the devastation of black civil society and
the weakness of black politics in New Orleans.

One further aspect of the aftermath to Katrina needs to be reviewed. The
demonization of the black victims of Katrina in the media further weakened
the black community's ability to influence policy and shape both the local
and national discourse that surrounded the aftermath to the disaster. This
demonization derived from several sources: the media, civic leaders, and the
ingrained stereotypes of African Americans that are rooted in a long history
of subjugation and attacks.

The media substantially contributed to the demonization of African
Americans. I have discussed some examples already. For example, many
media outlets portrayed the black victims of the aftermath and the evacuees
as irresponsible criminals deserving of little sympathy. Many in the African
American community have decried the former portrayal and in particular
pointed out that whites foraging for food were depicted as showing reasonable survival behavior, while blacks engaged in the same behavior were
portrayed as dangerous looters subject to being justly shot. There were also
pervasive stories in the media, later proved to be untrue, of massive gunfire
aimed at citizens, police, and the National Guard. Several accounts also suggest that the stories of the violence, although not the suffering, that occurred

at the Superdome and Convention Center were also inflated.[47] We have seen that these depictions of the black citizens of New Orleans as a dangerous and out-of-control population persisted well into 2006—this was a central theme of the multiple news stories from the summer of 2006 about how the evacuees were responsible for a huge rise in violent crime in Houston. By early 2007 Houston's Mayor Bill White was blaming the rise in murders in the city on the Katrina evacuees, even though experts pointed out that the rise in the murder rate was a national trend.[48] The constant portrayal of this population as criminals did much to reinforce the "suspicion" that the black citizens of New Orleans were responsible for their own problems. Indeed, there is evidence of this in the white public opinion data, in which a very large majority of whites responded that they believed the community by and large would not have been trapped if they had been less "stubborn."

Black New Orleans citizens and their supporters were also demonized as either hysterical or guilty of cynically playing the race card. The most common criticism of Spike Lee's excellent *Levees* was his reporting of the widespread belief (also documented by research in New Orleans by colleague Melissa Harris-Lacewell of Princeton) among African Americans that the levees had been bombed. Deep suspicions of the government are understandable not only given past misconduct, some quite recent (such as the Tuskegee experiments; the vicious COINTEL program aimed at both the Civil Rights and Black Power movements; and the well-documented evidence of attempts to discourage and mislead black voters in the 2000, 2004, and 2006 national elections), but also of a dubious history in the last century of how city officials handled the levees in at least one hurricane early in the twentieth century.[49] Yet even reporting the deep suspicions in the black community was deemed as irresponsible behavior as opposed to an opportunity to discuss racial history and mistrust. A critical function of the dominant public sphere in a society with a racial order is to monitor, discipline, and if necessary label as illegitimate and exclude contrary and critical viewpoints that emerge from the racially subordinate public and that raise claims of racial injustice.

For example, despite substantial evidence that blacks fared worse than whites in the aftermath of Katrina, writers such as John Biguenet for the *New York Times* and Cathy Young in the *Boston Globe* dismiss claims of black disadvantage out of hand, with the latter accusing those who made such claims as unconscionably playing the race card. James Taranto in the *Wall Street Journal Online* managed to combine charges of black hysteria with those of playing the race card. Responding to analysis by social scientists and political commentators (all black) of survey results demonstrating both the degree to which blacks saw the response to Katrina as illustrative of the nation's deep problems with racial inequality, as well as the monumental degree to which blacks and whites disagreed on how to analyze the aftermath, Taranto dismissed both black opinion and the analysts by labeling the former as being extraordinarily out of the reasonable mainstream of "American" public opinion, and the latter as being hard leftists trying to manipulate misguided blacks for their own political ends.[50]

Finally, there were portrayals by both civic leaders in New Orleans and Texas as well as media pundits who were all too willing to label the black population as so undesirable that all notions of launching efforts to aid them were doomed from the start. Charles Murray, of *The Bell Curve* fame (a book he coauthored, arguing that the genetic inferiority of blacks and other groups necessitated a change from an egalitarian state to a state that recognized that many "Americans" were by nature inferior), stated in the *Wall Street Journal* that Katrina had led to the "rediscovery of the underclass." He argued against federal aid being extended to the largely black poor victims of New Orleans because, as he claims: "You name it, we've tried it. It doesn't work with the underclass. . . . Five years from now, the official evaluations will report that there were no statistically significant differences between the subsequent lives of people who got the government help and the lives of people in the control group."[51] Murray was hardly alone in his harsh assessment of the storm's victims. Popular conservative talk show host Glenn Beck (now on FOX television) called the "small percentage" of citizens that remained in New Orleans "scumbags."[52]

The adoption of these demonizing narratives by the media provided sufficient cover for authorities to hinder black victims from receiving aid, whether it was armed police preventing New Orleans residents at gunpoint from crossing the bridge to relative safety or, as was described earlier, preventing both private citizens and the Red Cross from bringing aid to the city's residents.[53] These narratives also serve to reinforce the racial order in the ideological sphere, just as the actions of developers and federal officials reinforced the material aspects of the racial order.

DEMONIZING NARRATIVES ARE JUST ONE OF THE MANY legacies of Jim Crow that still haunt and shape the American racial terrain. With the enforced segregation of Jim Crow, exclusion became the racial principle around which society was organized, and dual civil societies became inevitable. This is especially the case since the symbolic fields of black and white civil society became as different from each other after Katrina, as reflected in public opinion data. By symbolic fields, I mean the patterns of interpretation that serve to filter events and other phenomenon through racialized lens and map these events onto sets of meanings. Coercion and segregation became the main tool through which social stability, or at least a version of it, was maintained. It should be noted that norms and values, markets, and white voluntary associations were as much tools of exclusion, segregation, and coercion via blacks as the state. White civil society was an integral factor for maintaining black subordination through coercion. In the South, organizations such as the Ku Klux Klan enforced Jim Crow through extra-state and at least implicitly state-sanctioned violence. By the era of the Civil Rights Movement, White Citizens' Councils were playing a more important role policing black transgressions against the racial order, although the Klan and its informal counterparts were still engaged in rampant terrorist violence. In the North, block clubs and other neighborhood organizations, parishes and congregations, and "civic" organizations such as anti-busing groups all policed the color line in order to maintain segregated neighborhoods, beaches, parks, schools, youth athletic leagues, and streets. In cities such as Chicago, Boston, and New York, racial exclusion was enforced with collective violence well into the last decades of the twentieth century. The point is that both in the South, where segregation was legally sanctioned until the mid-twentieth century, and in the North, where state sanctioning was much less explicit, white civil society was a necessary component in enforcing the separation of the races in nearly all facets of society. Consent, even in the North, became at best a secondary tool for ensuring black subordination. Just as black opinion was (and largely still is) excluded from the dominant public sphere leading to the development of the black counter-

Table 8: Interactions between Blacks and Whites by Category of Activity

Did respondent interact with whites/blacks while engaged in the following activities?	Blacks	Whites
Religious or voluntary organization?	33%	23%
While working on community projects	22%	13%
While at work?	75%	64%
Recreational activities?	49%	43%

public, black subordination under Jim Crow led to black exclusion from civil society and the formation of black civil society. Both the exclusion from civil society as well as exclusion from the "public of publics" led to a near total lack of access to the policy-making arena. This deadly combination has left black communities especially vulnerable to economic, political, and other disasters—a vulnerability that was magnified by the natural disaster of Hurricane Katrina and the human-constructed disaster of the aftermath to the storm.[54]

A contemporary legacy of the system of American apartheid known as Jim Crow is the shadow of segregation that still can be seen in many community organizations within which African Americans work.[55] Overall, as a minority group, most blacks (86 percent) must frequently interact with whites, but only slightly over half of white Americans (54 percent) frequently interact with blacks (see table 8). The picture becomes starker when we examine under what circumstances blacks and whites interact. Most of the interaction between blacks and whites occurs at work and recreational activities. Very large majorities of blacks and whites do not interact within voluntary organizations or sacred organization, nor collaborate on community projects. The very core of what Iris Young described as the self-organizing sector of civil society remains hyper-segregated, resulting in fragmentation. As Cathy Cohen points out, the segregation of these institutions also means that without a connection to the public sphere, black communities had limited mechanisms for influencing either white and "official public" opinion or public policy.[56] Both results are consequences of a civil society in the United States that remains fragmented, which has placed the New Orleans black community in an even more precarious position in the aftermath of Katrina.

There is even stronger empirical evidence demonstrating the extent of the racialization of publics of publics in the United States and the consequences

of that racialization on opinion formation. The extent of how racialized publics are in the United States emerges when we more carefully examine the
Katrina data. The simple racial difference displayed in the opening of this
chapter could well be masking class, gender, regional, or other cleavages. To
establish that race is the underlying cleavage that structures such monumental differences in the evaluation of Katrina's aftermath, I tested how much
power a respondent's race had after controlling for a number of other political and social characteristics.[57] Even after controlling for a number of other
variables, race was by far the most powerful variable for predicting one's response for all of the Katrina questions. The magnitude of these effects can
be estimated by seeing how much a respondent's answer to a question would
change by merely switching the respondent's race from white to black after
controlling for the other variables. The results are illuminating. After holding the other variables the same (income, age, gender, region, and education), changing a respondent from white to black:

- Raised the probability 33 percent that the respondent believed that New Orleans
  residents did not evacuate because they were trapped due to resource constraints.
- Raised the probability 64 percent that the respondent believed that the federal
  government would have moved faster if the majority of those in distress had been
  white.
- Raised the probability 50 percent that the respondent believed that Katrina exposed problems about racial inequality in the United States.
- Raised the probability 46 percent that the respondent believed that Kanye West's
  remarks were justified.
- Raised the probability by 37 percent that the respondent disapproved of the way
  the war in Iraq was being conducted.
- Raised the probability by 25 percent the respondent believed that the president
  didn't care about the interests of people like them (this latter probability would
  have been higher in every other year of the study as white approval of Bush had
  begun to decline by 2005).

The evidence strongly suggests that race systematically structures these
sets of responses, and that in turn these responses are the product of multiple public spheres—or for the case of African Americans, the black coun-

terpublic.[58] Jean Cohen points out, however, that multiple publics do not in and of themselves signify an exclusionary set of publics. Multiple publics are a mark, according to Cohen, of any pluralistic society—one can have both multiple publics and multiple different types of publics.[59] The key, however, is that these multiple publics comprised of "readers, listeners, viewers, and now cyber-communicators scattered around the national and international society" must also be part of a larger "public of publics," which allows them to contribute to what Cohen calls "public opinion in general" and what Habermas calls the will-formation process.[60]

In a racially fragmented civil society, however, the black counterpublic formed in response to the dominant publics has its roots in the relative political, economic, and social powerlessness that African Americans have had historically and continue to have in this era. The relative powerlessness of the black counterpublic has made it difficult for the consensuses that developed within it to be interjected within mainstream publics.[61] The extreme racial polarization found within the data is indeed an indication of lack of success that the black counterpublic has had in influencing white mainstream publics. The reverse is also true, of course; black publics remain relatively resistant to white opinion, but it is white opinion that molds public policy, and it is white opinion that gets coded as "normal," "rational," and "reasonable." Indeed, as Nancy Fraser and Michael Warner both argue, counterpublics are by their nature subordinate to their dominant counterparts (in this case, subordinate to white-dominated civil society, public spheres, and counterpublics) and, as Fraser argues, have subaltern status. Warner makes this point when he states, "Dominant publics are by definition those that can take their discourse pragmatics and their lifeworlds for granted, misrecognizing the indefinite scope of their expansive address as universality or normalcy."[62] But the effect of this misrecognition is that alternative discourses become marginalized and, in this case, with real consequences for the shape of political power and the distribution of life chances in post-Katrina New Orleans.

The relative powerlessness and lack of resources that disadvantaged the black community of New Orleans was manifested in the aftermath of the hurricane. Residential patterns structured by the intersection of race and poverty tended to confine blacks to poor and vulnerable neighborhoods. The same lack of resources made it more difficult for African Americans to leave the city and arrange for substitute housing whether they stayed or left. The immense racial wealth gap that disadvantages the black middle class makes it more difficult for middle-class African Americans to not only restart small businesses and rebuild residences, but to even contemplate how to return to their city.

The aftermath of the storm cruelly illustrated Habermas's admonition that "the capacity of the public sphere to solve problems on *its own* is limited," and the same can be said of civil society more generally.[63] But in the aftermath of the hurricane, the state failed in its responsibility to its citizens, and those who were poor and black disproportionately suffered the consequences of the state's failure. The lack of the black counterpublics' ability to influence white opinion also makes it more difficult for black publics to influence the state through the vehicle of black politics. Black opinion has the best chance of affecting discourse when black politics is in its most heightened state, as we have seen during periods of massive black mobilization, either through the electoral system (such as during the Reconstruction period after the Civil War) or through vibrant social movements (such as during the Civil Rights and Black Power movements). Far from being part of a democratic solution for addressing black disadvantage, the dominant American public sphere actively contributes to black marginalization.

It is also during these periods of strong black political mobilization that blacks have generally had their most success in forging alliances with other social forces attempting to influence both public opinion and policy-making. A critical theoretical and pragmatic question for black politics, one that has existed since before the founding of the Republic, has to do with how alliances can be formed with other forces, involving both who these others might be and on what basis the alliance is possible. This is a critical question if the human disaster and malfeasance that followed Katrina is to be more effectively countered the next time a disaster confronts black communities, either locally or nationally.

Another crucial component of African Americans' exclusion from dominant civil society and its associated public sphere has been their historical demonization as an inferior and dangerous people unworthy of either full citizenship or membership in civil society. African Americans have not only since slavery been deemed to be a "criminally" dangerous threat to white society, but have also, according to President Woodrow Wilson, presented "black dangers to white civilization."[64] As Mariane Ferme argues for the African case, "Civil society in this sense was presumed to be civilized society, from whose ranks the uncivilized were excluded."[65] The demonization of black citizens and their speech that occurred after Katrina was not only in keeping with long-standing historical practices, but once again highlighted how the dominant public sphere's exclusion of blacks makes African Americans more vulnerable in times of crisis.

President Wilson's view that blacks represented a dangerous element within the body politic has a long historical tradition. At the time of the founding, many could not even imagine the possibility of blacks entering civil society, let alone black politics. A founder who had sufficient imagination was Thomas Jefferson. He saw the prospect of blacks entering the polity and society of the United States as an utter disaster. He predicted that blacks would want vengeance and considered them moral, intellectual, and aesthetic inferiors of whites. Thus they were unfit both as citizens and as members of civil society. Specifically, in *Notes on the State of Virginia*, he argued:

> To these objections, which are political, may be added others, which are physical and moral. . . . Comparing them by their faculties of memory, reason, and imagination, it appears to me, that in memory they are equal to the whites; in reason much inferior, as I think one could scarcely be found capable of tracing and comprehending the investigations of Euclid; and that in imagination they are dull, tasteless, and anomalous. . . . The opinion, that they are inferior in the faculties of reason and imagination, must be hazarded with great diffidence.[66]

Jefferson's followers continued this argument well into the twenty-first century: the difference between blacks and whites meant that we could never share the same political community. Blacks could never be citizens; the Declaration of Independence did not apply. Jefferson worried about what would really happen after emancipation. With liberty, of a sort, would African Americans keep the promise that they had issued for decades—no justice, no peace? Indeed, this promise was kept in the 1950s, 1960s, and early 1970s.

Jefferson's view on blacks as inferiors who could be admitted to civil society and polity only at the great risk to the white race, particularly white women, is the central theme of the early twentieth-century film, the most powerful of its era, *Birth of a Nation*. It was in the context of praising this film that President Wilson made his comment about blacks being a danger to white civilization. Michael Rogin claims that one of the major consequences of the success of the film and book trilogy by Thomas Dixon upon which it is based is that "blacks became a sign of the negative American identity."[67]

The views of Jefferson and Wilson are still with us, albeit in muted form. There is less public speech that blatantly refers to blacks as inferiors, but those and similar sentiments were still very present as late as the 1990s. For example, there was still substantial white support in the 1990s for the view that blacks are inferior to whites. Fifty-four percent of whites in a national survey conducted in 1990 were perfectly comfortable stating that blacks are less intelligent than whites.[68] Too many Americans believe that they can identify a black criminal by merely looking at a black person. In what they thought was the privacy of their office, the top corporate officials at Texaco indulged in vile racist dialogue while discussing an anti-discrimination case that had been filed against them.[69]

The contemporary demonization of blacks goes beyond the themes of black inferiority and criminal threat. It also extends into the realm of the political. As we saw in earlier in the chapter, when an African American political consensus, such as on how to interpret the aftermath to Katrina, is markedly different from the white consensus, the black viewpoint is labeled malicious, out-of-bounds, self-destructive, and is otherwise held up to ridicule. Rogin points out that in some periods holding such different perspectives leads to social and political isolation as it has for blacks in this period. He argues, "Those who stepped beyond the bounds of legitimate controversy faced not so much punishment by the state as estrangement from the social mass."[70]

In a way, this demonization of a set of social policies and set of political ideas by first labeling them black, and second declaring them outside of the bounds of acceptable political discourse, is a form of racial demonization with political implications more insidious than the use of the Willie Horton ad by the 1988 Bush campaign. For example, it seems reasonable that racism should be considered as at least a plausible partial explanation for social outcomes that affect blacks. The silencing of any voice that might want to consider race as even a partial explanation for the racial inequalities and racial conflict that plague this society seems at least curiously ahistorical, if not sinister. This was at the heart of the ridicule that black opinion was subject to after Katrina—the view that the response to the aftermath was racialized and that blacks suffered disproportionately. It went against a deeply held taboo set of beliefs that for the great majority of whites, the race "problem" had been solved and all that remained was a "Negro" problem—a problem of a pathological population that caused itself and others great harm.

Claiming that the speech of the demonized is outside acceptable grounds of discourse is not limited to claims about the "problems" with demonized "citizens." Many liberals, including many on the left, argue that in this case black demands should be excluded because they raise particularistic demands, not the universal ones that should be the subject of democratic deliberation—particularly of the type advocated by theorists such as John Rawls and Habermas. Indeed, many left-leaning social theorists such as Todd Gitlin, Fred Cooper, Richard Rorty, and Rogers Brubaker have all claimed that the weakness of the U.S. progressive movement is due to the focus on the particularistic demands first of blacks, and then of other "identity" groups, starting in the late 1960s.[71] More centrist commentators such as Theodore White and Tom and Mary Edsall have specifically claimed that with the shift to black power, black discourse left the realm of the acceptable and could be safely, easily, and justly ignored by white Americans and their political organizations.

This set of claims was not new in the latter third of the twentieth century—the same claims were made by southern politicians in the period following the Civil War in response to constitutional amendments and legislation designed to protect the newly freed ex-slaves. White leftists at the turn of the last century admonished black progressives for raising particularistic issues such as lynching (which was at its terroristic height during this period) or Jim Crow instead of "universal issues" (such as worker rights for white males). What changed in the late 1960s was that African Americans and others lost for that time the constant political battle to have their claims recognized as intrinsically political, of universal concern to those who wanted to build democracy, and ones that should be central to, not excluded from political discourse.[72]

This defeat was due in part to the shift to a neoliberal black politics that reinforces the interpretation of black claims as merely those of just another special interest group. This move also coincided with the hegemonic dominance of the "public of publics" by the right, whose domestic agenda was not only to move black issues from the agenda, but also to render such claims unjustifiable and outrageous. Interestingly, Martin Luther King Jr. and, in some ways even more so, Malcolm X insisted that their claims be seen as universal claims based on human (for Malcolm not civil) rights, and both also were quite clear in labeling white resistance to black claims as being particularistic and interest-based. Both framed their movement's demands in much more universal and political terms than most black leaders use today. Political theorist Linda Zerilli explains the consequences of liberal demonization of black speech and political demands. "The issue at stake here, after all, is the sense of exclusion that some groups experience in relationship to the structures and institution of liberal democracies which, in their view, not only fail to represent their interests, but more importantly, which block their access to the spaces of political life."

Rogin points out the danger for demonized groups when these various facets of demonization combined: "The criminalization of political differences, the collapse of politics into disease, the spread of surveillance, and the stigmatization of dissenters as social pariahs have all played important roles in the suppression of radical politics. They have done so not merely through the pressures of public opinion, as in Tocqueville's analysis, but through the armed force of the state."[73] A group that is mentally inferior, prone to crime, and holds unacceptably radical and purportedly mistaken political opinions is not a group you want to invite to your political discussions about the future of a nation. It is a group that you can feel relatively comfortable in freezing out of political discussions about the future of a city or region after a massive disaster. There is also a more dangerous implication for blacks in the aftermath of Katrina. A demonized population, one considered outside the bounds of society and the polity—one, as Ferme argues, that is viewed as not fully civilized—is also a group that is owed very few obligations by state or society. Demonization of black Katrina survivors, already members of a demonized group, makes it easier to ignore their interests and plight as planning for the future is conducted and claims in the present are adjudicated. If whole groups of people are declared outside of the polity and whole sets of ideas and policies are declared subversive and suspect, not only do the prospects for racial discourse and reconstruction rapidly diminish, but the democratic institutions of America are endangered.

In a racially ordered society, civil society and public spheres are often the source, not the democratic solution, for racial oppression and disadvantage. Liberal theory has certainly been interpreted in practice by the founders and their successors (both those in politics and those in the academy) to mean that the obligations, rights, and privileges of polity and society do not apply to those who by nature are deemed outside of civilization (modern theorists have recently also begun to document how this view is also deeply present in eighteenth- and nineteenth-century European liberal theory and practice).[74] Therefore, we cannot count on the theorized sites of democratic practice and discourse to "self-correct" and act to include racially excluded populations in a society still substantially governed by a hierarchical racial order that structures civil society and public spheres.[75] Only sustained political struggle both on the ground and in the ideological realm can hope to break the racial order, including changing processes of socialization so they no longer routinely reproduce narratives of demonization. Only then will we be able to begin to realize the democratic promises of a "public of publics" that includes historically demonized African Americans.

WHAT LESSONS DOES THE AFTERMATH TO KATRINA PROVIDE progressive and black activists? A simple lesson to be learned, one that the American left has not learned in over a century and a half, is that in America, race and class both fundamentally matter. Katrina teaches us about the savagery of class disadvantage, as Reed argues in the *Nation*. But Katrina also teaches that racial disadvantage in the United States cannot be reduced to class disadvantage or regarded as in some sense secondary to class oppression. This is a lesson Reed often forgets, and the white left has never learned. Forgetting this lesson leads Reed to make the following prediction shortly after the hurricane devastated the Gulf Coast:

Class will almost certainly turn out to be a better predictor than race of who was able to evacuate, who drowned, who was left to fester in the Superdome or on overpasses, who is stuck in shelters in Houston or Baton Rouge, or who is randomly dispersed to the four winds. I'm certain that class is also a better predictor than race of whose emotional attachments to the place will be factored into plans for reconstructing the city.

Reed also argues in the same article, "Race is too blunt an analytical tool even when inequality is expressed in glaring racial disparities. Its meanings are too vague. . . . A racial critique can lead nowhere except to demands for black participation in decision-making around reconstruction."[76] One would think that by now the progressive community would have learned that the instruments of race, class, and gender are all too blunt for analyzing the complicated patterns of oppression in this country. For example, a critique that took race as a central, but not the sole, axis of disadvantage in post-Katrina New Orleans would make several demands beyond "black participation in decision-making." One demand would have been for participation in decision-making; a more basic demand from the same "black" perspective would have been for evacuees in the Katrina Diaspora to have the absolute right to vote in the 2006 spring municipal elections and for the state to provide the mechanisms necessary for dispersed evacuees to easily cast their votes. More generally another demand would be for the "right to return." The right to return must be coupled with a demand for the evacuees' neighborhoods—most of which are not only black, but poor and working class as well—to be rebuilt. Indeed, black activists partnered with the unions to provide not only for the rebuilding of black working-class neighborhoods, but also for the jobs to be provided during reconstruction and afterward to be unionized. There is a century-long radical tradition within black politics that has successfully combined organizing around race and class—it has been much less successful in organizing around gender issues. The aftermath to Katrina has highlighted once again that nothing in the United States has sufficiently changed to warrant shifting progressives attention from the systemic disadvantages that stem from either race or class—systemic disadvantages that would still entail profound economic, social, and political changes in the United States if they were addressed.[77]

The left will never be successful unless it can be considerably more nuanced in both theory and practice as it attempts to negotiate intersections of race, class, and gender. It is not just that disadvantage multiplies for some groups due to intersectionality, but it means that political responses must (1) understand the often complex nuances of how structural disadvantage is expressed within a given context; (2) be clear that in some circumstances one or the other of disadvantages might still be more prominent than the others (one could argue that race and class jointly and race separately were the most prominent set of disadvantages expressed as a result of the Katrina aftermath); and that therefore (3) our understanding of the complex range or intersections should lead us not to denigrate activists and communities that are dealing with some slice of a wider set of disadvantages; but that (4) given the history of the U.S. left, we should criticize those who, due to their privileging of one or more set of disadvantages, misread and deny the salience of selected disadvantages—as the white left and its allies systematically do with racial disadvantage and as the mainstream of the black movement has done with patriarchy.

Data presented in the previous section show, for example, that it is the racialization of public spheres and counterpublics that explains blacks' and whites' opinions on both how to interpret the aftermath and what policies to pursue in the future. Neither class nor gender played anything close to as powerful a role in shaping opinion after Katrina. It was the black elderly who were the most likely to die, and the black poor the most likely to be trapped and dispersed throughout the nation. The data from earlier in the chapter showed that those who were in the camps in Texas were mostly very poor and overwhelmingly black. We know from decades of research that the majority of those who will attempt to rebuild shattered poor and working-class communities and families will be black women, who face a number of additional obstacles due to systemic disadvantages that flow from the intersection of race, class, and gender. Yet a MoveOn memo dated Tuesday, August 29, 2006, which called for mobilization around the first anniversary of the hurricane, did not mention race, blacks, or racial disparities as one of the many talking points, nor indeed within the entire memo. The MoveOn memo captured the white left's version of what we found among whites in our public opinion study—the aftermath to the Katrina disaster has nothing to teach about racial equality in the United States. The MoveOn memo was as deracialized as the entire set of white responses presented in this study. The left and progressive movement is often complicit in reinforcing the national silence on race through both their denial that race remains (or ever was) a fundamental cleavage of oppression in the United States, and their fear of alienating some whites if racial justice is pursued too vigorously—and thus another sterling opportunity to both mobilize and address staggering racial injustice is lost.

Progressives should also draw a lesson from Katrina that reliance on civil society to rectify inequalities is a mistake. Progressives need not be shy in demanding state action, on a massive scale if need be, to address the political, economic, and social equalities both illuminated and exacerbated by Katrina and its aftermath.

The aftermath to Katrina also provides important lessons for black activists. The late political theorist Judith Shklar, in her book *American Citizenship*, argued that two key components of one's standing as a citizen in this country are the right to vote and the opportunity to earn. Both have been undermined in the wake of Katrina—and the result is being politically engineered just as the more general disenfranchisement of African Americans in the South was engineered a century ago. The mechanisms are not so different—elections rules are crafted that disproportionately disadvantage blacks, often based on blacks' relative lack of material resources. I would argue that the rules for the mayoral election shared at least a family resemblance to mechanisms such as the poll tax, which proved so successful at the turn of the previous century.

The devastation of the associational base of black civil society in New Orleans and the consequent severe undermining of the black counterpublic was a predictable consequence of the hurricane's aftermath, given the lack of resources and power possessed by the local black community. More surprising, some might argue, has been the demonstrated weakness of the national black counterpublic. This weakness has been demonstrated in at least two major ways. First, if we reflect on the data I first presented in this chapter, it is clear that the framing that African Americans possessed—that the aftermath of Katrina reconfirmed as of 2005 the still existing deep racial inequalities in this country, and that the government's slow and inept response was due at least in part to racially induced indifference to the victims—was rejected by a majority of white Americans.[78] It is particularly surprising that the proposition that Katrina exposed once again the deep racial inequalities that plague this nation was rejected, given that at the time of the disaster much of the mainstream media such as CNN, NBC, and the other major networks explicitly promoted such a framework in much of their coverage. Yet by the time our survey entered the field in late October 2005, that frame had been rejected by a majority of whites. By January 2006 columnists such as Cathy Young of the *Boston Globe* were labeling discussions of the disparate racial impact of Katrina "racial paranoia," while James Taranto of the *Wall Street Journal*, as stated earlier, was labeling black opinion on Katrina as misguided and "unhelpful" at best.[79] The national black counterpublic was not powerful enough to insert the framework for analysis that was represented in the overwhelming majority of black opinion as a legitimate framework for consideration. Blacks lacked the political power both locally and nationally to make their viewpoints legitimate and subject to national discourse within the publics of publics. One reason for this lack of success, I argued, was due to the subordinate nature of black public opinion. An associated reason was the power of demonizing stereotypes that are easily mobilized during incidents such as the aftermath to Katrina and which infest the talk shows and other media outlets that provide a dominating source for many white Americans' racial outlooks. Without the ability to affect the discourse in the "public of publics," the policy process and mainstream politics more generally cannot be affected. And subordinate groups cannot have their counterpublic's opinion represented in the "public of publics" without generating substantial political power. Blacks and their allies were not able to generate sufficient political power either through or outside the electoral system.

The second way that the weakness of the black counterpublic was manifested was in its inability to mobilize sufficient political power to influence the rules of the game of the election—and by implication, the future shape of the rebuilding of the city. It was not for a lack of sympathy or concern among blacks, including the black middle class. Black professional associations raised generous funds, and across the nation black students organized to spend their vacation time in rebuilding efforts. But much of black leadership has bought into the neoliberal ideology that defines organizational activity as lobbying, that is built on individualist leadership models, and which emphasizes civil society as the sole route to group advancement. Again ironically, public sphere theory in its current incarnation provides a pragmatic road map (to the degree it does so at all), which at least in the Habermasian version reinforces a set of strategies that when practiced by themselves are a political dead end. Further, the range of contrary voices within the black counterpublic is more constrained than it has been at any time since the turn of the last century. The lack of mobilization was linked to a distinct lack of allies available to African Americans during the Katrina crisis. In the past, black politics was capable of not only mobilizing black communities, but also of generating and mobilizing allies from other communities.

The lack of black political mobilization highlights another key political aspect of the Katrina saga. Katrina has not proved to be the transformative historical event some may have anticipated. Bill Sewell outlines the criteria for coding a set of events in history as one of a transformative "historical event."[80] These criteria include provoking a cascade of subsequent major events; changing major political, cultural, and/or social structures; and the transformation of modes of power as well. The aftermath to Katrina neither transformed major structures nor launched a cascade of critical events in the same way, for example, that either the taking of the Bastille did for what became revolutionary France (Sewell's example), or Rosa Parks and the Montgomery Bus Boycott did for the U.S. Civil Rights Movement. But why not?

Some of the conditions that could transform an event like Katrina into a historic event were in place. There are new forms of public spheres, cyberbased in many cases, as Jean Cohen points out; and a long debilitating war combined with a fiscal policy that has shifted economic hardship not only to the poor and working class, but also to the middle classes, has stressed and dislocated a variety of cultural, economic, and social structures—another precondition identified by Sewell. These conditions were taken advantage of by the immigrant rights movement, but not by activists and citizens who were most affected by Katrina. Further, it may be the case that this warrants and is producing further investigation. Black political identification may well have been strengthened by the events that occurred in the wake of Katrina.[81] Finally, Katrina and its aftermath was the type of event that was local in scope, but that resonated well beyond local or even regional boundaries. Nevertheless, in the end Katrina and its aftermath neither produced a cascade of events nor transformed hierarchical social structures.

The protests of the NAACP leadership, as righteous as they may be, stand in pale contrast not only to the hundreds of thousands who have hit the street in support of immigrant rights (a set of events that may well qualify as a historic event in Sewell's terms), but also contrast sharply with the vigorous militant mobilizations of the last century. The vigorous mobilizations of the Civil Rights and Black Power movements were produced through the strategies that emerged out of the theoretical debates that raged within the black counterpublic and were executed by the organizations and social forces within black civil society. For subordinate populations, the lesson has been forgotten; political power and political mobilization are needed not only to win rights, but to safeguard them as well. The work of black civil society has never proved to be sufficient to secure black rights without being paired with active, mass, independent political action. This is particularly the case when demonization of African Americans leads to nearly 60 percent (59 percent) of white Americans stating that the reported disenfranchisement of blacks in the 2000 presidential elections was either "not so big a problem," "not a problem at all," or a "fabrication of the Democratic Party."[82] The demonization of African Americans extends directly into the political realm as a large majority of whites either believe that it doesn't matter much if blacks are disenfranchised or that charges of disenfranchisement are fraudulent. The lack of urgency in assisting dispersed blacks from voting in the 2005 New Orleans municipal elections reflects this same disregard for black citizenship rights and underscores the importance for blacks to maintain an independent capacity to mobilize outside of the electoral system.[83] What Katrina has to teach us, neoliberal fantasies aside, is that while much has changed with the status of African Americans, that status is still precarious enough that vigorous mass political action remains a necessity, not a luxury. I'll conclude with the words of Frederick Douglass from 1857:

> Power concedes nothing without a demand. It never did, and it never will. Find out just what any people will quietly submit to, and you will have found out the exact measure of injustice and wrong which will be imposed upon them, and these will continue till they are resisted with either words, blows, or both.[84]

3 THE OBAMA CAMPAIGN AND THE MYTH OF A POST-RACIAL AMERICA

The depths of despair reached after Katrina seem to have been matched by the heights of (semi-)euphoria gripping African Americans in the early fall of 2008. But how deeply did the Obama campaign transform black opinion? Does the racial gap in American public opinion persist even though African Americans became more optimistic? More generally, does black euphoria suggest that President Obama's election marks the advent of a post-racial America?

This chapter begins with sketches of the racial politics of the campaign and the early days of the Obama administration. It was during the campaign that African Americans became the most optimistic about the prospects for achieving racial justices in the United States. Many, mainly white, observers also argued that Obama's election convincingly demonstrated that the nation had entered a new post-racial phase. Even during the campaign, however, there were signs suggesting that this optimism might be misplaced and that the Obama era may herald a dangerous new chapter in American racial politics.

I use the public opinion data to challenge the claim that America has entered a new "post-racial" era. I probe the contemporary state of racial dynamics and public opinion, concentrating both on changes that have appeared in black public opinion and on the resilience of the racial gap in American public opinion. In the conclusion to this chapter and throughout the remaining chapters of the book, I examine the extent to which the Obama phenomenon has transformed the very nature of black politics.

CAMPAIGN NOTES

On March 18, 2008, in the shadow of the Liberty Bell, Barack Obama delivered one of the most memorable speeches on racial conflict that the American people have ever heard from a candidate for president of the United States.[1] Race had not been a central theme of the Obama campaign up to that point. Indeed, quite the opposite. A firestorm had erupted around statements made over the years by Obama's Chicago minister, the Reverend Jeremiah Wright, forcing then-candidate Obama to detail his own views on race in America. This was one of a series of episodes that defined the racial politics of the 2008 campaign. Another involved bitter, racially tinged exchanges between the Hillary Clinton and Obama camps during the primary race for the Democratic nomination. Having won the nomination, Obama and his campaign became the target of increasingly shrill and racist attacks from both the mainstream and fringes of the conservative movement. Each of these episodes forced Obama to publicly define his views on race through both his actions and inactions. This section analyzes aspects of these events to better understand how black public opinion, as well as racial politics in the United States more generally, began to be transformed as the result of the campaign and the early days of the Obama presidency. These episodes also illustrate the continuing challenges that confront black politics. I start with the furor over the racial politics of Reverend Wright.

REVEREND WRIGHT AND BLACK POLITICAL IDEOLOGIES

Candidate Obama was mistaken. He was mistaken in his comments concerning the Reverend Jeremiah Wright, the Chicago preacher who had been Obama family's pastor and in the midst of the campaign became the subject of fierce attacks in the media. The problem was not, as he put it, referring to the 1960s, that Wright "has a lot of the baggage of those times." The problem was also not, as one newspaper characterized Obama's position on his minister, that Wright was stuck in a "time warp," in a period defined by racial division. No, the real problem was that the views for which Wright was being roundly criticized in the dominant media are well within the mainstream opinion of the black population. As public opinion researchers know, despite all the oratory about racial unity and the transcending of race, this country remains deeply racially divided—especially in the realm of politics. During the campaign, it was President Obama who demonstrated that he was out of step with the mainstream of black America.

The problem is that mainstream white America has a problem with the politics of mainstream black America. Most white people, and the mainstream media, tend to be horrified (in a titillating voyeuristic type of way) whenever they "look under the hood" and see what's really on blacks folks' mind. Generations ago James Baldwin described this white perception of blacks, blending poetry with a hint of the sinister. It is not the open hostility of a Bigger Thomas—Richard Wright's doomed and violent character in *Native Son*—that white people fear, writes Baldwin.

> It is the others, who smile, who go to church, who give no cause for complaint, whom we sometimes consider with amusement, with pity, even with affection—and in whose faces we sometimes surprise the merest arrogant hint of hatred, the faintest, withdrawn, speculative shadow of contempt—who make us uneasy . . . ; who to us remain unknown, though we are not . . . unknown to them.[2]

By 2008 it was the belief of nearly 80 percent of whites that blacks had already or would soon achieve racial equality. Just three years earlier, more than 80 percent of blacks believed that racial justice for blacks in the United States would either not be achieved at all or not in their lifetimes. In March 2003, with polls showing strong support among whites for an invasion of Iraq, a large majority of blacks declared themselves opposed to military intervention. We saw in chapter 1 that this opposition only strengthened in the ensuing years. Results from my survey, in the field during the week that the United States went to war, showed that a very large majority of blacks thought it one's patriotic duty to protest against the war they opposed. A majority of whites felt that protest was unpatriotic. This same type of divide appears in evaluations of the aftermath of Hurricane Katrina, of President Bush during the first six years of his administration, of Clinton during most of his administration, and of Reagan for the entirety of his two terms.[3] It is possible for whites and blacks both to react to this divergence with astonishment, bearing as it frequently does on what should be fundamentally consensual realities. Yet, as Baldwin suggests, blacks are on the whole well aware of white political orientations, while most whites most of the time remain blissfully unaware of black political views—and are horrified when they find out the "truth."

To express this point in more specific terms, Reverend Wright's blend of leftism and Afrocentrism remains one of the classic patterns of black political ideology. His philosophy is very similar to that of a number of honored black theologians, including the esteemed Reverend James Cone of Union Theological Seminary. Indeed, one could argue that Reverend Wright's criticism of racial dynamics in the United States and American foreign policy is milder than the biting criticism of American capitalism and imperialism found in the speeches of Dr. Martin Luther King Jr. during the last years of his life. Through the 1990s, 70 percent of black Americans believed the country to be unfair to blacks and the poor.[4] This is all to say that the black community has been and remains angry about race relations in this country. The black community was angry about the bankrupt foreign policy that the nation has pursued since before 9/11. Blacks were and are angry about what is perceived to be the political and moral blindness of white Americans. With the exception, perhaps, of black conservatives, this anger is spread across the black ideological spectrum. Black nationalists, black leftists, black feminists, and black liberals may differ on their solutions for America's ills, but they all generally agree on the need for dismantling a well-entrenched racial hierarchy.

So Barack Obama was wrong. Reverend Wright does not represent outdated thinking. The last time a scientific survey of black political ideologies was conducted, a large segment of the black population fell into the category of those who believed in the principles of liberalism, yet held no hope, the survey indicated, that this country would ever live up to its democratic and liberal creed. Even in the Obama campaign–generated euphoria found in the fall of 2008, half of blacks remained bitterly pessimistic about African Americans' future in the country. And nearly all blacks still believed that racism was a problem in the United States. The critical views expressed by Wright are all too rooted in the present. The racial divisions that Obama seeks to transcend with his message of hope and unity are not a feature of the past, but a deep structural fixture in this nation's present.

President Obama will be continually called upon by the mainstream media to prove that he is not a black nationalist like Minister Louis Farrakhan or an Afrocentric leftist like Reverend Wright. The suspicion will always be that he holds opinions closer to those expressed by Wright than the ones he voiced in the campaign. And the temptation will always be to distance himself from black opinion in order to reassert his liberal bone fides as the "post-racial" president of all Americans. But if President Obama wants to see the euphoria his election generated in the black community sustained, he will have to realize that he cannot run away from the issue of race and racial division. He will have to find a language that both addresses our hopes for the future and recognizes the difficulties and divisions of the present. As reassuring as it may be to white Americans, a denial of the past and a refusal to discuss the ongoing injustices of the present will not, even in the short term, lead to a blissful racial utopia.

It is supremely ironic, and might sound surprising, that Barack Obama, the centrist candidate who sought to bury race as an issue by attempting to bury his own mildly black nationalist former pastor, quite likely owes his election to the continued power of black nationalism. To make this claim credible, we first need some definitions. Black nationalism is the political ideology that takes race as the fundamental dividing line in the United States. Black nationalists believe that the first political, cultural, economic, and/or social priority is for black people to come together. Further, black nationalism calls for various degrees of political, economic, cultural, and/or social separation from white people. Race, in this view, becomes a primary determinant for making political judgments. For a century and a half, black nationalism has provided the main ideological challenge to the liberal, social democratic sensibilities that have usually dominated black politics. It is likely that Senator Obama's support among African Americans would have remained divided without the continued ideological influence of black nationalism.

Black nationalism is not equivalent to black solidarity. While black nationalists call for black solidarity (solidarity being defined here as black people coming together to defend each other and engage in collective action), so do black activists of other ideologies. Black liberals such as Frederick Douglass, Ida B. Wells, W. E. B. Du Bois, and Martin Luther King Jr. all called for black people to come together to struggle for justice, but none of these figures was a black nationalist. Black liberalism, in contrast to nationalism, is a broad political ideology that emphasizes support for individual rights, is generally pro-capitalist, and claims to be inclusive and tolerant of others. The black variant of liberalism is also much more egalitarian, more social democratic, than that found in mainstream America.[5]

While Obama himself falls in the liberal ideological camp, the black movement that developed in support of his campaign had more than a few of the markings of black nationalism. Early in the campaign, Obama and Clinton were dividing the black vote. That changed with the caucuses in Iowa and the primaries in New Hampshire and South Carolina. Black support for Obama swelled for several reasons. First, as many observers have noted, African Americans earlier that year were much more skeptical than whites about Obama's ability to attract sufficient numbers of white voters. This began to change after the Iowa caucuses and the New Hampshire primary. Second, like many Americans, African Americans were somewhat unfamiliar with Obama, despite his having won a Senate seat from Illinois. While these two factors would have undoubtedly increased Obama's share of the black vote relative to Senator Clinton's (and, in the early stages, to John Edwards's), they do not, even taken together, fully explain the massive swing to Obama among African Americans.

Jesse Jackson, in his two bids for the presidency over two decades ago, did not receive the type of support from blacks that President Obama achieved until his second campaign in 1988. Jackson was better known and more warmly perceived among blacks in the 1980s than Obama was before his post-caucus surge in popularity. Yet according to exit polls, Jackson received "only" 77 percent of black votes in the Democratic primaries nationwide, with a low of 68 percent in southern states and a high of 82 percent in northwestern states. It was only in the 1988 primary campaign that Jackson dominated to the extent that Obama did in the 2008 campaign, routinely pulling 90-plus percent from black voters. So why did Obama outperform Jackson among blacks his first time out? In both cases there were sitting Republican presidents (Reagan and the junior Bush) whom opinion polls showed blacks intensely despised. And in both cases a substantial portion of the black political elite had pledged their support to a white Democratic leader with reasonably good ties to black communities (senators Mondale and Clinton).

However, the attacks against Obama by the Clinton campaign and its surrogates—such as Bob Johnson and Andrew Young—sparked massive black outrage, which quickly evolved into broad African American support for Senator Obama. Closing ranks around an African American leader perceived to be unfairly under attack is a long and honorable tradition, reaching back to the nineteenth century, and is a hallmark of black solidarity. As noted, black solidarity need not be nationalist. Nevertheless, the support Obama began gathering after the South Carolina primary betrayed more than a hint of nationalism. As my former colleague the philosopher Tommie Shelby argues, one of the strengths of black nationalism as an ideology is that it provides a way for blacks to take collective action and defend African American political leaders under attack.

Black nationalist ideology was also the source of some dangerous tendencies that emerged during the campaign. Nationalist campaigns tend to severely limit discussion and dissent. The argument goes, "We can't criticize the brother, because that would harm the brother." This tendency began to appear among some black Obama supporters when it seemed that the attacks of the Clinton campaign might have worked to deny Obama the opportunity to become the first black president of the United States. The suggestion was made that to be "authentically black" meant to support Obama. One dangerous feature of black nationalism is that difference of opinion is often suppressed in the name of the twin nationalist shibboleths of authenticity and unity. This same phenomena was used to criticize black critics of both Clarence Thomas's nomination to the Supreme Court and the Million Man March during the 1990s.

This line of thinking reduces the collective critical discourse about Obama's campaign, when there was much to be critical of. Finally, another key component of many nationalisms, and certainly a prominent feature in black nationalist circles (as well as among other black activists), is homophobia. The Obama campaign called on the Reverend Donnie McClurkin, a Grammy-winning gospel singer and stalwart in the fight against "the curse of homosexuality," to take part in the South Carolina primary campaign, prompting pointed criticisms by some members of the black gay and lesbian community.

My colleague Larry Bobo at the TheRoot.com has argued that one of Obama's strengths is that he had pulled together a "center-left" coalition, one that had been increasingly marginalized for some time in Democratic Party politics. Bobo's claim is probably true. What is not true is that Obama himself represented the "center-left" in terms of his own politics. Whether we are speaking of reforming health care or reducing carbon emissions, his domestic program is generally located at the center of the American political spectrum—which is the center-right of the black political spectrum. The same can be said of his foreign policy. Obama's politics are considerably to the right of most African Americans, as well as progressives more generally. Yet the nationalist surge in support of his campaign had a dampening and chilling effect on the willingness to criticize Obama, particularly from the left.

None of this means that blacks should not have voted for President Obama. Nor does it mean that even a majority of blacks voted for him due to nationalist sentiments. Nevertheless, there are good reasons to consider what developed during the presidential campaign as a new black nationalism. To understand why, we need to turn back to Shelby. The first point is that this new nationalism is located for the first time within the mainstream of black liberal politics. Second, it fuses nationalist discourses with liberal philosophy—which is why it can coexist relatively comfortably with the politics of traditional liberals such as Ted Kennedy. Thus we have here a middle-class black nationalism (similar to middle-class black nationalism of the past) with the potential for supporting substantial benefits to the black middle class, while leaving behind the large segment of black America that continues to be deeply disenfranchised. These are the people for whom the "American dream" largely remains an "American nightmare"—as Malcolm X described it. Just as black nationalism historically served as an effective critique of black liberalism, the black left has historically served as the most effective critic of black nationalism.

It is important for those on the black left not to abandon politics in disgust, as we have done too often in the past. Instead, it is the duty of progressive blacks to remain involved in black united fronts, while continuing in the tradition of Du Bois and Dr. King to provide a trenchant critique of both America and its political leaders, and fighting for a black politics that continues to struggle for social justice.

This was, after all, the main point of many of Reverend Wright's sermons.

(OCCASIONALLY) RACIST WHITE LIBERALS

The black quest for social justice, however, has often been frustrated by racist attitudes on the white left. Black leaders listened in disbelief and anger when they were told at the end of the nineteenth century that key segments of the socialist and labor movement refused to organize against lynching because it was a divisive issue that would undermine the unity of the working class. They were told that blacks suffered no special oppression and had no separate demands that needed to be addressed. Whether the issue was lynching at the turn of the last century or the Katrina disaster at the beginning of this century, large segments of the white left have adopted one of four unhelpful positions. First was the view that blacks constituted a backward part of American society—a group whose issues simply did not appear on the progressive agenda. Second, blacks were accepted as an important part of the proletariat, but racism was not seen as an important issue, and it could wait to be resolved until after working-class victory was achieved. Third, a variant of the second position was the one noted in regard to lynching: racism is recognized as a serious problem for blacks, but issues of central concern to blacks qua blacks are divisive, and so addressing them needs to be postponed. Fourth is simple ignorance and hostility displayed toward the purported distractions produced by black movements and activists.[6] During the Obama campaign, many white liberals and some progressives evinced hostility toward the African American supporters of the candidate that fell comfortably within the racist traditions of the backward segments of the left. Princeton historian Sean Wilentz, a vigorous Clinton supporter during the 2008 primary campaign, occupied this fourth category.

Wilentz leveled an odd charge against Barack Obama. He accused the then-senator's campaign of attempting to hijack the Democratic presidential nomination by arguing its claim to the nomination based on having more pledged delegates than candidate Clinton, as well as a larger percentage of the popular vote. Wilentz urged that Clinton be regarded as the winner of the nomination contest because she would have won easily had the rules been different. Availing himself of technical political science terminology, he claimed that Clinton would have "stomped" Obama if the contests had been run under the same winner-take-all rules that governed Republican primaries. Wilentz did not ever consider that perhaps, just perhaps, Obama would have run a different campaign if he had been operating under a different set of rules. Wilentz made no attempt to be objective. For several months during the primaries, his main task was to demonize Obama and his campaign at every hysterical opportunity.

Incredibly, in the February 27 online edition of the *New Republic*, Wilentz made the obscenely fallacious, but evidently for many seductive, charge that the Obama campaign had been polluting political discourse by shamelessly playing the race card.[7] In this view, the regular invocations of Obama's past cocaine use, Bill Clinton's egregious comparison of Obama's campaign to Jesse Jackson's runs for the nomination in the 1980s, Andrew Young's sly attack on Obama's questionable status as a "black man," or Bob Kerrey's clumsy claim that Obama was educated in an Islamic madrassa—all of these racialized assaults were innocent and isolated incidents, so that to claim otherwise was playing the race card. These are but a few examples of the way in which discourse was manipulated in an attempt to reverse the truth about campaign strategies. There was also the matter of Clinton's "3 am Red Phone Call," the accusation (again by Wilentz) that black Democratic insider and CNN commentator Donna Brazile was making "wild charge[s]" when she said she found the tone of former President Clinton's remarks about Obama "depressing." Which, indeed, they were. Then-senator Clinton also made remarks that many people interpreted as belittling the accomplishments of the activists and leaders of the Civil Rights Movement. In her defense, Wilentz accused another leading black Democrat, Representative James Clyburn of South Carolina, of being bullied into aiding the Obama campaign when Clyburn, a veteran of the Civil Rights Movement, cautioned the Clinton campaign that "we have to be very, very careful about how we speak about that era in American politics."

As many experts on race and politics noted at the time, "playing the race card" would not have benefited the Obama campaign. The widespread idea was rather that race should be downplayed, based on a recognition by the strategists that a racial debate would make life much more difficult for candidate Obama. And it also would run the risk of fracturing a party badly in need of unity if it was to have any chance of defeating John McCain in November. It may be that no one was more mindful of this circumstance than the Obama strategists themselves, who were attempting to run a campaign that would transcend race.

I think my many colleagues and friends who were urging, or at least contemplating, a "black-out" (black boycott of the election) were mistaken. The stakes were too high to sit this one out or to use our votes for a candidate with no chance of winning. No progressive would seriously argue that the world, the nation, and the black community would not be far better off today if Bush and the Republican Party had not stolen the 2000 presidential election. During the 2008 campaign, was I advocating, as so many leftists have for over a century, that black people must be patient and wait "their turn" for some greater good, that black people overlook the racist nonsense espoused by so-called liberals in the name of some largely chimerical unity? No.

I urged that progressives take a harder road than either dutiful acquiescence or an election boycott at the national level. The need signaled by the Obama campaign was for black activists and other progressive forces to forge a comprehensive political platform that they could demand political candidates to live up to. The need was—and is—to organize teach-ins and community forums around the key issues, domestic and foreign, which are critical for turning the nation around and putting it on a progressive track that organizations such as ARC '09 conducts in the Midwest. We should be organizing in our communities around these issues and making it clear that candidates in 2010 and 2012 who do not support these political positions will be opposed. I was under no illusion during the campaign that either Democratic candidate would aggressively pursue a progressive and redistributive social justice agenda under current conditions. Barack Obama as well as Hillary Clinton, Al Gore, and other likely party leaders are all centrist Democrats—a category of politician whose politics, to my mind, are not congruent with the needs of the disadvantaged. In four years, we must be in a position where we either have a sitting president who is responsive to a progressive agenda or be in a position to nominate and elect more responsive candidates.

Progressive organizing and debate must include as a central focus race and the continued workings of white supremacy. The discourse on race, both on the left and more generally, must be transformed to such an extent that inflammatory attacks such as Wilentz's are discredited on their merits and no longer have the ability to convince those who are naive or (often willfully) ignorant on matters of race. We can no longer allow discourse around events like Katrina, as well as other devastating examples of the deadly force racial inequality still has on black communities, to be whitewashed by either the left or right. It may be the case that President Obama's own racial politics make this task even harder than it already is.

THE RACIAL POLITICS OF BARACK OBAMA

"I'm not somebody who believes that constantly talking about race somehow solves racial tensions." President Barack Obama made that statement rebuking Attorney General Holder for calling the United States a "nation of cowards" when it comes to discussing race. A number of black leaders were made uncomfortable by the comment, and on multiple grounds. First, many failed to understand why the president felt the need to rebuke Holder in the first place. Aside from the fact that what Holder said was true, he had already taken significant flak from the press and pundits for the statement and there seemed to be no need for the president to intervene. In addition, it is among the many actions (and inactions) committed so far by the administration signaling its aggressive refusal to come to grips with the nation's continuing racial divide. These black leaders agree, as do I, with john a. powell, director of the Kirwan Institute for the Study of Race and Ethnicity, who said, "A lot of people around Obama seem to think race is the third rail, and it's best to avoid it. Their major approach is 'We're going to do something for everybody.' But that's not really a solution."[8]

Obama's racial policy seems to be made up of three components: avoidance, trickle down, and, whenever talking about race becomes unavoidable or policies must be implemented, reconfirmation of the president's racial moderation. When asked about race, Obama tends to deflect the question, shifting the focus to the myriad crises afflicting the nation. When directly confronted with questions about how the dire crises that confront the black nation will be addressed, the administration's answer tends to be that their policies will help all of America—suggesting that the benefits will "trickle down" to the black community. Faced with the choice between joining the World Conference against Racism's follow-up to the Durban conference and allegedly appearing soft on Iran, the administration refused to participate.

The one time Obama has not been able to avoid race was during the Jeremiah Wright firestorm when he addressed the nation on March 18, 2008, from Constitution Hall in Philadelphia.

It was an amazing speech, a brilliant speech. It was brilliant both in substance and in delivery. He told a convincing, moving story about his own racial history. He was able to paint a truly hopeful, yet pragmatic, picture of why people should come together across races. He attempted to explain why he would not renounce Reverend Wright, because that would mean renouncing the black church and the black community. (Of course, later on, when the Wright story would not go away, he did just that.) In conclusion, Obama tried to shift the conversation to the set of critical domestic and foreign policy issues that progressives have wanted to tackle for years.

But the speech was too little. It was too little in that while addressing race, it equated white racial resentment (which scholars know is really just a polite label for white racism) with the black anger and skepticism that are the results of past and current racial discrimination. I suspect most blacks will give Obama a break on this score, at least for a while. But candidate Obama's comments did not satisfy those large segments of white America that harbor racial resentment. It was too little when he argued that we can move forward toward racial justice for all without the "need to recite the history of racial injustice." It was too little because even though he strongly and correctly argued that today's racial disadvantage is based on the white supremacy of the past, we know that many, many whites do not connect the situation of blacks today with injustices of any sort, whether past or present.

If current black disadvantage is to be explained, the history of racial injustice must be retold. It was an unfortunate moment when Obama said that blacks have been unwilling to come together in multi-racial coalitions. It was white liberals who walked away from the great multi-racial populist and labor coalitions of the late nineteenth and early twentieth century, during the Civil Rights era, and in more recent times. Each time with the predictable result of sparking greater support for black nationalist movements, such as those of Marcus Garvey, the Black Power Movement, and Minister Farrakhan.

What does this all tell us? If I am wrong, and I could be, then the nation may be ready to move forward on race, or at least to put race aside and tackle the issues that affect working- and middle-class people of all races. Many people I have communicated with about the speech, some black, some not, are convinced already that I am wrong, and that his brilliant speech was effective. It restored hope among his supporters and convinced many who had been skeptical that there was more to the man than just hollow rhetoric. All the while, however, the appearance is that only a black candidate as "politically white" as Obama can win high national office.

What do I mean by "politically white"? Here is where Obama's mistaken judgment about Reverend Wright comes in. At issue here is not how liberal or conservative African American politicians with national ambitions might be. The question is what kind of ties they have with grassroots and activist members of the black community, who hold conventional black political attitudes, and whether they are willing to break with them. We all know (or are) black nationalists, former black socialists, black feminists, liberals substantially to the left of most Democrats, and even the occasional black conservative. The great majority of us are exceedingly unlikely to denounce these family members, friends, and fellow congregants. We may not talk about them in mixed company (as Obama hinted in his speech) because we know what type of ugliness will follow, but neither will we cut them loose.

Why?

It is not only because often when we look at them we see ourselves, or our former selves, but because we understand the deep, continuing effects of structural black disadvantage; because we have personally experienced slights that remain a quotidian part of the black experience. If the Obama administration continues to treat racial issues, particularly those of importance to blacks, as toxic, the consequences will be what one might expect. We can expect a black community much more disillusioned with American politics than it was in the fall of 2008, and a nation that is continuing down a reckless course toward racial disaster.

AN INCREASINGLY VICIOUS RIGHT WING

Wide segments of the right, particularly on broadcast television, and the extreme right started pouring tankers of fuel on what had been the smoldering embers of white racial resentment as soon as it appeared that candidate Obama could win the election. The attacks were ratcheted up as it became increasingly clear that he likely would capture the presidency. For example, after the final presidential debate, both Karl Rove and *Slate*'s "Poll Tracker" electoral maps projected that if the election were held that day, Obama would win the presidency with 313 electoral votes, a massive electoral college victory. On that same day, the Associated Press reported that perhaps as many as 100,000 people attended an Obama rally in St. Louis, Missouri, making it the largest rally so far.[9] Charles M. Blow, an op-ed columnist for the *New York Times*, said that the election was already over, and if he was wrong he would drink Liquid-Plumr in penance. The next day, in a devastating critique of the McCain-Palin campaign, General Colin Powell endorsed Obama for president. This was the same day that the Obama campaign reported having raised an overwhelming total of $150 million in September.

On the following Monday, several sources reported Obama's lead shrinking both nationally and, more importantly, in key battleground states.

What was going on? Half a century ago, Malcolm X warned that when "we" started winning by their rules, "they" would change the rules. The desperate and despicable tactics of the McCain-Palin campaign vividly illustrated the lengths that the reactionaries who had dominated for most of the last quarter century would go in order to maintain power. There was less than one week left, but the racist attacks were stepped up to an unprecedented level. Many of these attacks were not only a threat to Obama's campaign, but, much more importantly, a threat to a just participatory democracy and an anti-racist civil society. The clear intent on the part of some pundits was to push the nation down a course leading to racial disaster. Even though President Obama achieved an overwhelming victory, there is a real danger that long-lasting damage has been done to the American polity by some of the reactionary tactics of parts of the media and the GOP.

Some GOP local chapters incited nothing short of racial hatred, with discernible effects across the country in energizing the racist dregs of the nation. Outside Chicago a local CBS News affiliate reported shortly before the election about a sign that had been erected portraying Obama as Bozo the Clown. The sign was surrounded by barbed wire and emblazoned with the familiar circle with a negative slash through it. The caption read, "No Brozos."[10] Photographs circulated on the Internet showing a white male with a T-shirt reading "N**gers Please. It is called the White House."

The GOP itself was complicit in evoking racist stereotypes. In California a local volunteer group produced an image of Obama's picture superimposed on a $10 food stamp—surrounded by pictures of ribs, watermelon, and fried chicken. The local party apparatus responsible for the flyer claimed unconvincingly that no one had realized the images were offensive. "It was just food to me," offered the head of the volunteer group. "It didn't mean anything else." Nevertheless, a local black Republican activist called the flyer "awful." In Virginia a local GOP official wrote a flyer ridiculing Obama's potential appointments and much of black America at the same time. Obama's "platform" would include hiring Ludacris to "paint the white house black," read the flyer. An Obama administration would increase foreign aid—"mostly to Africa" so that "the Obama family there can skim enough to allow them to feed their goats and live the American Dream." Obama's drug policy would be to "raise taxes to pay for drugs for Obama's inner-city political base." Referring to the torture technique used by U.S. interrogators in the name of the "war on terror," a GOP official in Sacramento, California, called for his troops to "waterboard" Obama. Another Virginia GOP group produced a flyer using Osama bin Laden's eyes, with the skin color darkened around them, pasted onto an anti-Obama poster. The text stated, "America must look evil in the eye and never flinch."

The group's claim that the flyer was not meant to be anti-Obama per se, in an environment in which Obama was constantly being linked to bin Laden, was preposterous. Nor was the fearmongering limited to state or local Republican groups. As Election Day neared, the McCain-Palin campaign and the RNC produced automated telephone calls (robo-calls) that were so vicious and untrue that several leading GOP figures denounced them. The goal of all of these attacks was to trigger enough racial resentment and animus to provoke white voters to turn away from Obama even if they agreed with him on most issues. The National Republican Trust PAC even resurrected Reverend Wright, something the McCain campaign had previously declared it would not do, as another racial issue designed to have whites vote their racial fears instead of their material interests.

Voter suppression was another phenomenon that threatened to deeply undermine the democratic process and the election's outcome. Salon.com had an excellent state-by-state summary of the efforts that the GOP conducted to disenfranchise likely Democratic voters—particularly black voters. And once again, the battleground states were the key focus. In Indiana, Pennsylvania, and Ohio, the GOP targeted predominantly black counties. Voting-rights activists claimed that 50 percent of those targeted in Florida were black and Latino. In Texas there has been a long-standing effort by some Republican officials to prevent students at heavily Democratic-leaning historically black colleges from voting legally. Once again the sanctity of the democratic process itself was sacrificed in the name of preserving a reactionary racist political order.

GOP operatives viciously stepped up their racist attacks going into the last week of the campaign. The chairwoman of a New Mexico GOP group called Obama a "Muslim socialist." A co-chairman of McCain's campaign, former Oklahoma governor Frank Keating, called Obama a guy of the street who not only was a former drug user, but a leftist whose politics were once "very extreme." And perhaps most horrifying was an attempt by Ashley Todd, a McCain volunteer, to create a do-it-yourself racist event. Todd claimed that a black man had assaulted and robbed her, and then carved a "B" into her face because she was a McCain supporter. She later recanted and admitted she had fabricated the entire incident. And even the "B" was backward.

Racialized attacks continued from the campaign into the early months of the Obama administration without losing a beat. Senator Jim DeMint, a South Carolina Republican, was horrified that President Obama has become the "world's best salesman of socialism." He grimly argued that conservatives will have to "take to the streets to stop America's slide into socialism." And if that is not alarming enough, former Arkansas governor Mike Huckabee had shrilly declared that the president's policies would be loved by "Lenin and Stalin." Two of the most vicious stereotypes involving blacks and politics stoked fears of black Muslims and black communists, evoking the Nation of Islam as well as more traditional black Muslims, on the one hand, and memories of the Black Panthers, on the other. President Obama was being portrayed as both.

These assaults came not only from the right, and they were not restricted to the then-senator. The July 21, 2008, cover of the *New Yorker* depicted both Barack and Michelle Obama using vicious racial stereotypes. In line with its title, "The Politics of Fear,"[11] the cover suggests that both the 1970s-era armed black radical and twenty-first-century black Muslim are now flag-burning collaborators, posing an imminent and deadly threat to the Republic. And while the *New Yorker* claimed the cover was supposed to be ironic, people on the not-so-fringe right treat these images as absolute truth. They view the first couple as the avatars of the imminent advent of tyranny and speak coldly of the violent steps necessary to preserve the Republic. The decision makers at the *New Yorker* had every reason to believe that their liberal readership would understand the irony that the cover sought to provoke. Yet in this current media environment, they also should have realized that the image would be used for and widely interpreted in a manner far different than intended. They had the responsibility to understand how others, not just their intended audience, would interpret the image and what the image's overall impact would be.

Perhaps most sickening of all, Fox News' Glenn Beck dedicated one of his shows during the week of February 23, 2009, to "war gaming" the coming civil war against Obama-led tyranny. While claiming at the beginning of the February 23 to show that "the views in this program are not predictions of what will happen, but could happen," by the end of the program Beck's guests were walking a knife edge between prediction and advocacy of armed insurrection.[12] They start mid-program talking about the "Bubba effect." Conservative whites, according to Beck's former military and intelligence agency guests, will withdraw from society and start "profiling . . . those that enter their space that are threatening to them." Who are these threatening people? Those that "are not going to look like a bubba." When Beck tries to "moderate" the discussion by asking how to "defuse" what his guests are now describing as an armed insurrection, a "civil war," they reply, "Well, I don't think you would want to defuse it, Glenn. . . . All of the problems we have talked about in one way or another are the result of the American government either overspending or overreaching." His guests conclude by stat-

FIGURE 2: The infamous *New Yorker* Obama cover.

ing, "But to be frank with you, you know, Civil War—history repeats itself. And I don't think that you will have brothers fighting each other like we did back in the Civil War. We've learned our lesson."

Not to be outdone, Rush Limbaugh on his May 11, 2009, program made the racial connotations of the charges against the Obama administration even clearer. Echoing National Republican Congressional Committee head Representative Pete Sessions, a Republican from Texas, that Obama was intentionally trying to wreck the economy and "inflict damage and hardship on the free enterprise system,"[13] Limbaugh spouted the following incendiary claims:

> The deterioration reflects lower tax revenues and higher costs for bank failures, unemployment benefits, and food stamps. But in the Oval Office of the

White House none of this is a problem. This is the objective. The objective is
unemployment. The objective is more food stamp benefits. The objective is
more unemployment benefits. The objective is an expanding welfare state. And
the objective is to take the nation's wealth and return it to the nation's quote,
"rightful owners." Think reparations. Think forced *reparations*. Think *forced
reparations here if you want to understand what actually is going on*.[14]

President Obama opposes reparations for African Americans, as many
commentators have pointed out. In August 2009, in the middle of the general election campaign, he publicly stated his opposition to reparations.
Since becoming president, he has continued to demonstrate his opposition.
One of the reasons offered by the State Department for the United States
not attending the follow-up to the World Conference against Racism was
the pro-reparations language found in the pre-conference documents. Facts,
however, do not deter any of the wild claims raining down from the right,
warning that the Obama administration is leading the nation into a tyranny
that will leave "Bubba" no choice but to water the tree of liberty with the
blood of patriots.

The fringe right is listening. A memo from the Department of Homeland Security was leaked in mid-April 2009, indicating the danger of violence being initiated by right-wing extremists, motivated by, among other
things, the election of a black president. As Charles M. Blow of the *New York
Times* stated, "While only a tiny number of conservatives and veterans are
members of hate groups, nearly all hate groups do indeed follow far-right
ideology."[15]

What is it that has the right so fired up? For some, simply losing to a
black man is anathema. For most of the right, the return to a relatively sane
and fairer tax policy provides ample reason to advocate at least nonviolent
revolt. The dismantling of the Reagan-era thinking and policies that have
sustained the American right as a movement for more than a generation is
unacceptable. On one level, the prospect of liberal tax reform gives the right
an easy rallying point. Obama's attempt to have the rich bear a larger—and
fairer—share of the tax burden is being labeled "class war" by many on the
right and a few so-called moderates. In a sense, they are right; this is old-
fashioned, social-democratic redistributive politics—which in the United

States is mistaken for class warfare. This type of politics used to be the central feature of the Democratic Party's political economy from the days of the New Deal to those of the Great Society. Thirty-plus years of conservative Republican and Democratic presidents have led to a national memory loss about what a progressive economic program—one that benefits the vast majority of citizens—looks like.

In a deeper, more profound sense, however, the right's shrill complaints about the advent of class war are deeply hypocritical. In the 1980s some conservative elites were more honest about the dynamics of "class war." I had a brilliant conservative colleague in graduate school who once remarked that both British Prime Minister Margaret Thatcher and Ronald Reagan were waging class war, but that Thatcher had won her battles while Reagan had not yet been fully victorious.

What this era's American conservatives are refusing to acknowledge is that for eight years Bush led a looting of the American treasury through tax policies, Iraq War contracts, and the deregulation of financial institutions that further enriched the wealthiest families and favored corporations, the result of which is a horrific national debt and a global economy in shambles. That was class warfare, and we saw economic inequality rise to astounding new levels under this regime. The right has been waging the most vicious class war for a generation. Their problem, to quote Malcolm X, is that "the chickens have come home to roost." Obama is no more a socialist than was FDR. Like Roosevelt, he views it as his mission to save capitalism, despite its richest elites. That task requires both more regulation and a quick correction of some of the worse economic injustices of the past thirty years of conservative rule.

But the right is refusing to go quietly. Conservatives are embarked on a smear campaign to discredit and destroy the new Democratic president. At the Conservative Political Action Committee conference held during the end of February 2009, we heard that Obama was not really born in the United States (this was before the "Birther" movement had gained the national attention that it soon would), and his election to the presidency was therefore illegitimate. Alabama Senator Richard Shelby was caught endorsing this preposterous claim back in his home state. We have already noted that allegedly sober and responsible Republican leaders, not content with calling Obama a socialist, were comparing his policy proposals to those of Lenin and Stalin. Conservative leaders urged their supporters to take to the streets, to "build a civil rights movement" to take the country back—as if it were being occupied by a foreign power.

After the inauguration, racial slurs remained pervasive at the local level as well. The mayor of Los Alamitos, California, had to resign after he was exposed circulating a cartoon of the White House where the lawn had been overrun with watermelons. In an environment in which a segment of the nation's political elite was openly questioning the president's legitimacy or comparing him to some of the nation's worst enemies of the twentieth century, it is not surprising that the editors of the *New York Post* could publish an editorial cartoon identifying the author of the president's policies as a vicious chimp. As late as early 2010, an aspirant to the Republican nomination for senator from New York was exposed sending e-mails attacking President Obama using the most racist stereotypes of "primitive" and "savage" Africans.

The attacks of the right could intensify in volume over the next several years, and it is very possible that we will start seeing a conservative mass movement hit the streets as suggested by Beck's war game scenarios. Corporate warriors from many sectors, not just the health-care industry, have lined up to run a massive disinformation campaign to subvert President Obama's policy initiatives. The scope of the effort is likely to exceed the campaign that successfully targeted the Clinton health-care plan in 1993. By the summer of 2009, some grassroots white southerners now opposed the president's health-care initiative. Why? Because they "heard it was only for blacks." Racial resentment has once again become a powerful, if ugly and immoral, weapon for undermining a progressive agenda. Progressives must not relax now or confine ourselves to critiquing aspects of the president's policy that we find problematic. If we are to win the "class war" that is coming this time, we must defeat attempts by the right to monopolize public discourse.

Another avenue of attack by the right will be the claim of "playing the race card" when African Americans suggest, no matter how innocently, that economic or racial disadvantage is a reason to support the stimulus package and other mildly progressive components of the president's domestic program. Even black schoolchildren are not exempt from scorn and attack. The *Washington Times* called Ty'Sheoma Bethea irresponsible for writing the president to request that her crumbling school be afforded resources so that she and her fellow students could pursue their dreams of success. The *Times* turned her letter on its head by arguing, "What is on display is not responsibility but irresponsibility. This is the new reality in America, that those with political pull will benefit, those without will not. . . . Connections are replacing competence as a measure of a person's worth."[16] They have transformed an earnest schoolgirl requesting a reasonable public education into a political operative cynically using her powerful political "connections" to unfairly gain patronage-based largesse. These attacks continued with Glenn Beck arguing that any church advocating social justice was in fact advocating "Nazism or communism." These attacks are beginning to work within some segments of the population; an April 14, 2010, *New York Times*/CBS News poll found that Tea Party supporters believe Obama supports "blacks over whites" and is "disproportionately directed at helping the poor rather than the middle class or the *rich*."[17] It should not be surprising that the same *New York Times*/CBS News poll found that Tea Party supporters were less than 1 percent black or Latino.[18]

There is still a role for old-school, black grassroots mobilization—to put pressure on the president and other elected officials as well as to counter the right's version of populist mobilization. FDR once told progressive members of Congress that he agreed with their policy agenda, and their job was to force him to implement it by mobilizing political support for their agenda. This is another lesson blacks and other progressive forces can borrow from the New Deal. We need not only to counteract the vicious lies and attacks of conservatives, but we also have to galvanize enough political support that Congress and the president feel compelled to initiate, pass, and implement a progressive agenda.

The tumultuous days of the campaign and the early Obama administration were characterized by presidential politics racialized to a degree that we have not seen in at least a generation. I have already begun to show how African American opinion shifted in the short years between the aftermath of the Katrina disaster and the Obama campaign. What I explore next is the degree to which the racial politics of hope, avoidance, and hate have trans-formed, if at all, the long-standing deep chasm between black and white public opinion.

If Obama's election means anything, it means that we are now living in post-racist America. That's why even those of us who didn't vote for Obama have good reason to celebrate.

Dinesh D'Souza[19]

Dinesh D'Souza, the author of the 1995 book *The End of Racism*, is one of a gaggle of conservative pundits who found the silver lining of a post-racial society in the otherwise devastating Obama victory. Vindication! That is the cry we hear, "I was right all along."

I don't think so. White Americans overwhelmingly believe that D'Souza is not in touch with reality when it comes to the end of racism in the United States. Ninety-three percent believe that racism remains a problem in this country. Blacks certainly also do not agree with the proposition that racism is no longer exists in the nation. Ninety-eight percent still believe that rac-ism plagues the nation. D'Souza might counter that the apparent agreement between blacks and whites signals a new unity across the races—surely a harbinger of the racial harmony that would be associated with a post-racial America?

Not quite, as a little more probing reveals continuing deep racial divisions in public opinion including in perceptions of racism in American. Seventy-one percent of blacks believe that racism remains a major problem, but only 32 percent of whites agree. The bitter divides in public opinion that marked the aftermath to Katrina, the racialized and at times racist 2008 presidential campaign, and wildly different material conditions between large segments of both races (more on the latter in the next chapter) have all served, by and large, to maintain the large gap between black and white public opinion.

As seen in table 6, very large differences between average black and white public opinion persist. A wide gulf remained evident between black and white opinion in 2008, even with the black shift toward more optimism on the prospects of black racial equality. Nearly 50 percent of white Americans (49 percent) believed that blacks had already achieved racial equality—a sentiment with which only 11 percent of African Americans agreed. Given the large differences on the perceptions of racial equality, it is not surprising to find a very large difference between blacks and whites as well on the perception of whether racial discrimination remains a serious problem. Large differences remained in beliefs about whether the U.S. government should apologize to blacks and Japanese Americans, respectively, for slavery and the World War II internment camps. Similarly, large gaps appeared on questions concerning whether felons who have served their time should be allowed to vote and the suitability of profiling as a security policy. A very large gap persisted in how warm blacks and whites felt toward then-candidate Obama.

For many of these beliefs, there was a larger difference of opinion among whites than among blacks. One example was how warm white respondents felt toward President Obama. White opinion was spread out over a wide range, while black opinion was strongly concentrated around high levels of affective warmth. What explains white warmth toward Barack Obama?[20] Being from the South had a large impact on affective warmth toward Obama, even after controlling for other factors such as party affiliation, gender, age, income, and other variables. Just being from the South reduced white warmth toward candidate Obama by nearly 10 degrees. Similarly, strong Republicans were also nearly 10 degrees cooler toward Obama than strong Democrats. It was often speculated that young white Americans were more enthusiastic about the president than their older cousins. That speculation was borne out, as white respondents twenty-five years old or younger were on average 5 degrees warmer toward the president.[21] More educated white Americans felt slightly warmer toward Obama than less educated whites. Interestingly, those who trusted television more than other sources of information were 5 degrees warmer than those stating greater trust in other news sources. On the other hand, the substantial number of white Americans (nearly 30 percent) who do not trust any news sources were 5 degrees cooler than those whites who trusted some news source. Gender and income had no discernible effect on white warmth toward President Obama.

If Mr. D'Souza wanted any evidence that we do not live in either a post-racial or post-racist society, he need look no further than this bit of data. When asked, "Would you or someone you know closely not vote for

Barack Obama for president because of his race?," 30 percent of the white respondents answered yes. What are the characteristics of white Americans who would have been less likely themselves or who had a close associate who would have been less likely to have voted for Obama because he was black? The main demographic trait characterizing this group was being from the South. Southern whites were 8 percent more likely to respond positively to the question that they or somebody they knew considered race alone enough to disqualify Obama for their vote.

Analyzing white responses to one of the most charged issues in American racial politics provides further insight into the factors that influence white racial attitudes in the age of Obama. Only 23 percent of whites (as opposed to 74 percent of blacks) believed that the U.S. government should apologize to African Americans for slavery. This is a significantly smaller percentage of whites voicing this belief than we saw earlier in the decade, when 30 percent supported a government apology to blacks. Those most likely to support an apology were non-southern, poor whites who believed that black racial equality was not likely to be achieved in the near future. More specifically, white southerners were 10 percent less likely to support an apology. White Americans who believed that blacks would not achieve racial equality soon were 30 percent more likely to support an apology than those who believed racial equality has already been achieved. The most affluent whites were 20 percent less likely to support an apology than the least well-off white Americans. Somewhat countering the influence of income was education. The most educated whites were 14 percent more likely to support an apology than the least educated.

The racialization of black public opinion takes a different form than it does with whites. For African Americans, how racialized one sees the world is profoundly influenced by how strongly one sees one's own fate linked to that of the race, which in turn is driven by how deeply embedded one is in black information networks. For example, blacks who reported believing that their fate was strongly linked to that of the race were 37 percent more likely to believe that racial equality for blacks would not be achieved in their lifetimes than those who did not believe their fate was linked to the race. Similarly, the perception that discrimination is still a major problem appears 12 percent more frequently among those with strong linked-fate beliefs than those who do not view their fate as linked to the race. Young people are also 9 percent less likely to perceive racism as a major problem as compared to their older cohorts. Highly educated blacks were 23 percent more likely to see racism as a major problem than their least educated cousins.

What drives perceptions that the fate of individual African Americans is linked to the race? As hinted at above, those who are most exposed to black media are nearly 20 percent more likely to believe in linked fate than blacks with less exposure to black news sources. The young are 8 percent more likely to think their fate is linked than their elders. Both the highly educated (22 percent) and the most affluent (14 percent) are more likely to view their fates as linked than, respectively, their least educated and least affluent counterparts. Women are somewhat less likely (7 percent) to view their fate as being linked to that of the race than are black men. While it is true to say that highly educated, affluent young males who are embedded in black information networks are the most likely to believe their fate is linked to that of the race, it is more important to remember that nearly three-quarters of all blacks still believe their fate is linked to the race. Black public opinion, as is white opinion, is still strongly shaped by racial considerations.

BARACK OBAMA, DESPITE HIS BEST EFFORTS TO AVOID IT, WAS immersed in a campaign that was highly racialized. Indeed, Obama not only had to operate in a racialized environment, but also endured implicit and explicit racist attacks during both the campaign and now throughout his presidency. Given the racialized nature of the political environment—a factor that has not changed since the Katrina disaster—we should not be surprised that American public opinion also remains highly racialized. Both white and black Americans perceive continuing high levels of racial discrimination, even though they substantially disagree about the degree to which racial discrimination remains a major problem. Thirty percent of whites still report knowing someone who would not have voted for the president because of his race. It is hard to understand how these findings are consistent with any version of a post-racist world we might wish to imagine. It is hard to understand how one can believe that we live in a post-racial society if we do not even live in a post-racist society, as D'Souza argued. Unfortunately, too many white Americans suffer from snow blindness and therefore hold the

Table 9: African American Exposure to Black Media Sources, 2008

	Used at Least Once during Past Month
Black television news	65%
Black talk radio	57%
Black newspaper	44%
Black-oriented blog or website	22%

illusory belief that they and the country more generally operate according to color-blind principles.

Blacks in 2008 continued to view politics through a racialized lens. How strongly one feels one's fate is linked to that of the rest of the race and how deeply embedded one is in black information networks shape black opinion. As seen in table 9, a majority of blacks are still at least partially embedded in black information networks. This embeddedness, as we have seen, still significantly contributes to African American's racialized view of American politics.

Finally, as discussed in chapter 1, a large number of blacks still view themselves as constituting a nation within a nation. Even though many blacks are more optimistic about black prospects at present than they were before, it will take a greater transformation in the politics of race than we have seen thus far to break the pattern of viewing American politics through a racialized lens.

As to how desirable it would be at this point in time for the pattern to be broken, I have my doubts. Certain, in any case, is that the gap between black and white public opinion will continue to have important consequences for black politics in the near term. Blacks remain isolated from whites in public opinion. The process of demonization of black politics and black discourse described in chapter 2, although contested, is still alive and well, as the Reverend Wright incident highlights. And as the incident around the follow-up to the World Conference against Racism shows, the ability of blacks to influence the policy process on matters of special concern to African Americans remains severely limited. Even relatively moderate black Democratic insiders voiced disappointment with the administration's decision not to participate. It also appears that areas of concern such as urban policy are relatively low on the president's agenda. While African Americans were more hopeful at the time of the 2008 election than they were at the time of Katrina, there is still plenty of hard work to be done, and black politics remains dangerously weak in its ability to influence both discourse and policy.

The glittering spectacle of the president's campaign should not obscure two critical and continuing truths about racial politics in the United States. First, despite relatively high levels of black euphoria, it is obvious to most African Americans that we do not live in a country that has come close to achieving the status of "post-racial." Politics and society remain racialized, and all too many blacks, particularly poor African Americans, are still systematically disadvantaged by a racial order that continues to shape all aspects of American life. Second, President Obama's victorious campaign did not represent a revitalization of an independent black politics capable of mounting the sustained campaigns needed to successfully rejuvenate the quest for racial and other forms of social and economic justice.

In the next chapter, I will begin to probe the material foundation for African Americans' continuing racialized view of the nation and its politics. The changing material reality facing African Americans has transformed black politics—a transformation that in turn poses its own sets of hazards and obstacles for those attempting to rebuild a vibrant black politics.

4 BLACK POLITICAL ECONOMY AND THE EFFECTS OF NEOLIBERALISM ON BLACK POLITICS

We finally cleared up public housing in New Orleans. We couldn't do it, but God did.
Representative Richard Baker, Louisiana 6th District [1]

Black public opinion in the early Obama age was more optimistic than it had been in decades. In addition to the symbolic gains highlighted by the election of Barack Obama, are there economic reasons for blacks to be more optimistic? Is the political optimism grounded in improved possibilities for the good life for black citizens within this country? In this chapter I begin by using a number of vignettes to highlight some of the political implications of contemporary black political economy. The second half of the chapter begins by briefly reporting key indicators of African Americans' economic status. I report both on the absolute state of the black political economy and on the economic condition of African Americans relative to that of white Americans. From there we move to an examination of economic divisions among African Americans. Building on the lessons gleaned from the vignettes, the chapter concludes with a deeper discussion of neoliberalism, and how neoliberalism has shaped the economic and political terrain that black political movements must now navigate.

What ties these vignettes together is how the processes of race-inflected neoliberalism structures the political terrain, actors' ideologies, and citizens' perceptions of what is "possible" and what are "acceptable actions and policies." Also tying them together is how neoliberal economic transformations shape and reshape communities, life chances, and political conflict. Within each vignette the economic and/or political character of the physical space of each community is transformed by neoliberal processes, which in turn transform the life chances of those communities' residents. Gentrification and the transformation of American cities along more European lines, where the once industrial and poor central city is now the site of new attractive and affluent neighborhoods with a complete array of services, has transformed black electoral politics, as seen in one district in Chicago. On the other end of the economic spectrum, we will see how deindustrialization and economic devastation induced by globalization made a very different Chicago community more vulnerable to economic "development" that no longer provided the living wages, affordable housing, and benefits that jobs in the community once provided. Spaces that had once been dedicated to manufacturing production, which provided communities with good jobs, are now the sites of massive retail consumption where the only jobs provided do not pay a living wage. In New Orleans, as in Chicago, race-inflected neoliberal ideologies and technocratic practices transformed the political character of spaces, making it more difficult to build broad progressive coalitions capable of fighting for social justice. As we will see, the Katrina vignette provides a particularly vivid example how these neoliberal practices—combined with old-fashioned racism and racial terrorism—helped to radically alter the shape of the racial order and break the social compact that had been in place since the battles of the New Deal and Civil Rights Movement.

These vignettes are also tied together by demonstrating how neoliberalism's restructuring of the economy has sharpened already existing class cleavages, further undermining the myth of a "monolithic" black community, and by extension making even more difficult the task of building unified black political movements. Neoliberalism ideological orientations provide a temptation for the new growing black middle class to abandon traditional notions of a black politics centered on mass mobilization and egalitarian, state-centered, and contentious politics. Further, neoliberalism offers the new black middle class the promise of riches and status in return for adopting neoliberal conceptions of a sterile and extremely limited notion of politics, and agreeing to the premise that poverty is primarily the result of pathological behaviors of communities and individuals. A battle is being fought for the political and moral soul of the new black middle class. Appropriately, our vignettes begin with an election in Chicago that echoed themes central to the Obama campaign.

DURING THE SAME CAMPAIGN SEASON THAT BARACK OBAMA campaigned for president of the United States, five candidates vied for the state assembly seat that was once held by Barack Obama. Both the presidential and the local campaign were indicative of important transformations in black politics, and more generally racial politics in the United States. Specifically, both elections were evidence of a change in America's and Chicago's racial climate that enabled some black middle-class, technocratic, super-credentialed, and, perhaps most importantly, safe candidates to become now more acceptable to whites than even in the recent past. At the same time, the Chicago election particularly accentuates increasing class cleavages among African Americans, further problematizing the concept of a singular black political community.

Obama's former district was one of the most racially and socioeconomically diverse in the state. While still a majority black district, it was also undergoing intense gentrification, which was attracting many new affluent residents of all races. Gentrification on Chicago's South Side, as compared to other areas in the city or to cities such as Boston, is distinct in that affluent blacks have made up a major segment of the new gentrifying population. The racial aspects of the electoral contest took on added interest as well, in that affluent whites were moving back into the central city. Reversing a decades-long trend of white flight, white voters were now taking up residence in neighborhoods that had been largely industrial and/or part of the historic Chicago black community of Bronzeville. The class dimensions of the race, however, were in many ways more decisive in determining the campaign's terrain than race. In Chicago, class politics has been known to trump racial politics around issues such as whether (poor) neighborhood children should be "allowed" to go to extra-resourced magnet schools in their own neighborhoods.

William Burns, one of the two top vote getters, was a University of Chicago alumnus who had worked for Obama in the early days and was the very model of the new class of "cosmopolitan" black politicians. His most competitive opponent, Kenny Johnson Jr., equally smooth, was a protégé of the Jesse Jackson political family. The election was unsurprisingly about the intersection of race and class in a Chicago neighborhood. But it was also more complicated than that. Two of the candidates defeated in the primary relied during the campaign primarily on support from working-class and poor African Americans. In addition, however, one was a machine politician, and the other had a background in city housing and school administration. Machine politics had rarely benefited African Americans of any class, especially after the party-based patronage machine was dismantled, so that a reform dynamic worked to complicate the politics of class in the election.[2] Overlaid on this already complex narrative of class, machine politics, and reform was also a generational split. Burns and Johnson were both young technocrats, and the candidates who identified themselves with reform, technocratic excellence, and an up-and-coming new generation of African Americans. They both crafted appeals utilizing neoliberal rhetoric to appeal to the new affluent constituencies moving into the district. These two candidates each attempted to make strong bids simultaneously for both traditional black voters and the new affluent residents of the district. Both candidates forged multiple appeals to the electorate—appeals designed to attract voters across not only racial cleavages, but also across growing class cleavages within the black electorate.

Also reflected in the political context was Chicago's changing political terrain. Following nearly a century of extremely active and well-organized independent mobilization and participation in (machine-based) electoral politics, organized black politics declined after the sudden death in office of Mayor Harold Washington on November 25, 1987. Since then, black politics in Chicago has been marked by demobilization of the black community and dominated by a group of well-connected families, including the Sawyers, Jacksons, and Strogers. With the partial exception of the Jacksons, who had strong ties to the civil rights and progressive communities primarily via Jesse Jackson Sr., this has also entailed embracing neoliberal policies and ideologies calling for the suppression of active community political engagement.

It was in this environment that the four black candidates and one non–African American vied for the 26th District seat. The eventual winner was Will Burns—the young but experienced politician, well connected to state and city Democrats, the local NGO and foundation community, and the powerful academic community centered at the University of Chicago. Burns's campaign was well aware of the changing demographic makeup of the district. The campaign actively reached out to newcomers to the district, but also worked extremely hard to garner support from longtime, generally less affluent, African American residents. Burns was one of two candidates who believed they needed to build wider coalitions across race and class than local black politicians had needed to build in the past.

As Amanda Wall shows, candidates and their staffs clearly recognized intersection between race and class as critical political terrain. Burns was portrayed as a "new" black politician—middle class, with an elite education, who was also able to get "down with the people." Accordingly, Burns's strategy was based on appealing to middle- and upper-income voters of all races based on "competence" and education, while appealing to working-class and poor black voters through both quasi-nationalist appeals, key endorsements from black leaders with impeccable racial credentials, and identification with Obama, not only as someone who had worked with Obama in the past, but also someone cast in the same mold as his mentor, Barack Obama. This was a risky strategy as black politicians in general, and in Chicago specifically, have more often based their appeals on racial calls for unity and/or portraying themselves as a man or woman of the "people." As his staff pointed out, Obama too had experienced some difficulty in certain low-income black wards, which Burns eventually lost and which were won by another black politician with a similar profile but a different mentor.

Kenny Johnson Jr. garnered the second highest tally of votes. He was widely seen as having strong ties to Chicago powerhouses Jesse Jackson Sr. and Jesse Jackson Jr., and he won an endorsement from both of them. When asked to describe the district he was running in, Johnson first mentioned the class composition of the district's various neighborhoods, and only then did he bring up racial diversity. Johnson's campaign strategy was similar to Burns's, geared to appeal to the class and racial diversity of the district, with the one significant difference that Johnson emphasized his entrepreneurial business experience, as opposed to Burns's emphasis on his advanced educational attainment, as a way to build a broader coalition that cut across racial and class lines. Both portrayed themselves as new "independent" modern black politicians with support from key black establishment icons.

The other two black candidates had not adjusted to the changes in the district, and particularly not to the large influx of racially diverse affluent voters. Phillip Jackson (no relation to Jesse Jackson Sr. and Jr.) chose to run a campaign emphasizing his long-standing role as a community activist dedicated to the advancement of the black community and particularly his advocacy on behalf of black youth. Thus he made no direct appeal to affluent sectors of the district. He ended up garnering only 18 percent of the primary vote. The unelected incumbent (whose predecessor had died in office), Elga Jeffries, was well aware of the changing demographics of the district and how the twin factors of the demolition of one of the most densely popu- lated and infamous strips of public housing in the nation, combined with the rapid influx of affluent residents, fundamentally changed the district for the foreseeable future. As her campaign manager, Bob Deneen, stated, the traditional poor black base was being "gentrified out."[3] Like fellow candidate Phillip Jackson, she emphasized her deep ties with the institutions and lead- ers that had served the earlier version of the district so well and stressed her efforts on behalf of her poor black constituents. Like Jackson, she made little attempt to reach out to the newer residents, whom she regarded as inter- lopers. Even her campaign manager, referring to the more affluent, racially mixed part of the district, said, "[She] pretty much didn't want to talk to the people on the north end, [and] without that vote she couldn't win."[4] The one non-black candidate, Paul Chadha, was the one candidate for whom the racial terrain proved much more difficult to traverse than the terrain of class. Chadha's strategy was to target primarily the affluent white residents of the district around the issues of property taxes and thus had little chance of gathering enough support district-wide to make his candidacy credible.

The interplay of race and class in the 26th District highlights one type of black politics we will see more of in political campaigns of the future that involve multiple black candidates, as class divisions are mapped onto other cleavages. There will certainly be campaigns in which the racial aspects are more central than the class aspects, but as we have seen increasingly over the past several electoral cycles, the dynamics of electoral campaigns have become more complicated as class, ethnic, generational, and other cleav- ages among blacks result in a more contingent, and often more contentious, intra-racial politics. The transformation of space as some areas gentrify due to the economic changes that occur in global cities such as Chicago restruc- ture local politics, accentuating the political ramifications of increasing class cleavages among blacks.

ANOTHER TYPE OF POLITICS THAT HAS EMERGED OUT OF neoliberal transformation of the American economy involves translocal movements' attempts to block the siting of big boxes—especially, but not exclusively, Walmarts—in poor urban neighborhoods.[5] The big box corporations seek to take advantage of the combination of devastated local economies and what they perceive to be the relatively less powerful minority communities in these same localities. Much of the scholarly literature has understood these confrontations as non-white communities coming into conflict with the labor movement or the emergence of class conflict within these non-white communities. Close examination, however, reveals complex and shifting alliances and cleavage lines forming around these struggles—often uniting a wide range of groups that rarely united in the past. William Sites, for example, lists a broad range of interests that have opposed Walmart entering urban communities—particularly those with a large non-white population. The anti-Walmart alliances have included, according to Sites, labor, feminists, small businesses, and other older commercial concerns, environmentalists, nearby residents, and civil and immigrant rights organizations.[6]

The relationship between "the" black community and the movements opposing Walmart moving in has differed depending on city. In Southern California, black and Latino communities united to prevent a Walmart from being located in Inglewood.[7] In Chicago, black elected officials, civil rights–identified organizations and personages, and the black ministerial community split down the middle. Some sided with unions and other anti-Walmart forces. Others sided with Walmart. Walmart poured money into black civil society. As part of its strategy to neutralize potential black opposition, Walmart funded church projects, community groups, and some civil rights organizations.[8] One result, according to Sites, was the building of a "network of ministers" willing to advocate on behalf of Walmart. These ministers remained actively supporting Walmart's initiatives well into 2010. Through such practices Walmart was able to co-opt institutions and organizations within the black community that often in the past had been important forces in political coalitions fighting for economic justice.

Walmart poured money into Los Angeles–area civil rights organizations as well, including La Raza, MALDEF, the Urban League, United Negro College Fund, and the NAACP. NAACP locals in both Chicago and Atlanta ended up supporting Walmart's efforts to move into each metropolitan area. The propensity of some civil rights organizations and church leaders to take Walmart's money frustrated some activists as they saw community leaders "take the money" despite militant posturing.[9] The grounds for some leaders' support of Walmart was sometimes more complicated since they were not so much bought off but were in agreement with Walmart's argument.[10] Regardless of the reason that many community leaders supported Walmart, this support was one element in some initial successes in the Los Angeles area. For example, Walmart was successful in Baldwin Hills, working with black community leadership.[11] These efforts were accelerated as Walmart donated $300,000 to the NAACP in 2001 and $150,000 in 2003, resulting in what some characterized as a "deafening silence" on the part of the organization.[12] In total, Walmart spent $1 million in Inglewood as part of "outreach and mobilization efforts" to influence residents of a city of ten thousand people.[13] The short-term results of Walmart's largesse would be far different, however, in Inglewood than Chicago.

Walmart was able to point to the exceedingly large numbers of job applicants they had received in Chicago and elsewhere, with eight to fifty applicants for every potential opening. The Chicago aldermen (city council members) of the two black neighborhoods proposed as Walmart sites also heavily emphasized the extreme economic deprivation of their wards as their prime reason for supporting Walmart. Virginia Parks and Dorian Warren argue that it was neoliberal processes that led to Walmart selecting the specific Chicago site around which the conflict developed. The previous occupant was a factory that was moving to Mexico in order to reduce labor costs.[14] As Parks and Warren point out, "On no grounds was a Wal-Mart job equal" to one of the old factory jobs, so Walmart was hardly proposing an "acceptable replacement." Sites describes how what devastated the urban communities that Walmart targeted in the first place were forces unleashed by the neoliberal transformation, including "First World capitalist liberalization [which led to] globalization, mass immigration, accelerated deindustrialization, state rescaling, [and] urban entrepreneurialism."[15]

These forces profoundly transformed the spatial character of the Chicago site. The space of the proposed Walmart was transformed along multiple dimensions.[16] First, its relation to capitalism radically changed. In contrast to the neighborhood's former economic life based on manufacturing, the proposed new economic engine would be massive consumption, with the attendant downward pressure on wages and benefits, as well as the imposition of intense new pressures on small businesses. The space was also transformed in terms of the meanings and identities that were and are associated with it. To both residents and non-residents, areas that are seen as robust working-class neighborhoods have a different set of meanings associated with them than those marked as "blighted."

Another result of these economic processes was that in Chicago there was a further intensification of the economic devastation found at the intersection between race and class. Chicago has no low-income white neighborhoods, and 93 percent are high income. There are no high-income Latino neighborhoods, with the majority (57 percent) of Latino neighborhoods classified as low income. Black neighborhoods show the greatest economic diversity, although a large majority, 62 percent, is classified as low income. Nine percent are classified as high income, and 30 percent as medium income. Blacks are the only one of the three groups with neighborhoods in all three categories—although blacks also have the largest percentage of neighborhoods classified as falling into the lowest category.[17]

It was this pattern of racialized economic disadvantage, combined with the success that Walmart and its allies had in framing the conflict as between "white labor outsiders" and an economically devastated local black community, that has led many scholars to see in these struggles a disconnect between community activism, on the one hand, and labor activism, on the other. This disconnect, Parks and Warren claim, leads to "fragmentation [that] results from political processes, discourses and institutions that create 'fragmented interests' rather than 'universal publics' around issues of economic rights and security."[18]

Prior to these "fragmented interests" identified by Parks and Warren, however, is a racial order that shapes both the state and civil society. Specifically, the racial order undermines the ability of labor and community activists to broadly unite. The difficulty in uniting these activists and their movements is partly due to a relatively privileged, and predominantly white, sector of the labor movement in cities such as Chicago, which excludes non-white minorities, blacks in particular, from their unions. This practice has contributed historically to fragmentation along racial lines in labor movements, civil society organizations, and with regard to state policies. As seen in chapter 2, this racial order has also been associated with the fragmentation and racialization of public spheres, including the supposedly overarching "public of publics." A consequence of the evolved, neoliberal, form of the modern racial order has been (as we see clearly in the Obama era) the peeling off and bringing into the neoliberal governing alliance black elites among politicians, clergy, community leaders, and some, but not all, civil rights leaders.

Some neighborhood black activists bemoaned what they saw as an abandonment of a rich heritage of black working-class organizing—linking this abandonment to a loss of memory of black activism and unionism of just the previous generation. One black neighborhood activist railed: "I've never seen so much ignorance. They had no sense of all the history of African Americans in unions. A. Philip Randolph, ever heard of him? So they're going to side with the corporate enslaver, like 'Wal-Mart will save us Negroes!' "[19] Neoliberal amnesia affects black communities by erasing histories of struggle, not by, as for many whites, erasing the history of black oppression or denying current black disadvantage. As we will see, black amnesia about past struggles, however, does not necessarily dramatically change black political opinion. For African Americans, loss of hope and knowledge of past struggles can be just as damaging to black aspirations for justice as the form of racial amnesia found in white communities. Part of the problem, according to Dorian Warren, was that "black-led labor activism" has declined and the labor movement "needs an honest discussion about race."[20] The instantiation of the racial order in the Chicago area was associated with a significant segment of black leadership either explicitly or implicitly supporting Walmart's efforts.

The racial order, however, shapes, not determines, local outcomes. In New York and the Los Angeles area, African Americans and other people of color are well embedded in the leadership of the local union movement. In Los Angeles, the United Food and Commercial Workers International Union (UFCW) had built alliances with organizations based in black and Latino communities and had a number of black women as the public face of the organizing in Inglewood. The anti-Walmart forces were able to mobilize both black elected officials and the black and Latino church communities to their cause. In Inglewood, black women workers were central in the opposition and mobilized support in the black community by explaining concretely to their neighbors the personal and community-wide ramifications of a Walmart victory, thus circumventing one of the obstacles facing activists in Chicago. Further, the general strength of the labor movement in Los Angeles meant that powerful institutionalized forces were to some degree able to counter Walmart's savvy and well-financed public relations and lobbying campaign. Using the combination of grassroots strength and labor strength, anti-Walmart candidates won the sufficient city council seats in Inglewood's 2003 election to solidify the anti-Walmart forces on the city council. This was a relatively rare example of a black and brown community holding accountable elected officials who were too tied to corporate interests. All of these factors contributed to a victory at the polls for the anti-Walmart forces in April 2004.[21] Walmart's travails in Inglewood and more generally in large metropolitan areas with strong labor movements affected Walmart's strategic focus over the next years.[22]

Yet even in Chicago, a very large segment of the black population still overwhelmingly opposed the city policies being enacted on behalf of Walmart and other big boxes seeking to move into black communities. Walmart, other big box firms, and their allies in Chicago in and outside of local government tried to prevent an ordinance being passed in June 2005 that would require big boxes in Chicago to pay a living wage. Support for the ordinance was very high among registered voters in the city, including an overwhelming 91 percent of black registered voters. After it initially passed the city council with a "veto-proof" majority, Mayor Daley vetoed the bill anyway, and pro–big box forces launched an intense media campaign attempting to paint the ordinance's supporters as white outsiders who were not concerned about the welfare of poor blacks in Chicago. After the campaign had been aggressively waged for over a month, support in the city remained strong, although having dropped somewhat below its June level. Even after the explicit racial framing of the debate by the big box supporters, a very strong majority of 81 percent of black registered voters remained firmly in support of the living-wage ordinance.[23] Parks and Warren argue that the strong support among blacks was due to blacks' continued support for economic redistribution.

> The two competing frames, "jobs and development" and "redistribution," were presented in these statements:

> *This ordinance will drive away the jobs and economic development that are desperately needed by Chicagoans. We just can't take that chance.*

> *Profitable retailers should pay enough for families to make ends meet. We must make sure these companies, who will make a lot of money from us, pay a fair wage and provide benefits.*

> . . . Among blacks, 15.9% agreed with the "jobs and development" frame while 76.3% agreed with the "redistribution" frame. Thus, similar to national support among African Americans for redistributive policies, black Chicagoans also supported, by a 3 to 1 margin, a local redistributive policy as a response to the proliferation of big box stores in black communities.[24]

Despite the continued strong support for the living-wage ordinance, Daley's veto was sustained, as three aldermen who had previously supported the bill switched their vote.

This survey evidence shows that scholars such as Sites, in arguing that "union and minority community residents are often positioned on opposite sides of local development issues,"[25] mischaracterize the conflict and the reason for the defeat of the anti-Walmart forces. Given the survey evidence, it is impossible to draw any conclusion except that the majority of African Americans in Chicago still strongly support the redistributive, social democratic politics and ideologies that have marked black politics since the Civil War and Reconstruction.[26] African Americans, in either Inglewood or Chicago, were not by and large buying Walmart's argument that it was contributing to black economic empowerment. Not only did Walmart jobs not pay nearly as much as the manufacturing positions that once supported black workers in places such as the Chicago neighborhood that was the proposed site; unionized grocery jobs, jobs similar to the ones that Walmart was proposing to bring to the community, paid one and a half times more than jobs at Walmart.[27] It was several black "leaders" and elected officials, not the "black community" as a whole, that drank the toxic neoliberal Kool-Aid.[28]

Given the overwhelming black grassroots opposition, why did the anti-Walmart forces fail? Why did many black members of the council support Walmart when their constituents did not? Why did organizations such as the local NAACP and civil rights leaders such as Andrew Young support Walmart, unlike Young's former colleague, the Reverend Jesse Jackson, who remained a staunch Walmart opponent? Even the combination of the desperate economic circumstances and the attempt on the part of the mayor and his allies to frame the struggle as one pitting white outsiders against the black community proved insufficient to undermine massive black opposition to big boxes, which promised jobs but did not provide a living wage, economic security, or decent benefits. Why was the black community not able to hold its elected representatives accountable?

Many of the answers to these questions, the last one in particular, can be found in the failures of black politics in the continuing aftermath of Hurricane Katrina. The lack of an independent black progressive movement, whether left or progressive nationalist, and of independent black progressive political organizations has deprived black citizens of the institutional forces needed to hold their "leaders" accountable. As Martin Luther King Jr., W. E. B. Du Bois, Malcolm X, and many other leading activists pointed out generations ago, the black elite, particularly the middle-class black elite, is very prone to compromise and forging alliances with the powers that be in any given era. What is different in this era is the lack of organized black political forces to hold black elites and leaders accountable. Further, this organizational weakness has made it harder to forge alliances with forces outside of black communities. In cities such as Oakland, Detroit, New York, and indeed in Chicago, black progressive forces in the past were able both to organize effectively within their own communities and on that basis to forge strong alliances with a variety of progressive forces outside of black communities.

What is also new is how the transformation of space as a result of neoliberal economic processes transformed black politics. Just as the transformation of a formerly black working-class neighborhood into at least a partially gentrified neighborhood necessitated a new black politics based on neoliberal appeals in addition to traditional racial messages in Chicago's 26th District, the transformation of a black working-class neighborhood into a devastated neighborhood made that neighborhood more vulnerable to both corporate and political manipulations as grassroots political capacity to resist had been weakened. These same weaknesses that undermined progressive politics in Chicago during the big box conflict would also continue to undermine the efforts by the black community of New Orleans and its allies to craft a just and fair rebuilding of the devastated city.

Local governments have been creating legal barriers—legal, in the sense they created laws—to prevent people who are African-American from returning.
Lucia Blacksher[29]

A luta continua . . .[30]

Current and former black residents of New Orleans were faced with something old and something new, as the aftermath to the Katrina disaster stretched from months into years. The something old was a coordinated and vicious assault by all levels of the state, corporate elites, and white civil society to put blacks back "in their place"—to reverse the decades of progress that blacks had achieved in the Deep South through the mass struggles of the Civil Rights Movement and hard, old-fashioned individual and collective effort. The something new came in the form of neoliberal practices and ideology that were used both to implement and justify (often in "non"-racial terms) a new campaign of black political and economic disenfranchisement.

A basic aspect of this campaign was to try to deny poor blacks the ability to live in the city or its neighboring suburbs and parishes. For example, St. Bernard Parish instituted a series of new regulations and practices to keep poor blacks out—going so far as to pass an ordinance that "prohibited homeowners from renting their properties to anyone who was not a bona fide blood relation without first obtaining a permit—a loaded concept anywhere, but particularly in St. Bernard, where the white majority owned 93 percent of the pre-storm housing."[31] Earlier the parish had implemented a year-long ban on both the development and reestablishment of affordable housing.

While forced to drop the blood-kin proviso, new more modern techniques were used to ensure the same result. An appalling permitting process kept the parish white where neo–Jim Crow measures would not. The something old was still available when modern techniques and practices failed to work. When police and bureaucratic harassment failed to dissuade black renters, some black landlords were jailed and a string of arsons destroyed the rental properties of others.[32]

In Jefferson Parish, the site of the infamous armed blocking of the bridge at Gretna, an African American couple had crosses set aflame and the letters KKK burned into their lawn. Jefferson is the "old stomping grounds," in Lizzy Ratner's phrase, of Klan leader turned politician David Duke, and while whites there resorted to some very old-school intimidation, their goals differed little from those of some of their more technocratically inclined, although equally racist, neighbors. Indeed, even in Jefferson Parish, politicians were modern enough to use all available tools to achieve racist ends. While the night riders engaged in their traditional terror and the police at the bridge and elsewhere were not far behind, the politicians blocked affordable housing to guarantee that the "lazy" and "ignorant" would not reside in the parish. The demonization of the black citizens of New Orleans continued well after the rest of the nation "forgot" Katrina in the form of technocratic political debate as well as legislation, regulations, and campaigns of bureaucratic harassment, all designed to maintain the suburban parishes as lily-white monuments to segregation. Welcome to our brave neoliberal world—which combines the terror of the Klan with police brutality and technocratic maneuvering, all justified by a neoliberal ideology that implicitly reserves democracy and liberal rights only for those pre-coded as "rational" and "worthy" citizens.

As Ratner points out, even where race is not the issue, class is. Residents of New Orleans East, which she characterizes as "a traditionally middle-income African-American community with pockets of immense wealth and poverty," also used bureaucratic measures to try to prevent an influx of the black poor. This was one of the communities trying to block affordable housing before the hurricane struck. While in New Orleans East no one displayed the Confederate battle flag and violence was not used, officials there were every bit as strident in the use of regulations and legislation to prevent more of the black poor from moving in. The same neoliberal justifications were also used elsewhere in New Orleans to block low-income housing.

The need for rental housing was intense not only due to the massive storm damage done to poor and middle-income neighborhoods, but also because of policy decisions made in the wake of Katrina. One controversial decision was to destroy thousands of units of public housing and not replace them. Three thousand formerly occupied units were demolished, as well as 1,500 more that were unoccupied at the time of the storm. In the immediate aftermath of the storm in particular, the veneer of rationality and the language of sober policy-making—which has long masked initiatives that negatively affect blacks and the poor, and disproportionately the black poor—were thin or nonexistent. For example, the dean of Louisiana's congressional delegation, Richard Baker of the Louisiana 6th District, said a month after the storm on national television, "We finally cleared up public housing in New Orleans. We couldn't do it, but God did."[33] The hurricane had already destroyed 50,000 rental units—and FEMA would also shut down 3,700 trailers.[34] The destruction of affordable housing to this extent, combined with the decision not to replace the missing units, meant that poor former and current citizens had scant opportunity to find a place to live.

Katrina did not cause white political forces to resort to these techniques, as they were being used before the hurricane struck. The disaster, however, multiplied the effectiveness of these tactics—particularly given the dispersal of the most potent political force able to challenge them—the black community of New Orleans. The strategies adopted after the storm to prevent the poor, and especially the black poor, from returning are continuing to work. According to federal, state, and local officials, half of the city's former elderly and disabled, as well as the working poor (and their children), have not returned to the city. Policy Link—a policy institute—estimated that "barely" 40 percent of the city's former poor residents can now afford housing in the area. The situation was dire enough that the United Nations called for an immediate halt in the destruction of public housing.[35]

But housing is not the only sector in which neoliberal arguments were used to justify the draconian and anti-democratic policies underlying massive post-Katrina transformation. The elected school board in New Orleans remains in control of only five public schools, out of ninety-three, as the great majority have been turned into charter schools. State Superintendent of Education Paul Pastorek was reported on NPR as saying that "he could imagine the possibility that someday all New Orleans schoolchildren could be attending charter schools."[36] While Pastorek, according to Carr, later modified his statement to say that he was indifferent as to who operated the schools, the state takeover has been marked by a shift away from local democratic control and has been accompanied by a growing lack of transparency in decision-making. Here again the tropes of efficiency and rationality were used to dismantle democratically governed institutions. Nevertheless, in at least one of the schools in what had been the black Ninth Ward, students' performance has actually declined under the new regime. The state's takeover was greatly enabled, of course, by the chaos and destruction caused by the storm. But the ability to maintain the takeover is due at least in part to the hostility that the previous school board had generated among significant sectors of the New Orleans citizenry. Alleged lack of competence as well as the perception that previous boards had engaged in corrupt practices led some citizens to celebrate the takeover of the system, regardless of whether it was done in an anti-democratic manner. The lack of improvement in the students' performance, however, has eroded whatever initial support the takeover may have had in some black communities and has led to increased demand for accountability on the part of the new administration.

The conditions described above and the machinations of suburban communities and the newly empowered white community of New Orleans have led one black city official to declare that "among many African Americans [there is] justifiable paranoia."[37] This paranoia led to a mobilization that almost defeated a citywide vote on the master plan. Blacks, given their recent experience and the resurgence of open racism within the region, were understandably worried that the plan would be used to prevent the rebuilding of their neighborhoods. And this concern seems borne out in that 64 percent of white residents say they prefer that some neighborhoods not be rebuilt.[38] While the city has slowly grown back to three-quarters of its former size, and blacks once again make up a majority of the residents, though a smaller one, black political power has not been rebuilt to its previous heights. New Orleans now has the first white-majority city council since 1985[39]—which was soon followed by the election of the first white mayor in several terms.

The council, as well as white-dominated institutions and media, have embraced the language of rationality and neoliberalism to justify having a city with a "smaller footprint"—which would entail the further suppression of black political power and the barring of the poor from the city and region. It is precisely this discourse—sometimes conducted in public, sometimes behind closed doors—that led former mayor Marc Morial to issue this cautionary statement:

> [Before the storm] there was a multiracial effort . . . to come together around big things, despite some pushing and shoving along the way. Katrina changed that. The idea that a plan is confected by a handful of people while 80 percent of the people were gone, and it would eliminate whole neighborhoods, seems to have created distrust.[40]

The effort Morial describes "to come together" was hampered before and after the hurricane by a vicious struggle waged by various racist forces to maintain white supremacy in New Orleans. J. Phillip Thompson of MIT describes the racial order within which those who wanted to rebuild on an equitable basis had to work:

> The race conflict was spatially and politically transformed, and coded, into tensions between "the City and the State" (read: "African American city" in "white state"). This largely explains why New Orleans was so vulnerable prior to Katrina, and why rebuilding is so difficult post-Katrina. Concentrated in the surrounding suburbs, resentful of the African American community's assertiveness, and of federal programs targeted to help the African American poor, the white-majority elected State officials determined to fiscally starve the mostly African American city.[41]

The AFL-CIO and many other individuals and organizations did attempt to intervene in order to rebuild the city and its individual neighborhoods and communities. Indeed, Phil Thompson argues that the wave of white (and other) young people who went to the city to help rebuild was reminiscent of an earlier generation of young people who headed to the South to heroically participate in the Civil Rights Movement.[42] Unfortunately, the

AFL-CIO initiative quickly faced significant obstacles. Some included the difficulties of working in a city that even before Katrina was extremely poor and had inadequate service provision. Another problem was the low educational level of many of the applicants eager to be trained for and work construction jobs. Yet another challenge faced by rebuilders was the low civic capacity present in New Orleans. Due to the lack of support for low-income housing, local civic groups had little experience and less capacity than was needed to rebuild housing in a city needing tens of thousands of new and rebuilt units.

As serious as these problems were, more serious was the resistance from local, state, and national political leaders. For example, Thompson relates how, shortly after a June 14, 2006, announcement by the unions and Mayor Ray Nagin of a plan to refurbish several hundred units in a public housing complex that had suffered relatively little damage—and despite massive local objections by the mayor and community—the Bush administration ordered those to be demolished.[43]

It was not just in New Orleans that neoliberal governance restored the "old" racial and class orders. In some ways, attempts in Mississippi to use the disaster to further a neoliberal corporate agenda were even more blatant than in the parishes of Louisiana. Even though the Mississippi Governor's Commission acknowledged that "[Katrina] had a particularly devastating impact on low-wealth residents who lacked an economic safety net," Governor Haley Barbour redirected $600 million of recovery aid to enhance the port of Gulfport, even though it suffered only $50 million worth of damage.[44] To do so, Barbour required a waiver from the Bush administration of the requirement by the Department of Housing and Urban Development that 50 percent of recovery funds be used to "benefit low- and moderate-income people."[45] The Republican governor had no visible trouble receiving the waiver, even though his own commission had stated that it was precisely the poor who were worse off due to Katrina. Naomi Klein cites the state-sanctioned looting of public treasuries by private entities that typified much of the aftermath to Katrina as a prime example of what she labels "disaster capitalism."[46] Disaster capitalism is yet another example of neoliberal governance turning as many opportunities as possible into dual opportunities to both dismantle the state and enrich powerful corporate interests. In the case of Katrina, disaster capitalism also enabled the partial restoration of an old pre–Civil Rights era racist racial order.

Katrina is an important example for us not only because of how it illuminates the complex intersection of race and class in this century. The aftermath to the disaster also reveals the extent to which neoliberal justifications are being used to reestablish the old racial and class orders. For example, in the name of efficient land-use policy and rational planning, attempts were made to build a golf course on land that had been the site of a poor neighborhood.[47] Even more telling, perhaps, was the quickness and glee with which the Bush administration immediately rolled back a slew of regulations protecting workers at the behest of their corporate friends in the Gulf—waiving a number of key regulatory provisions. These included OSHA health and safety regulations, even though the workers (many immigrants) had to work in a very toxic environment and with many toxic materials; requirements that contractors pay prevailing wages to workers on federal contracts; and affirmative action provisions. And officials were allowed to issue no-bid contracts and authorization to contractors to "lure" undocumented workers from Mexico and Latin America, indeed from as far away as India, without fear of employer sanctions. According to the 2008 Oxfam America report:

> While these federal waivers were eventually rescinded, they sent a powerful signal to the marketplace and set a low threshold for the future protection of workers' rights.

In more general terms, however, the need to rebuild the city and region has provided local corporations and contractors an extraordinary opportunity to take advantage of globalization processes to break the social compact, severely disadvantaging two sets of workers. Oxfam America reports:

> In what has become a disturbing trend along the Gulf Coast, an employer capitalized on the opportunity to hire cheap labor, but in the process shut out displaced local workers; they weren't offered the jobs or, if they were, they couldn't afford to take them. In addition, a flawed federal program, which should have helped the immigrants support their families, actually ended up pushing them further into debt.[48]

This nexus of intersecting pressures has resulted in African Americans losing many of the gains they had achieved through a combination of their individual hard work and efforts, as well as through the Civil Rights Movement. One black woman, for example, who had had a good professional job in Biloxi, Mississippi, was offered a job as a kitchen worker when she returned to the same establishment. She has been similarly rebuffed by other potential employers, in spite of her work history and credentials. This was a general pattern for blacks in the Gulf.[49] Many who had good working- and middle-class jobs before the storm were faced afterward with immense downward mobility—an instantiation of a racial order in the Gulf that had both modern elements (blacks being excluded totally from the labor market) and "traditional" elements (blacks regardless of excellence of credentials being confined to the lower levels of the occupational/income distributions). As the Oxfam report states:

> These factors may help explain why only 12 percent of African-American evacuees who returned to New Orleans after the hurricanes were able to find work when they came home, compared with 45 percent of white evacuees.[50]

The post-Katrina neoliberal remaking of the racial order in the Gulf also negatively affected both native and immigrant Latino and Asian workers. One Latina worker in Mississippi reported being reluctant to go out in public after Katrina because of police harassment and baseless prostitution arrests that ended only when she came up with a few hundred dollars for the "fine." She said, "Before Katrina, I felt like a normal person, not so different from everybody else. Now I feel ignored or discriminated against because of my race, gender, or language. *I don't feel free.* And I don't know what's going to happen."[51]

Employers recruiting contract labor to the Gulf Coast took full advantage of their employees' tenuous legal standing and the Bush administration's waiver of regulatory protections to establish horrific working conditions, reminiscent of those that sparked fierce labor movements a century earlier in Europe and the United States. Many workers and communities fought back. South Asian workers at Mississippi ports sued their employers about the appalling conditions under which they worked. Black women and men formed groups that both mobilized to make just demands on the state, while also attempting to provide the type of services the state should have been providing in the first place.

Unfortunately, tensions between black and Latino workers in particular made the work of building cross-racial/ethnic alliances more difficult. These tensions are the result both of structural factors shaping the racial and class terrain in the Gulf and the decisions, as much political as economic, of elites to use the hurricane as an opportunity to economically disenfranchise large numbers of black workers by exploiting large numbers of immigrant workers at very low wages and in very bad conditions. It is predictable that black workers and communities would resent an immigrant population that displaced them from good jobs by working for substandard wages under very bad conditions. It is predictable that Latino and other immigrants would have very poor views of a black population when their perceptions have been shaped by a globalized and Americanized media that demonizes black citizens.

At the same time, however, a public opinion study commissioned by Oxfam America highlights common concerns and interests among black and Latino communities, which could be the basis for building a unified movement.[52] The Oxfam study shows that between 2000 and 2007, the African American population in Orleans Parish declined from 66.7 to 60.2 percent, while the Latino population grew from 3.1 to 4.5 percent during the same period.[53] Potentially heartening is that both blacks and Latinos identified the same three critical problems—access to affordable housing and health care, as well as "receiving fair treatment from the criminal justice system."[54] More troubling, substantial majorities of both blacks and Latinos reported experiencing discrimination as a major problem due to their phenotype (a majority of blacks and about half of Latinos), educational level, or due to their language.

Unfortunately, the study also reveals significant obstacles standing in the way of building black/Latino alliances in the Gulf. While a majority of blacks "felt very comfortable" hiring (65 percent), working for (51 percent), or working with Latinos (68 percent), large percentages of Latinos did not feel very comfortable hiring (27 percent), working for (19 percent), or working with blacks (29 percent). Similarly, 59 percent of blacks, but only 32 percent of Latinos, stated that they were "very comfortable" living in neighborhoods with, respectively, Latinos and blacks.[55] Perceptions about labor market competition between blacks and Latinos play out differently, and at least in one direction the feelings are shaped by class. While neither Latinos nor middle-class blacks tended to agree that "Latino workers limit job opportunities for African- Americans," poor blacks were much more likely than either of the other two groups to agree that Latinos in fact did limit black opportunity. In focus groups, this belief among blacks was tied to the perception that Latinos were willing to work for very low wages, less than a living wage for a family in the United States. Furthermore, 60 to 63 percent of both black and Latino respondents reported that lack of trust of the other group presented a major barrier to building alliances between the two groups.

More optimistically, despite the lack of trust, over 80 percent of both groups believed it was important to form alliances between the two groups.[56] Both groups also stated that civil society, specifically the church and grassroots community organizations, would be instrumental in helping to bring the two groups together. This is true as far as it goes. What we also need is accountable political leaders who do not seek just to further their own careers by inciting tensions between the groups in name of bourgeois (pseudo-)nationalism.

All of these conflicts, struggles, and processes continue to be reflected in the fragmented and racialized publics of New Orleans. Years after Katrina, a dispute broke out between representatives of the black media and black elected officials with the large white-oriented radio stations. According to one reporter, "Members of the black media say the city's more popular stations largely champion the white point of view."[57] After the hurricane hit, the radio station WBOK converted from gospel to talk radio, based on the owner's belief that black perspectives were missing from the airwaves in New Orleans. One black member of the city council agreed and accused a white talk show host of being racist. According to one black media source, a major dividing line had to do with black talk radio emphasizing race as a major cause of the myriad problems facing New Orleans, while white stations, though agreeing on the problems, denied that race had anything to do with them. This should not be surprising because the divide in New Orleans media exactly parallels the racial divide in public opinion immediately after Katrina, as presented in chapter 2. One of the explicit goals of WBOK was to force "them" to "listen to us."[58] A central task for black politics in this period is not only to get those in predominantly white publics to "listen to us," but also to build political movements powerful enough so that the views of black publics become influential in the overall politics and policy-making within the polity.

The trauma produced by Hurricane Katrina and its aftermath continues to afflict the disadvantaged, particularly poor people of color, years after Katrina made landfall. Not only have poor people and communities received criminally inadequate support from the state to rebuild, but corporate elites and their allies have taken advantage of the disaster to roll back the democratic economic and racial advances gained over so many decades of blood, sweat, and tears.

In the following section, I first turn to a brief examination of relative and absolute black economic status. This section highlights key economic trends that have accompanied the political transformations described in the vignettes. This discussion will highlight the effects that global and national processes of economic transformation have had on African Americans and their communities. I conclude with a more in-depth discussion of how neo-liberalism has shaped black politics.

To be a poor man is hard, but to be a poor race in a land of dollars is the very bottom of hardships.
W. E. B. Du Bois, *The Souls of Black Folks*

Inequality matters. And of course race matters in the production of inequality, including economic inequality, as Cornel West first reminded us a decade ago. Du Bois suggested more than a century ago that economic inequality can have particularly devastating effects in a country as consumer and capitalist oriented as the United States. Economic inequality, however, does not exist in a vacuum. There are political, social, and structural reasons for continued high levels of absolute and relative black economic disadvantage. Much of this story is well known.[59] Super-profits derived from the super-exploitation of black labor through the systems first of slavery and then Jim Crow provided a critical foundation for American economic growth for nearly the first two centuries of the Republic.

The new twenty-first-century racial order has changed the face of black inequality. An aspect of inequality that has not always been appreciated, though it is all too visible in the modern black ghetto, is its spatial nature. Pioneering efforts by sociologists including William J. Wilson, Douglas Massey, and Nancy Denton—and as refined by others, such as Mario Small, Omar McRoberts, and Loïc Wacquant—have led to a better understanding of the spatial dimension of inequality as a central component of the racial order, specifically as the intersection between race and class. As black inequality has undergone a spatial transformation in the United States, African Americans, particularly the young, have become subject to a double stigma. First, as Wacquant shows, they are stigmatized for living in areas such as the South Side of Chicago (where I have lived and/or worked most of my life), which are labeled by outsiders as " 'no-go areas,' fearsome redoubts rife with crime, lawlessness and moral degeneracy where only the rejects of society could bear to dwell."[60] Second, as Devah Pager argues, black youth in particular, but increasingly all African Americans, are "marked" as likely criminals both by their "fellow" citizens and by the institutions of the state—especially the police.[61] Inequality, both in its economic aspects and in the ideological burdens that go along with it, determines life chances for the black poor as grim as any seen at any point in mid- or late-twentieth-century urban America.

In 1994 I wrote, "Large gaps between black and white economic status are still found in late-twentieth-century America."[62] Unfortunately, this statement still holds seventeen years later. African Americans across a number of key indicators uniformly confront worse economic conditions than their white counterparts. Two basic points must be kept in mind. First, in terms of absolute economic disadvantage, high levels of black unemployment and poverty are indicators of the economic disaster that continues to devastate poor black communities. Second, in relative terms, blacks continue to lag severely behind their white counterparts at the aggregate level in critical economic categories. While the black poor find themselves in much more dire circumstances than their more affluent cousins, the income gap between blacks and whites is also large at the upper end of the income distribution.

Looking in turn at poverty, unemployment, and income, in the following subsections I provide evidence of the continuing economic gap between black and white Americans. I then fill out a description of the evolution of the black political economy over the last twenty years. While by no means comprehensive, the sketch I provide should prove a sufficient basis for a better understanding of the economic context of the transformations I describe in black public opinion and black politics.

POVERTY

As table 10 shows, African Americans have not begun to close the poverty gap with whites. Although the black poverty rate has declined for the past twenty years, it remains three times as severe as that of white Americans. According to data collected before the onset of the worst economic crisis the nation has faced in decades, one out of four African Americans still resided below the poverty level. It can be assumed that the number now is higher.

Ironically, in cities such as Chicago, black suburbanization has served mainly to relocate areas of poverty once concentrated in the "central city." As

Table 10: Black and White Poverty Rates, 1986–2006

	Blacks	Whites	B/W
1986	31%	9%	3.4
1987	32%	9%	3.6
1988	31%	8%	3.9
1989	31%	8%	3.9
1990	32%	9%	3.6
1991	33%	9%	3.7
1992	33%	10%	3.3
1993	31%	10%	3.1
1994	29%	9%	3.2
1995	28%	9%	3.1
1996	27%	9%	3.0
1997	26%	9%	2.9
1998	24%	8%	3.0
1999	23%	8%	2.9
2000	23%	7%	3.3
2001	23%	8%	2.9
2002	24%	8%	3.0
2003	24%	8%	3.0
2004	25%	9%	2.8
2005	25%	8%	3.1
2006	24%	8%	3.0

a result of the demolition of public housing in Chicago proper, a heavy concentration of poverty has been substantially transferred to the south suburbs. We have seen this pattern in places from Oakland, California, through the Midwest to the eastern seaboard, of poor urban residents being forced out of the inner city by a variety of mechanisms, including the destruction of public housing and gentrification. Thus, for many poor African Americans, moving to the suburbs is not a mythic fulfillment of the American dream, as it was for millions of white Americans of earlier generations. Instead, it is often accompanied by continued poverty combined with fewer social services, more costly yet fewer transportation options, and thus amounts merely to a relocation of what Malcolm X called an "American nightmare" from city to suburbs.

UNEMPLOYMENT

One of the reasons for continuing high levels of black poverty is continuing high levels of black unemployment. For most of the past twenty years, as table 11 shows, blacks have suffered double-digit levels of unemployment. Since the 1950s it has generally been the case that black unemployment was at least twice that of white Americans. By November 2010 (not shown in the table), black employment had soared to 16 percent as compared to a nearly as catastrophic 13 percent rate for Latinos and a still devastating, but much lower rate of 9 percent for white Americans.[63]

The same changes in the American political economy responsible for continued high rates of black poverty—deindustrialization, spatial mismatch, the shrinking of the government labor forces at all levels, deproletarianization—have played an even more proximate role in sustaining high rates of black unemployment. Also involved here, however, is old-fashioned racial discrimination, as clearly demonstrated by the recent study "Are Emily and Greg More Employable than Lakisha and Jamal?: A Field Experiment on Labor Market Discrimination."[64] The researchers found that employers were much less likely to call back job seekers who have "black-sounding" names (such as Lakisha and Jamal) than those with "white-sounding" names, even though applicants had identical résumés. The researchers show that this finding holds across occupational categories involving a range of skill and education requirements. After considering several alternative hypotheses,

Table 11: Black and White Unemployment Rates, 1986–2008

	Blacks	Whites	B/W
1986	15%	6%	2.5
1987	13%	5%	2.6
1988	12%	5%	2.4
1989	11%	5%	2.2
1990	11%	5%	2.2
1991	13%	6%	2.2
1992	14%	7%	2.0
1993	13%	6%	2.2
1994	12%	5%	2.4
1995	10%	5%	2.0
1996	11%	5%	2.2
1997	10%	4%	2.5
1998	9%	4%	2.3
1999	8%	4%	2.0
2000	8%	3%	2.7
2001	9%	4%	2.3
2002	10%	5%	2.0
2003	11%	5%	2.2
2004	10%	5%	2.0
2005	10%	4%	2.5
2006	9%	4%	2.3
2007	8%	4%	2.0
2008	10%	5%	2.0

the authors demonstrate that not only is racial discrimination the most par-simonious explanation for employers' behavior; it is also the only hypothesis that fits the results.

With or without "black-sounding" names, however, being black simply makes it harder to get a job. As Devah Pager recounts:

> Blacks are less than half as likely to receive consideration by employers than equally qualified whites, and black nonoffenders fare no better than even those whites with prior felony convictions. The sheer magnitude of these findings underlines the continuing significance of race in employment decisions.[65]

One reason for this phenomenon, Pager argues, is that young black males are assumed to have criminal backgrounds regardless of the evidence to the contrary.

High rates of black incarceration contribute to this stigma, thus worsening employment prospects for all blacks. But they have a more direct effect on black joblessness as well. Bruce Western argues that black unemployment rates are even higher than recognized officially, due to the "hidden joblessness" that comes of incarceration. Employment, according to Western, has no effect on white incarceration rates but does have a significant effect on black rates. "Between the mid-1980s and the late 1990s," he claims, "employment rates for black dropouts fell 7 percentage points, increasing their chances of going to prison by 11 percent. The declining wage and employment rates of young less-skilled black men through the 1980s and 1990s is thus estimated to have increased their chance of imprisonment by about 20 percent. In sum, there is strong evidence that deteriorating labor market status is closely associated with increasing rates of imprisonment."[66] Pager's study shows that the problem works in both directions—blacks with prison records find it very hard to gain employment. Black unemployment contributes to high incarceration rates, which in turn feeds the high unemployment rates.

The reasons for continued high black unemployment rates—rates that are higher than the rates listed here due to the current financial crisis—are many and varied. The basic point remains that high black unemployment rates continue to provide a grim marker of black absolute and relative economic disadvantage.

INCOME

Dividing the populations of black and white households into fifths, we see that in 2007, 20 percent of all white Americans received annual household incomes over $189,000, 40 percent over $106,000, and 60 percent over $68,000. The comparable numbers for blacks in 2007 put household income for the top 20 percent at over $125,000, for 40 percent over $70,000, and for 60 percent over $43,000. These statistics are displayed in more detail in figure 3.

Even after controlling for inflation, it is clear that black households continue to lag profoundly behind white households in received income. In both 1986 and 2007, the wage gap between blacks and whites is large. The only

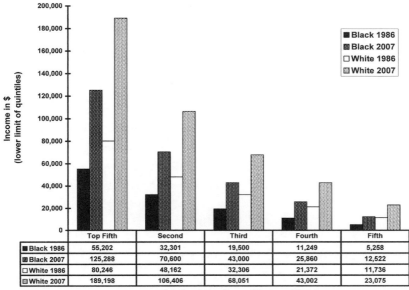

	Top Fifth	Second	Third	Fourth	Fifth
■ Black 1986	55,202	32,301	19,500	11,249	5,258
▦ Black 2007	125,288	70,600	43,000	25,860	12,522
☐ White 1986	80,246	48,162	32,306	21,372	11,736
▥ White 2007	189,198	106,406	68,051	43,002	23,075

Quintile of Pop Group (Black vs. White)

FIGURE 3: Black/white income quintiles, 1986 and 2007.

way for black incomes to reach parity with white incomes is to mentally shift the black quintiles over one slot. Thus, roughly speaking in both years, the highest-earning 20 percent of black households received approximately the same income as the second highest-earning white quintile, and so on. It should also be noted that not taking incarceration into account leads to understating the black/white wage gap and overstating black income gains,[67] and it also leads to overstating immigrant labor's downward pressure on native workers' wages. Indeed, once incarceration is taken into account, the yearly decline in wages due to immigration is estimated to be 1 percent, while the weekly decline becomes zero.[68]

Some analysts find the wage gap puzzling. Part of the puzzle is based on the view that the wage gap, particularly at the upper end of the income distribution, should be shrinking more rapidly than it has been. As Eric Grodsky and Devah Pager point out, black scores on cognitive tests (and educational levels more generally) rose during the 1990s, reducing the racial educational attainment gap, which should have led to a narrower gap at the upper end of the income distribution. Even though scores were generally rising, the fact that the black/white gap was narrowing led many scholars and policy makers to expect that the wage gap would also narrow. Yet the gap is larger between higher-income blacks and whites.[69] That the gap may be due in part to continued discrimination in labor markets does not seem to be considered by some analysts as a possible explanation for this conundrum.

As with the poverty and unemployment rates, the black/white income gap is a strong indicator of the persistence and depth of the gap between black and white economic status. Just as income provides a useful indicator for indicating the gap between the economic status of whites and blacks, it also is a useful indicator of the amount of economic inequality found among African Americans.

CLASS DIVISIONS AMONG BLACKS

As can be seen in figures 4 and 5, black income inequality was stable from 1986 through 2007.[70] That said, it is also apparent that the most affluent 40 percent of black households receive 75 percent of the income.

What has changed is how much income the top 20 percent is receiving. The lower limit for the top 20 percent of black households rose from $55,000 in 1986 to $125,000 in 2007. Even after using the Consumer Price

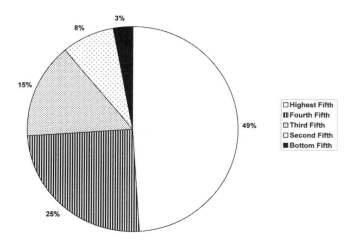

8% 3%

15%

49%

Highest Fifth
Fourth Fifth
Third Fifth
Second Fifth
Bottom Fifth

25%

FIGURE 4: Black income shares, 1986.

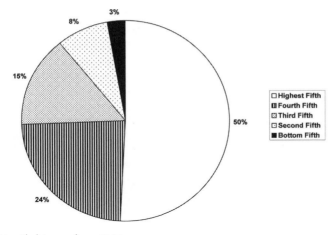

FIGURE 5: Black income shares, 2007.

Index to convert 1986 dollars to 2007 dollars to account for inflation, this represents a significant rise for those in the most affluent percentile.

The income disparities are even starker when we look at the most affluent 5 percent of black households (see table 12). Five percent of black households consistently receive 20 percent of black income, while the poorest 20 percent receive about 3 percent of black income. The most affluent 5 percent receive about four times the income they would have if income were distributed evenly among black households, and the poorest 20 percent of black households receive only about one-seventh of the income they would if income were distributed evenly among African Americans.

Class divisions among blacks are also exacerbated by incarceration. College-educated blacks are much less likely than black men without a college education to go to prison, and consequently have much better labor market and income prospects.[71] The life chances of unskilled African Americans with a prison record and college-educated African Americans are extraordinarily different.

In conclusion, poor and middle-class blacks still face discrimination in a number of markets relating to housing, employment, retail, and loans and other financial services. This discrimination feeds directly into economic disadvantage in the present, in the form of diminished employment prospects,

Table 12: Percent of Income Received by Most Affluent 5% of Black Households

	Percent Received
1986	19%
1987	19%
1988	19%
1989	18%
1990	19%
1991	18%
1992	19%
1993	21%
1994	20%
1995	20%
1996	22%
1997	19%
1998	19%
1999	20%
2000	20%
2001	20%
2002	22%
2003	20%
2004	21%
2005	21%
2006	22%
2008	21%

for example, and in the future in terms of limits on the ability to generate, invest, and transfer wealth to succeeding generations. The plight of the black poor is particularly devastating, leaving once-stable working-class black communities and families increasingly isolated and disconnected from the mainstream economy. While the black middle class, particularly the upper-middle class, is doing better than ever (at least up until the latest financial crisis), the black poor are arguably worse off than they were a generation ago.

WHAT LESSONS ARE SUGGESTED BY THE VIGNETTES AND THE changes in black relative and absolute economic status? What are the political ramifications of the massive inter- and intra-racial economic disparities sketched in the preceding section? Given the financial crisis that took root in the fall of 2008, we can expect political conflicts to have an economic edge to them for the foreseeable future, while the ruling ideology will remain a "made in America" racially tinged neoliberalism. One kind of conflict will be over policies that are responsible for shaping cities and regions in a time of severe budgetary constraints. Another will be over the heart and soul of the disadvantaged, as various political and economic interests compete to be recognized as advocates for the poor. As class divisions solidify among African Americans, we can also expect black politicians to increasingly make class-based appeals, both implicit and explicit, to different class segments within the black community. This trend will become more pronounced as affluent African Americans increasingly become part of the gentrification process and take up temporary residence side by side with poorer black neighbors, before eventually pushing out the less fortunate, most often also black, earlier residents of changing neighborhoods. Each of the vignettes as well as the economic data substantially undermined the idea of a unified black "community." Political projects and movements can be created that attempt to unify African Americans around various causes. In the future, however, the idea of "the" black community cannot be assumed, but must be articulated politically.[72] In summary, the three vignettes are vivid examples of how neoliberalism has transformed black political economy.

I use the term "political economy" for three reasons. First, the idea that there are "free" markets is a myth—although one that is particularly central to the neoliberal ideology of our time. Markets do not exist in a vacuum. They are embedded in the dense networks of political and social relations that shape them, dictate how markets function, determine who can participate in them and at what level, and determine how goods are allocated within markets. As Karl Polanyi explained over half a century ago, Western capitalism has never been characterized by unfettered free markets.[73] American labor markets, to take but one example, have been structured for most of the history of this nation by racism or, more precisely, structured by the racial order, as described in chapter 2.

Second, political institutions play a central role in shaping the economy and the economic fortunes of marginalized populations such as the black poor. Often when we think of political economy, we are envisioning the political institutions, the rules and regulations, that govern markets, economic entities, and consumer behavior. We also envision the political consequences that flow from perceived political management of the economy, such as the electoral consequences of high unemployment and/or inflation rates. When thinking about communities, we should also ask if the government is acting as an investor. To what degree are public schools supported? Are public hospitals and clinics being supported? Or, in poor black and Latino neighborhoods, are they being shuttered? Is there adequate public transportation allowing people to get from where they live to where the jobs are? Or, as in many black urban communities, do we find public transportation services facing new cuts, even as they have struggled to absorb the previous ones? What is the level of general public investment in community services? As Loïc Wacquant shows, American levels of public investment in poor communities, as compared with France and the United Kingdom, are exceedingly low.[74] By providing or withholding public services, government invests to one degree or another in human and social capital, which in turn determines citizens' absolute and relative ability to enter and compete in markets.

Finally, I use the term "political economy" in a third, less conventional sense. I use "black political economy" to refer to the political solutions and political movements, as well as the economic solutions and policies, that are required to overcome the economic disadvantages facing African Americans, particularly those facing poor African Americans.

I also focused on neoliberalism in this chapter because what Lisa Wedeen calls "the global processes of neoliberal reform" have profoundly shaped both black life chances and black politics.[75] Neoliberal processes, policies, as well as the elites who have embraced neoliberal ideology have all reshaped both the black political economy and black politics, including the relative and absolute economic status of African Americans. The argument I advance in this chapter is that neoliberal processes as analyzed by such scholars as Wedeen, William Connolly, and David Harvey, and described in particular by Harvey, have remade economic, political, and social orders on a global scale. The central point I want to make for the American case is that these processes have also reshaped, even as they were in turn shaped by, the American racial order.

Wedeen's explication of the various meanings given the term "neoliberalism" is a good starting place for my purposes. She explains:

> Neoliberalism is used to refer to four different political-economy phenomena:
> (1) macroeconomic stabilization (policies that encourage low inflation and low

public debt, and discourage Keynesian countercyclical tendencies); (2) trade liberalization and financial deregulation; (3) the privatization of publicly owned assets and firms; and (4) welfare state retrenchment.[76]

All four processes have played a major role in transforming American society, including the economy and politics, starting with the Nixon administration forty years ago. These transformations accelerated during Reagan's tenure. Particularly important for understanding how neoliberal policies have decimated many black communities, especially poor black communities, are points three and four, the privatization of public assets and the reduction or elimination of state services. I would add to these four processes a fifth critical feature of neoliberal regimes that Wedeen identifies, this one involving neoliberal ideology, norms, and sets of practices that in turn justify the political use of the language of "rationality," "efficiency," and "technocratic expertise."

Another key aspect of Wedeen's analysis has important lessons for the U.S. case. In addition to the inter-state variation that is to be found in how neoliberal policies are implemented and the effects they have on the local society, economy, and politics, she emphasizes variation on the intra-state level.[77] Local variation is also to be seen in the type and intensity of resistance to neoliberal policies, including whether resistance appears at all. Further, she makes the point that the shift to a neoliberal regime does not entail the stereotypical shift from the provision to the non-provision of welfare state services in all regions or localities, since in some states or regions within states such services were never provided in the first place. This regional variation is evidenced in the United States in that, with the very brief and partial exceptions of the democratic governments of the Reconstruction era in the South after the Civil War, the participation of the South and the Southwest in the American welfare state has consistently been at lower levels than the rest of the nation. Yet the more marked pattern in the United States has been that groups, specifically racial groups, have been excluded explicitly and implicitly from the benefits of the welfare state. This American version of the intra-state variation in the implementation and effect of neoliberal policies appears, for example, in New Orleans in Katrina's aftermath. The American racial order continues to take a somewhat different form in the South than in the rest of the country, once again often under the rubric of "states' rights" justifying the truncation of black human rights in the old Confederacy. In the aftermath of the storm, neoliberal policies and the justifications offered for them blended with old-style, occasionally violent racist practices. Just as the American welfare state at the time of the New Deal was deformed and undermined in the South by legal requirements to conform to the racial order of Jim Crow, this southern variation involved imposing a neoliberal regime in a particularly virulent form in the aftermath of Katrina.

Finally, Wedeen points to a "recalibration of the state's role in the national imaginary" as a key aspect of the implementation of neoliberal policies.[78] How this recalibration is viewed by the populace, however, depends on the view of the state embedded in the discourse of each major public or counterpublic. For decades now, the consensus black understanding of the proper role of the state has differed greatly from that of the majority of white Americans. African Americans historically, unlike their white counterparts, have by and large supported a strong central state that both regulates the economy and redistributes wealth from the rich to the poor. One consequence of the neoliberal transformation of black politics described in this chapter is the increasing abandonment on the part of black elites of precisely this mainstream black understanding of the role of the state and, on that basis, the form that politics properly takes. By the latter, I mean that from the country's founding through the Civil Rights and Black Power eras, African Americans have embraced a robust engaged politics that included the building of mass movements, vigorous mass political debate within the black counterpublic, and the construction of independent and active black political organizations. Today black organizations and elites have all too often abandoned this legacy of political activism in favor of a politics that relies on low levels of political participation and lobbying, with what mass political action that does develop being centered on individual candidates rather than independent political movements organized around issues of central concern to African Americans. In the big box vignette, we saw how some black elites in Chicago allied with the neoliberal state in order to facilitate Walmart's penetration of a poor black neighborhood that had already been negatively affected by neoliberal processes of globalization.

What David Harvey cogently describes as the neoliberal state can be seen as deeply complicit in the New Orleans and Chicago big box vignettes. Harvey characterizes as a "neoliberal state apparatus" one "whose fundamental mission was to facilitate conditions for profitable capital accumulation on the part of both domestic and foreign capital."[79] Local city government in Chicago and government on the local, state, and federal levels in the Gulf Coast certainly performed this role to the benefit of capital. What Harvey and others overlook is the central role that the resurgence and reformation of white supremacy played—and plays—in securing the victory of neoliberalism in its rawest, most vicious, powerful, and imperialist form in the United States.[80] Harvey himself points out that a key aspect of neoliberalism as it appears in the United States concerns the way it is able to resuscitate racist appeals to convince white workers in particular, but even large segments of the white middle class, to "vote against its material, economic, and class interests."[81] What he and others, such as William Connolly, miss is not only how race is deeply implicated in the mobilization of white working-class support for a reactionary economic agenda, but also how it structures the very nature of capitalism in the United States, including its current neoliberal incarnation.

Research on how neoliberalism—especially in the sense of a set of policies, but also in terms of ideology—affects black politics in the United States is beginning to emerge.[82] This research is attempting to rectify contemporary theorizing on neoliberalism, which tends to ignore race, racial orders, and racism—unless it is to dismiss the concerns of non-whites and their movements as "identity politics." The theoretical analyses of scholars such as Ira Katznelson and William Sites suffer from a lack of knowledge of black (and more generally non-white) political mobilizations in the twentieth century.[83] They lament the historic fragmentation of urban political movements due to the separation of work and community in the United States, with the consequent separation (and rising hostility) between community and labor organizations and movements. In particular, Sites and others point to how this fragmentation has been racialized, with the non-white community movements coming into opposition with urban labor movements. Aside from the obvious problem that for nearly half a century urban-based labor movements have included heavy non-white participation—particularly black and Latino—often under Latino and black leadership, there is a broader historical problem with this view. An examination of urban black political history reveals not only the frequent appearance of a strong alliance between labor and black community activism, but that in cities such as Detroit, Chicago, New York, and Atlanta, these movements are not only connected but are actually wings of the same movement. From the 1940s through the 1970s, the labor movement was not only an important site for the development of black political leadership in the urban centers of the nation. It also provided the basis for independent black political formations and movements. These were most spectacularly visible in Detroit in the efforts of black workers organizing in plants against both economic and racial exploitation. Cities such as Chicago, Detroit, Mahwah, New Jersey, and many, many more also were the sites of militant black worker organizing.

While the core of the Detroit organizing was in the auto plants, militant, often Marxist-inspired, black organizing also occurred in sectors as diverse as shipping, health care, and higher education. Often these movements had to take on corporate America, the state, and in all too many cases white-dominated unions such as the construction trade unions in Chicago and Pittsburgh, which actively prevented black workers from joining their ranks. In many ways the labor/community alliances that were formed in black, Latino, and Asian American communities in the late 1960s and throughout the 1970s were a dress rehearsal for today's labor/community alliances that critics such as Sites describe as "social unionism."[84] We do need to be clear, however, that the mobilization of white racism did serve to benefit the right and its corporate sponsors. The extreme income inequality described earlier in this chapter, Harvey argues, resulted from what "was from the very beginning a project to achieve the restoration of class power. After the implementation of neoliberal polices in the late 1970s, the share of national income of the top 1 per cent of income earners in the US soared, to reach 15 per cent (very close to its pre–Second Word War share) by the end of the century."[85]

Another consequence of the transformations analyzed early in the chapter and highlighted in the vignettes is the importance of the spatial dimension—the way that the racial and economic orders categorize places—in marking neighborhoods, individuals, and entire groups as the inferior and despised other. Wacquant describes the nature of this spatial marking:

> As a new century dawns, the incapacity of the governments of the advanced
> countries, that is, the refusal or reticence of their ruling classes converted to

neoliberalism to check the social and spatial accumulation of economic hardship, social dislocation and cultural dishonor in the deteriorating working-class and/or ethnoracial enclaves of the dualizing metropolis, promises to engender abiding civic alienation and chronic unrest which pose a daunting challenge to the institution of citizenship.[86]

Wacquant proceeds by outlining how the embracing of neoliberal economic and social policies by the nation's elites had multiple critical effects on poor blacks. First, as I argued in *Black Visions*, these policies served to deproletarianize working-class black youths by separating them from the labor market both through deindustrialization and the stigmatization described by Wacquant, as well as Pager and Western. Second, according to Wacquant, these policies brought about three interrelated blights: massive unemployment, the relegation of entire communities to decaying neighborhoods as private and public services were withdrawn as part of the neoliberal turn, and the intensification of stigmatization, as already described.[87] Harvey amplifies the latter point when he argues that neoliberal apologists "see [some] geographies and spatialities (and local loyalties) not only as disrupting order and rational universal discourse, but as potentially undermining universal morality and goodness, much as they undermine the basic foundational propositions of economic theory."[88] Thus through a neoliberal inversion, black ghettos and Latino barrios are viewed not as places of oppression but of immorality and inefficiency. We saw in some of the vignettes that the new spatial, political, and economic realities are resisted by urban political activism. Politically active ghettos and barrios are, as Harvey argues, particularly prime targets for demonization. America's ghettos and barrios are the domestic equivalent of countries that are marked by international neoliberal regimes as immature, ungovernable, and the site of battles between Good and Evil.

The rapidity with which increasing economic devastation hit cities such as Detroit and Los Angeles can be seen in the decline in manufacturing jobs. South Central Los Angeles (the iconic black ghetto of mid- to late-twentieth-century Los Angeles, now mainly Latino) lost 70,000 high-wage manufacturing jobs just between 1978 and 1982. The 200 firms that left South Central during this period moved either to the predominantly white outer suburbs or over the border to Mexico, where labor could be more easily exploited. The manufacturing jobs were to some degree replaced by low-paid service jobs offering inferior conditions. The employers of these new service firms had a strong preference for immigrant, mainly Latino, labor and an antipathy toward black labor. This transition in the local political economy was a major factor contributing to a 50 percent black male unemployment rate during the early 1990s.[89] This process was repeated in the major manufacturing centers in the East, Midwest, and West Coast—all areas that had a history of militant labor organizing, including significant participation by black (and other non-white) workers. The script that was implemented after Katrina, in other words, had already been tested in the quarter century of deindustrialization that preceded the hurricane. Blacks had always been economically disadvantaged in the United States. What was new about this process was that for the first time, beginning with deindustrialization, large segments of the black population were permanently pushed out of the labor force—they became economically "disposable." Even one of neoliberalism's main cheerleaders, Thomas Friedman, admits that due to neoliberal processes, "hundreds of millions of people on this planet . . . have been left behind by the flattening process."[90]

This economic devastation of black communities also has critical implications for black political participation. Cathy Cohen and I found that living in extremely poor neighborhoods significantly shaped African American public opinion, even after controlling for individual attributes such as income, ideology, and racial consciousness.[91] Blacks who resided in the very poorest neighborhoods (neighborhoods where more than 30 percent of the families had incomes below the poverty line) were significantly more likely to distrust traditional coalition partners of African Americans such as unions, "the working class," and the black middle class. They were much more likely than other blacks to feel that their community had insoluble problems and feel frustration in trying to solve these problems. They were much less likely to be tied to political networks of community and political elites. Not surprisingly, they were much less likely to participate in community politics and even engage in discussion with families and friends.

The combination of the social, political, and labor-market isolation of America's black inner cities with the increasing political salience of class in the black community has left the black poor with far less access to social, political, and economic capital, while at the same time leaving them in a state of relative political disengagement. The political hostility toward "mainstream" black and white social forces reinforces this isolation and makes capital formation even more difficult.

Finally, another aspect of neoliberalism has been the emergence of the custodial state and the transformation of both the meaning of citizenship and the rewriting of the contract between state and citizen. The new "contract" requires the (re-)segregation along lines of both race and class of those who are viewed to have "deficits." We saw this process play out most explicitly in New Orleans, but it is implicit as well in both Chicago vignettes. Neoliberal ideology states that if you are unable to succeed in the market, it is your own fault and is not the concern of others. The problem lies explicitly in your individual character and/or your group's "culture." Silently (although increasingly less so), many adherents of this ideology also believe that there may be a genetic foundation to the "deficits" as well.

This ideology was implemented with a vengeance by urban leaders in both the public and private sectors during the urban crisis of the 1970s. In one approach it was termed the "sandbox" strategy, suggesting that municipalities should merely try to police the perimeter of inner-city neighborhoods—the ghettos and barrios of America. The idea was to let the residents kill each other, and spank them like children when their misbehavior spilled outside of the sandbox and/or the residents made too much (political) noise. Combined with that strategy was the concept of "urban triage"—withdrawing services from declining neighborhoods in order to encourage the poor (mostly blacks and Latinos) to move out of the city. In the name of economic rationality, services and urban revitalization efforts were to be provided only to middle-class and affluent neighborhoods. Paul Peterson provided the "rational" theoretical groundings for these policies in *City Limits*.[92] He contends that local elected officials could only cater to the demands of corporations and affluent individuals and families because otherwise these sectors would move to cities with policies that would benefit them to a greater degree. As a consequence, Peterson argues, cities should not fight for desegregation or work to improve poor neighborhoods, as these policies would drive out those with the economic resources that were vital to the "interests of the city." Social justice, or even basic fairness, had no place in a city governed on "rational" economic lines. (Peterson does not discuss the "costs" that might ensue if militant movements developed that would demand fair and equitable treatment and services from local officials and the local state.) The concept of the "custodial state," introduced by Charles Murray and Richard Herrnstein in *The Bell Curve*, is a logical extension of the policies first implemented on a large scale in the United States during the 1970s. A custodial state is defined according to the authors as

> a high-tech and more lavish version of the Indian reservation for some substantial minority of the nation's population, while the rest of America tries to go about its business. In its less benign forms, the solutions will become more and more totalitarian. Benign or otherwise, "going about its business" in the old sense will not be possible.

To avoid this future, the authors argue that a variety of steps must be taken, most of which involve dismantling the social welfare and regulatory state and abandoning the "ideology of equality," because

> most of its effects are bad. . . . In everyday life, the ideology of equality censors and straitjackets everything from pedagogy to humor. The ideology of equality has stunted the range of moral dialogue to triviality. In daily life— conversations, the lessons taught in public schools, the kinds of screenplays or newspaper feature stories that people choose to write—the moral ascendancy of equality has made it difficult to use concepts such as virtue, excellence, beauty and—above all—truth.[93]

This infamous book argued that members of the underclass—composed primarily of the black and Latino poor—are cognitively deficient and should be viewed as children, incapable of rational thought and action. They must be taken care of and given a "valued place" suitable to their inferior gifts. Due to genetic deficiencies and cultural pathologies, they do not have the ability to function as rational liberal and equal citizens in a democracy.[94] Murray, as noted in chapter 2, was one of many who described the black citizens of New Orleans in these terms, and therefore argued that no aid should be extended to them. Neoliberal ideology shaped not only much of the nation's understanding of the people and events in the aftermath to Katrina, and served to justify the draconian policies that have dominated post-Katrina policy-making in New Orleans, but has also been used as a warrant for similarly draconian policies that have dramatically afflicted poor, particularly non-white, communities throughout the nation before and after Katrina.

Unfortunately, as we saw, many black (and other) politicians show signs of having drunk the toxic neoliberal Kool-Aid. What we have also seen, however, is that political and social organizing is under way in many communities. Part of what is missing from this organizing is coordination, analysis, and, especially, information sharing among communities—particularly those in different regions of the nation with a common heritage of black progressive organizing. Also missing is the type of community capacity— particularly democratic capacity—through which local black communities can engage in democratic deliberation and make democratic decisions about how resources should be used and, as necessary, movements mobilized. Traditionally, this capacity (albeit not always democratically) has been provided by politically engaged black sacred and secular organizations. Independent black political organizations need to be rebuilt in order to overcome the institutional deficit resulting from the decades of deinstitutionalization. This capacity is essential not only for generally strengthening progressive black politics, but also specifically for providing mechanisms by which the African American grassroots can hold new and old black elites accountable. Building these organizations will not be possible by relying on the political rhetoric of the past. It will be even more necessary than in the past, however, to continue to attack the deadly myth that individual initiative is the sole mechanism for black advancement. Once again, those engaged in rebuilding black politics will have to rethink what new roles and forms black political organizing should take and what demands should be made on the state. The conclusion to this book includes a thought experiment that explores one potential model for the shape these types of institutions might take. Next, however, I proceed by investigating the potential tactics, goals, obstacles, and opportunities likely to be embraced and confronted by black progressive movements at the start of this century as they attempt to build multi-racial alliances.

5 THE PEOPLE UNITED?

¡El pueblo unido jamàs serà venido!
The people united will never be defeated!

In the fall of 2008, I participated in a panel discussion at the University of Chicago on how to view race and the presidential election from perspectives of African American, Asian American, and Latino politics. Most of the presentations (including mine) were fairly routine—most of us discussed Obama's impact on voter attitudes, community mobilization, candidate recruitment, and perceptions of race and politics in the racial communities with which we were most familiar. There was one jarring note, however, when an expert on Latino politics termed Obama's candidacy "unfortunate," since it was Latinos' "turn" to take over the non-white political spotlight—and that blacks' turn had passed.

A perspective that privileges interracial competition over cooperation can also be found among black activists, elites, and academics. On a Listserv I belong to, one black academic has accused several others representing a wide range of ideological positions, including black nationalism, of betraying their race (his characterization, not mine). Their crime? They disagreed with his argument that the Latino population in general, and the Latino immigrant population in particular, was directly responsible for high black incarceration rates. His stated "logic" was that since Latinos allegedly take jobs from blacks, and unemployment rates are correlated with crime, then Latinos are responsible for black incarceration. Even if one buys into his set of dubious assumptions, this remains an embarrassing example, especially for an alleged social scientist, of confusing correlation for causation.[1]

At the grassroots level, California dramatically illustrates the potentially large political payoffs of grassroots coalitions uniting people of color, while simultaneously providing exceedingly grim examples of racial conflict. Interracial violent conflict in the prisons has been replicated in communities as some Latinos gangs have marked random black people living in the same neighborhood for death. Southern California also provides examples of black and Latino cooperation in winning progressive political victories, such as preventing a Walmart from being opened up in Inglewood. More generally, the Obama campaign won overwhelming majorities of both Latinos and Asian Americans in the general election (although the support from these groups had been weaker during the Democratic primary). It has been possible to build what a generation ago were inaccurately called "Third World" coalitions. Nevertheless, certain notable successes notwithstanding, the perception has certainly been that the level of conflict between communities of color has ratcheted up to such an extent that interracial violence among people of color is no longer surprising.

A generation ago, it was a common assumption among activists of color that building enduring and progressive coalitions between groups of non-white Americans was possible. During the period of racial insurgency, from approximately 1950 to 1980, alliances between non-white movements against racial and other forms of injustice seemed "natural." Indeed, many such alliances were built both among activists and grassroots communities. Nevertheless, this was no golden age, as conflicts between communities of color continued to occur throughout the United States. As compared to now, however, a different set of logics was at work. The assumption held by many activists, including more than a few nationalist groups, was that these alliances could be organized around mutual self-interest. Today this assumption is not nearly as widespread among grassroots communities of color, let alone among elites when their self-interest often dictates working against such alliances.

The cold truth is that African Americans will never numerically have enough strength on our own to win our demands for a just democratic society. We must have allies. The question for black politics across the decades has not changed. Who will make the most reliable and sensible partners for political alliances? Historically, the answer has been that other groups facing similar discrimination, oppression, and domination offer the best possibilities for alliances. For the black poor, both the black middle class and other poor people presented alliance possibilities.

In the past for African Americans as a whole, other groups suffering racial subordination, as well as poor people, were potential alliance partners. During the nineteenth and twentieth century, blacks, Native Americans, Latinos, and Asian Americans were all targets of virulent, violent racism. During the same period, blacks, Asian Americans, and Latinos in urban areas, when not fighting outright pogroms, were the object of scorn and discrimination from all classes of whites, including white workers. White radicals in the early twentieth-century American left either downplayed questions of racism and racial oppression in the manner of Sam Gompers or, like some of his more racist comrades in the Socialist Party, openly called for white socialists to support and indeed embrace white supremacy. Not surprisingly, the racism that black radicals of this era faced from within the socialist movement led many such as Hubert Harrison to leave white-dominated socialist organizations and to form black radical organizations.[2]

Solid working relationships had been developed by the time of the insurgencies of the 1960s and early 1970s in many regions of the country, even in Southern California, where black/Chicano relations had always been fraught. East of the Mississippi, black, Asian American, and Puerto Rican activists allied to fight police brutality; oppose the Vietnam War; organize on college campuses for black, Puerto Rican, and Asian American Studies programs; work within minority caucuses at a wide variety of workplaces; and organize radical cultural and artistic programs. The most widespread alliances between activists of color of that generation were found on the country's college campuses and between the revolutionary nationalist organizations emerging out of the barrios, J-towns, Chinatowns, and ghettos of America. These alliances eventually evolved into first regional, then national Marxist organizations, whose leadership was usually derived from those same revolutionary nationalist organizations.[3] In the Southwest and on the West Coast, similar alliances were formed, although the relationship between blacks and Chicanos were more fraught than the relationships between blacks, Puerto Ricans, and other Latinos had been in the Midwest and East.

Blacks during the era of twentieth-century black insurgency were also often in close alliance with progressive whites during both the Civil Rights and Black Power phases of the insurgency. These alliances were first and foremost based on a concern on the part of liberal and radical whites for social justice, as was evident in the great sacrifices many white men and women suffered during the violence aimed at the Civil Rights Movement. These alliances were also sometimes built on the basis of mutual self-interest. Alliances against the Vietnam War were built on both anti-war ideology and self-interest, particularly on the part of youths who were called on to fight a war that many thought was ill-considered if not immoral. Workplace alliances were also built on perceived mutual interests. But alliances with whites, particularly in the workplace, were often limited by the pervasive shadow of white supremacist ideology. In Detroit, for example, radical black workers had to fight both the auto companies and the UAW, who tried to convince white workers that their interests did not coincide with that of black workers. This battle was waged in workplaces and communities across the country.

Perceptions of interests are constructed. Whites throughout the country were told that their interests as whites trumped their class interests. This ideology had been successfully used in the past. Notably it was used to destroy the nascent interracial alliance of poor blacks and whites in the South during populist uprisings of the late nineteenth century as well as early labor movements and socialist organizing throughout the country during the same period. White supremacy limited, if not eliminated, the potential for mobilizing progressive whites and put alliances with them on a different footing, one under the shadow of white supremacist ideology, than the ones between peoples of color. In the past, powerful movements and movement organizations had been needed to overcome the widespread influence of white supremacist ideology—an ideology that today is demonstrably alive and well in the Birther, Tea Party, and allied movements of the extreme populist right. Once again white supremacist ideology provides a formidable barrier to alliances among citizens of all races with a reason to be disgruntled about the country's ills.

The racial terrain in the United States, however, has been substantially transformed since the last great upsurge in mass black political activism. A variety of factors contributed to the decline in both black insurgency and the alliances with other people of color that played a large role in that insurgency, particularly in the West and the East, and to a somewhat lesser degree in the Midwest. The decline in political cooperation between both activists and communities of color had both structural and political roots. Increased immigration into Latino and Asian American communities led to changes in those communities that made it more difficult to form alliances with African Americans. Many of these communities' newer residents had neither the shared history of discrimination nor interracial cooperation, and often possessed attitudes about blacks based on American stereotypes dominant in the global media that made it more difficult to maintain existing coalitions and working relations. Politically, the community, campus, and workplace activists who had been the glue and bridging agents between non-white communities and those communities' movements no longer played that role because they no longer performed the organizing necessary to do so due to attacks by the state; decisions by activist organizations to pull their organizers out of cultural, workplace, student, community, and other forms of organizing; and the eventual disintegration of activist organizations and networks. Their relative, but pronounced, absence meant that they were no longer present to either help these newly remade communities join together in various organizing efforts or help reframe, redirect, and/or negotiate the rising tensions between many of these groups.[4]

It should not be assumed that the same potential alliance partners of a generation ago remain the best alliance partners for today. What types of alliances are possible in this era, given the complex racial terrain found in contemporary America? Increased immigration, the decline in highly coordinated nationwide activism, especially on the part of progressives, and a growing tendency among some non-white political, economic, and academic elites to view relations between different groups of people of color as inherently conflictual have all served to radically reduce cooperation among people of color. Political and economic elites in particular, many of whom have adopted neoliberal ideology, see it in their active interest to demobilize communities of color[5] and, indeed, promote conflict among them. The promotion of conflict often serves elite interests by making more difficult the type of alliances likely to generate more radical demands. Elites are probably correct in their perception that their own individual success is inversely related to the level of mobilization and radicalness found in the communities they purport to represent. While there were certainly major tensions and some conflict between these groups even during the insurgency period, there were also much higher levels of cooperation than seen today in most urban areas.

This chapter focuses on the implications of the transformation of the racial terrain since the mid-1970s for rebuilding a robust progressive black politics.[6] I begin by discussing the current evolution of the racial order in the United States. Public opinion on race and immigration is then examined to see whether my speculations on the evolution of the racial order are reflected in the data. I then argue that there are several areas where the political interests of the majority of blacks, Latinos, and Asian Americans intersect, thus providing a basis for rebuilding on a firmer basis the alliances that on occasion proved fruitful to all of these groups a generation ago. I conclude by arguing that rebuilding these alliances is not only a necessary component of rebuilding a robust progressive black politics, but even more importantly a central component in building a more inclusive and just democracy in the United States.

A CRITICAL AND UNDER-DISCUSSED ASPECT OF THE DECLINE in cooperation is the radical remaking of the racial terrain that has taken place since the mid-1960s. It could well be that these changes have made it more difficult, if not impossible, to rebuild alliances that were so often productive a generation ago. If they are to be rebuilt, however, it will only be based on an understanding of how the racial terrain and the underlying racial order have evolved over the past three decades.

Traditionally, the racial hierarchy has been conceived as being arrayed along one dimension of racial status. On this scale, whites are considered superior to all races, and for hundreds of years of racial theorizing, blacks have been considered the most inferior race. Claire Kim, however, in her book *Bitter Fruit: The Politics of Black-Korean Conflict in New York City*, has persuasively argued that there is more than one dimension to the racial hierarchy underlying the American racial order. She describes a second dimension, one of civic ostracism. This dimension is characterized by an "insider/foreigner" logic. Kim argues that while whites have coded Asian Americans as superior to blacks, but inferior to whites, on the racial status dimension, on the civic ostracism dimension, "whites construct Asian Americans as immutably foreign and unassimilable . . . in a way that excludes Asian Americans from civic membership."[7]

Kim focuses her analysis on these two dimensions. But there is no theoretical reason to believe that the number of dimensions constructing the contemporary racial order is limited to two.[8] Following Judith Shklar and W. E. B. Du Bois, as well as numerous other commentators on the construction of American citizenship and that construction's connection to America's particularly individualistic capitalist ethos, I argue that a third dimension must be added as a central component in the construction of a model of the racial order—the dimension of economic status.[9] Shklar specifically argues that economic status—a key component of which is defined as economic independence—is one of the two primary determinants of one's standing as an American citizen. It only makes sense in "the land of the dollar" that a third dimension in the racial order is one's racialized economic status. Individuals and groups that are not economically successful are considered deficient. In this racial context, economic failure is seen at least in part due to the pathologies of the struggling group and, in the minds of too many American citizens, also as a result of innate racial inferiority. Consequently, a central task of black politics is to fight against the economic subordination and devaluing of black citizenship status that is a result of the racial order's economic subordination of African Americans.

Of course, some African Americans are rich, although very few are actually wealthy (having assets in reserve as opposed to "just" having high incomes). There are also all too many whites who are brutally poor. Similarly, there is variation among all of the groups. The economic status of Indian immigrants is substantially healthier on average than that of other South Asian immigrants. The same could be said of many East Asian immigrants as compared to the economic status of immigrants from Southeast Asia. The point is not even that on average blacks are economically much worse off than whites and are on average at the bottom of the American economic ladder, although this is certainly true. The key to understanding racial subordination is understanding that there are structural components of the racialized economy that systematically disadvantage African Americans due solely to their race (such as pervasive labor, loan, housing, and consumer discrimination aimed at blacks). Further, the racial order is associated with an economic ideology stating that blacks are supposed to be at the bottom of the economic ladder—that it is the right of white Americans to be at the top of the economic ladder. Political theorists such as Judith Shklar and historians such as Eric Arnesen have carefully documented how white status as citizens has been intrinsically tied to the economic subordination of blacks.[10]

There is no single metric along any of the three dimensions, let alone across all three dimensions, that would allow for definitive comparisons across racial groups. Any plausible ranking would have whites ranked at the top across all three dimensions, and blacks and Latinos at or near the bottom along nearly all dimensions (although, on the "foreignness" scale, blacks are not on the bottom). Is it more important that blacks are at the very bottom on two of the three dimensions, or that Latinos are low on all three? In the end, such questions have no simple answers. Not only do they depend on the subjective view of the observer, but more generally this question evades the larger democratic question of the lack of full inclusion for all non-white groups.

In America, whites have always been defined as the "norm." They remain the racial standard within the nation by which others are defined. Despite impressive economic gains by some Asian Americans, whites remain economically the most well-off economic group. In terms of the civic ostracism dimension, whites are always presumed to belong to the polity and civil society. Even African Americans, who have formed an integral part of the economy—if not the polity or civil society—since before the founding, still provoke doubts among some about whether they are "real" Americans. While whites are at the top across all dimensions, blacks are at or near the bottom on two, but not the third dimension, and Latinos are also near, if not at, the bottom of the racial hierarchy. Asian Americans have the most conflicted status, due to being relatively well-off as a group on two of three dimensions, but at or near the bottom on the third. A key point to understand is that where one sees a group placed in the racial hierarchy when discussing blacks, Asian Americans, and Latinos depends on what combination of dimensions one is discussing. Historically, these discussions have been centered on the economic and racial status dimensions, but Kim and others make a powerful and persuasive case for including a civic inclusion dimension as well.

How these three groups are arrayed across dimensions is not set in stone, nor is the way the dimensions are defined. For example, given the intersection of racial/ethnic and religious subordination found in modern France, analyzing the racial terrain there would require a racialized religious dimension. The same could also well be true in the United States if this analysis were focused on understanding the incorporation of Muslim Americans. Such an analysis would also have to pay attention to the racial dynamics within the American Muslim community, particularly between native-born (mostly black) and immigrant (largely non-black) Muslims. Even if we restrict ourselves to the three dimensions I propose, there would still be variation in group placement depending on our focus. A strong argument could be made that if we were analyzing the local racial terrain in south Florida, Latinos would rank higher on the civic inclusion dimension than blacks, given the strong inclusion of the Cuban American community and the marginalization of both the African American and Haitian American communities in the region. And, as argued previously, racial terrains and orderings evolve over time. Indeed, since *Bitter Fruit* was first published in 2000, pundits and conservative scholars such as Samuel Huntington have argued even more vociferously that Latino immigrant populations are unassimilable, joining Asian Americans, according to this type of account, as somehow immutably foreign.[11]

In a just, democratic America, every non-white group would be as fully included along all citizenship dimensions as whites. The civic ostracism dimension would be eliminated, as no racial or ethnic group would any longer be coded as "foreign." Similarly, and perhaps harder given the long history of institutionalized, structural, and hegemonic racism in this country, the elimination of the racial status dimension requires, first of all, the end of racialized stigmatization, but, second and more importantly, the end of structural racism, so that racial difference has no more impact on an individual's life chances than differences among white ethnics do at present. No longer would the color of one's skin, or one's accent, make one more liable to arrest and more subject to being charged with more serious crimes and sentenced to harsher prison terms. Third would be the end of the racialization of the economy, the economic status dimension, such that, for example, living in a black neighborhood would not mean that one's home appreciates at a slower rate, even though equivalent in all other respects to a home in another neighborhood, that having a "black-sounding" name would not decrease one's chances for employment, and that, in general, being non-white would not lead to systematic economic disadvantage and discrimination within a multitude of markets.

What the end of the racialization of the economy would not entail is each individual experiencing equal outcomes regardless of effort or talent. It does require that the economic decisions made by individuals, firms, and the state no longer be influenced by racism, and that steps, often difficult steps, be taken to ensure that all Americans, particularly poor people of color, have what they need to be competitive in a twenty-first-century global economy. America will only begin to actually be a fully democratic polity when all three dimensions are successfully eliminated from the American social landscape.[12]

Finally achieving what in another era would have been called (bourgeois) democratic rights would not entail full emancipation for blacks and others residents of the United States, but it would represent a massive step forward—the biggest step toward that goal since the victories of the Civil Rights and Black Power era. Winning full democratic rights would necessitate a similar level of mass insurgency as was seen during the Civil Rights era. Ira Katznelson argued many years ago that a special characteristic of black political movements was the degree to which they, unlike white ethnic or even worker movements in the United States, saw the world "holistically." What Katznelson meant by "holistically" was that African Americans, for example during the 1960s and early 1970s, saw tight connections among racial oppression, economic disadvantage, and American military (mis-)adventures. These connections are particularly sharply drawn in the speeches and writings of black leaders ranging from W. E. B. Du Bois, Malcolm X, and Martin Luther King Jr. Further, on a more theoretical plane, the configuration of the racial order with its intersection of race and class placing blacks at the bottom of both the economic and racial dimensions requires that full black racial emancipation also means a transformation of the American economic order as profound as the required transformation of the racial order. Thus, racial emancipation would partially lead to universal emancipation.

If racial emancipation of blacks requires full economic emancipation for blacks and others, why does this represent only a partial step toward full emancipation for everyone? The reason is, despite the continued myopic and dogmatic arguments of many Marxists, that racial and economic emancipation would no more necessitate the end of patriarchy or hetero-normativity than economic emancipation would or has meant the end to racial subordination.[13] There are multiple hierarchies of power, and while black emancipation would take us a long way toward full emancipation, it cannot take us all the way along that road in and of itself.

The intersection of race and class has led many black leaders, particularly Dr. King, to a vision of pragmatic utopianism. "Utopian," as can be seen in King's words, because of the insistence that a just America and black freedom can only be won when America is no longer militaristic, has ended racial oppression, and the economic system is truly transformed along humane lines, ensuring that poverty no longer exists and that each has the resources to fully develop their potential as human beings (and not just Americans; King's visions saw that for this transformation to be truly just, it must include the citizens of the world, not just of the United States). Even today strains of this ideological worldview can be detected in black public opinion, despite the capitulation of the great majority of black leaders to neoliberal ideology.

A better understanding of the nature of the current racial terrain provides a firmer basis for understanding the significance of President Obama's victory in the fall of 2008. Two of the three underlying axes of the racial terrain suffered significant symbolic disruptions as a result of Obama's victory. First, his status as a son of an immigrant from outside of Europe delivered a moderate symbolic blow to the civic ostracism dimension. It provided hope, symbolic as it was, that the children of other immigrants of non-European origin might soon experience being fully included in the civic and political life of the nation. Second, and far more dramatically, it provided an enormous symbolic blow to the racial status dimension—at least in political terms and at least for middle-class African Americans who have fully bought into the American dream.

What Obama's victory and, so far, his presidency have not done is even begin to address either symbolically or materially the racialized economy and the disadvantages inflicted in particular on poor people of color in this nation. Further, although the symbolic victories are not to be taken lightly, it remains the case that the material groundings for both civic ostracism and racial subordination remain strong and intact. Indeed, when Audra Shay, then running to be chair of the Young Republican National Federation (with the endorsement of Governor Bobby Jindal from her home state of Louisiana), responded supportively to a commentator on her Facebook page who declared it time to take "this country back from all these mad coons," she provided a sterling example of the strong racist counterattack that is under way in the country.[14] This counterattack was launched in order to maintain a white-dominated racial order. Despite the furor caused by the incident, Shay won the election. Similarly, Obama's childhood in Hawaii, as well as his Kenyan father's immigrant status, have provoked a series of lunatic attacks claiming that the president's claim of U.S. citizenship is fraudulent. For the "Birthers," as those making this claim are called, both Hawaii's status as a former colony with a majority non-white population and Obama's African and, of course, alleged Muslim heritage are sufficient to undermine the president's status as a citizen. These allegations continue in the face of a monumental amount of evidence that overwhelmingly prove (a word that as a social scientist I very rarely use) that the charge is baseless. What these charges do prove is that white supremacy is still alive, well, and capable of providing the foundation for the mobilization of many Americans. In any decent democracy, these charges would not matter in the first place. In any truly democratic state, a citizen's religious beliefs, or lack thereof, would be a private matter. What all of these incidents also show is that there are many committed to maintaining a white-dominated racial order, even though that order is under attack along multiple fronts, given a changing racial terrain that is transforming not just black politics, but American politics more generally.

IS THIS NEW RACIAL TERRAIN REFLECTED IN PUBLIC OPINION and, if so, how? One possibility would be that the multi-dimensionality of the racial space has put an end to the visible racial hierarchy in public opinion. If

Table 13: Race and Public Opinion, October 2008

	Blacks	Latinos	Asian	Whites
Warmth toward Obama (1 = cold, 100 = hot)	89°	72°	66°	51°
Racism still a problem? (Yes/Major problem?)	97%/71%	95%/56%	95%/38%	93%/32%
Blacks unlikely to achieve racial equality soon or ever? (Yes)	46%	24%	31%	22%
Latinos unlikely to achieve racial equality soon or ever? (Yes)	36%	24%	30%	28%
Asian Americans unlikely to achieve racial equality soon or ever? (Yes)	26%	23%	27%	16%
Should government apologize for slavery? (Yes)	74%	63%	47%	23%
Apologize for Japanese internment during WWII? (Yes)	67%	67%	72%	33%
Racial profiling makes nation safer? (Disagree)	41%	27%	31%	21%
Know someone who would not vote for Obama because he's black? (Yes)	21%	23%	21%	29%
Should felons who have served their time be allowed to vote? (Yes)	72%	52%	51%	46%

the existence of multiple dimensions had this result, the systematic ordering of public opinion data by group would be meaningless. We know that at least in part this is not the case. As we have seen in previous chapters, blacks and whites remain divided on many key political questions. A second possibility would be that blacks and whites continue to anchor the ends of the opinion distribution, with Asian Americans and Latinos falling in the middle. A third possibility would be that the space remains ordered, but blacks and whites no longer anchor the ends of the distribution. A fourth would be that the ordering changes according to which dimension is most salient for a given set of questions. Table 13 provides an example, listing a set of questions that strongly tap the racial status dimension of the racial space.

Not surprisingly, given our earlier discussion, blacks and whites consistently anchor the ends of the opinion distribution on questions that evoke race. Blacks are consistently the most racially progressive, and whites—often by a large margin—the most racially conservative. Blacks as a group are clearly the most pessimistic about the prospects of achieving racial equality. Even though in 2008 blacks were substantially less pessimistic on average about the prospects of blacks achieving equality than they were in 2005, they were still much more pessimistic about their prospects than any other racial or ethnic group. More telling perhaps, blacks are as or more pessimistic about the chances of Latinos or Asian Americans achieving racial equality than either Latinos or Asian Americans are about their own group's prospects!

Four racial patterns can be observed in the opinion data, reflecting what I am labeling the racial status axis. One pattern is the one just noted: blacks as a group are the most racially pessimistic as compared to the other three groups. An example of this can be seen in the questions on prospects for achieving racial equality. A second is seen in the responses to the question "Should the government apologize to Japanese Americans for their internment in camps during World War II?" Here whites are the clear outlier, with only a minority approving of an apology, while very strong majorities in all three non-white groups do approve. There is a 34 percentage point difference between whites and the next racial group. This same pattern can be seen, albeit less dramatically, in the responses to other questions as well. A third pattern appears in responses to the question of whether the "government should apologize for slavery." Here blacks and Latinos have on average similar positive responses to the question as compared to the other two groups. A fourth and fairly common pattern shows a steady drop-off in responses as we move from blacks to whites, which can be seen in responses to the question of whether racism still represents a major problem or not for the nation. Generally, along this axis, the average responses of each group reflect the ordering we see along the racial status dimension of the racial space. More specifically, and more precisely, the one consistent pattern across these questions tapping the racial status axis of the racial space is that blacks and whites continue to firmly anchor the opposite sides of the public opinion spectrum on matters that are strongly inflected with race.

A different pattern appears when one examines opinion data from questions that tap the "foreignness" axis of the racial opinion space.[15] Table 14 displays average group responses to questions that tap this dimension of the racial space. Several different racial patterns are seen in the responses displayed in table 14. One of them, as expected, given the racialization of opinions regarding "foreignness," is that on some questions blacks are the outliers—their responses far removed from those of the other three racial

Table 14: Race and Immigration, October 2008

	Blacks	Latinos	Asian	Whites
Government treats immigrants better than blacks? (Agree/Disagree)	56%/10%	11%/51%	19%/44%	25%/53%
Immigrants take jobs, housing, health care from native-born Americans? (Agree/Disagree)	44%/22%	53%/21%	23%/46%	47%/23%
Correlation between take jobs/ immigrants treated better questions	0.38	0.13	0.20	0.26
Differences between blacks, Latinos, Asian Americans too great to form alliances? (asked of half the sample) (Agree/Disagree)	14%/41%	39%/23%	39%/19%	14%/44%
Common problems facilitate alliances between blacks, Latinos, Asian Americans (asked of half the sample) (Agree/Disagree)	53%/07%	52%/08%	49%/12%	44%/12%

groups. In regard to whether the government treats immigrants better than blacks, for example, a small minority in each group agree with this assessment, while the figure among blacks is more than 50 percent. A different and perhaps more surprising pattern is seen, however, in responses to the question of whether immigrants are taking jobs and other critical resources from native-born Americans. Half or nearly half of blacks, Latinos, and whites agree with this statement—with Latinos as a group seeing racial competition for resources in the most zero-sum terms. In this pattern Asian Americans are the outliers, with a much smaller minority agreeing with the zero-sum description of racial group competition over vital resources.

These differences between groups do not only represent differences of opinion among the groups about immigration. How opinion is organized also differs. For blacks, there is a strong correlation between their opinion about whether immigrants are treated better than blacks and their opinion about the degree to which there is a zero-sum competition for resources. Latinos, on the other hand, see virtually no connection between the two questions: Yes, there is competition between immigrants and native-born Americans for vital resources; but, no, there is no connection between this competition and how one views government treatment of immigrants as compared to the treatment of blacks. Asian Americans are close to Latinos in not seeing a strong correlation between the two opinions, while whites are approximately in the middle between blacks and Latinos in how strongly they view the correlation.[16]

Different and separate patterns are seen in the experiment in which we asked half of the sample whether differences between groups were so great as to impede the formation of non-white alliances—that is, a rainbow coalition, albeit one that is silent on the question of white inclusion. The other half of the sample was also asked about alliance formation among people of color, but the framing was different. The question for this second subsample emphasized the common problems shared by these groups, and this alternative framing produced a different racial pattern on the question of alliance formation. The results suggest that a basis does exist for building political alliances among people of color, but the success of these formations very likely depends on whether a framing emphasizing common problems or differences between groups becomes dominant within and across groups.

Unfortunately, the sterile environment of a public opinion survey cannot replicate the messier reality of the streets. Consequently, we cannot answer the question of which message becomes the dominant one in the current political environment among grassroots people of color. Does the progressive emphasis on common problems resonate more among people of color than the nationalist view emphasizing differences between non-whites? A generation ago this battle was fought out on community street corners and in workplaces and at college campuses, as well as in the pages of newspapers such as the *Black Panther* or *Muhammad Speaks* and in the writings of groups ranging from the Congress of African Peoples to the Black Workers Congress. Today it is more frequently in the blogosphere and on YouTube, as well as the country's prisons and streets, that interpretations about group relationships among people of color are being formed. What the public opinion data do suggest is that there are multiple ways that issues can be framed. Some framings will make it more difficult to build alliances among people of color; other framings will facilitate such alliance building. For these alliances to be rebuilt, a shared sense of a common destiny, a shared sense of what constitutes social justice, and a shared intolerance for self-interested "community" elites who would sacrifice both "their" communities' interest and social justice for their own selfish self-interest must all be rebuilt. In the final section, I highlight a few of the possible arenas within which new alliances can be built.

ALLIANCES AMONG PEOPLE OF COLOR WILL NOT RESEMBLE those of previous decades, even if framings that emphasize common problems take root in each community. The communities in which those alliances were forged a generation ago had not yet experienced high levels of immigration. People of color were only too well acquainted with the oppression of the American racial order, whether it was the anti-Latino discrimination and abuses suffered in the Southwest or on the streets of New York; the internment of Japanese Americans during World War II; or the all too recent deprivations of Jim Crow. There were conflicts among groups over scarce resources, but there was also a common history of racial oppression and radical organizing (both leftist and nationalist). These were also communities that were familiar, if not necessarily comfortable, with one another.

By and large, the communities joining together in those alliances no longer exist. Immigration has massively transformed the Asian American and Latino communities and, although to a much lesser extent, the black and white communities. In 2006 the foreign born made up 40 percent of the Latino population, 66 percent of the Asian American population, 8 percent of the black population, but only 4 percent of white Americans.[17] Switching the focus to some of the nation's largest urban concentrations, we observe the same patterns. In 2006 the native-born population of New York was 63 percent, Los Angeles 60 percent, Chicago 78 percent, and Miami only 50 percent. The percentage of non-citizens in each of these cities ranged from 13 percent in Chicago to 26 percent in Miami, with both New York and Los Angeles near or at 20 percent.[18] The racial terrain in these and most other American urban areas, small as well as gigantic, has been fundamentally transformed by continuing high levels of immigration, particularly into non-white communities. Consequently, the demographic and, more importantly, the experiential basis for the alliances of a generation ago has been severely eroded as immigrant members, lacking the history of conflict and cooperation with blacks particularly that helped enable the coalitions of the past, assume a central voice in these communities. For many of these relative newcomers, what they know of African Americans has often been sadly limited to the images conveyed by mainstream media and Hollywood-dominated popular culture.

This is not to say that alliances cannot be built in this era. They can. The obvious and critical example is in organizing for economic justice. The big box and New Orleans vignettes in chapter 4 are indicative of the necessity and potential, as well as the problems, of forging alliances to ensure better and just outcomes for the nation's poor. It is imperative in this domain for grassroots blacks and Latinos to unite out of self-interest, given their placement at the bottom of the economic ladder. How the issue is framed is critical. Those whose interests are best served by keeping the poor at each other's throats fighting for crumbs will emphasize the differences and conflicts, particularly among communities of color. Those who wish to build progressive alliances on the Gulf Coast, for example, will need to point out how it is in the interest of both the immigrant workers suffering inhumane working conditions and black workers frozen out of the jobs they once had to come together in an alliance to challenge their common nemesis—corporate robber barons and their captive politicians. Such an alliance is the surest way to provide decent working conditions and employment opportunities for all. Higher levels of employment and better working conditions would have been possible as communities shattered by Katrina in Mississippi were being rebuilt if hundreds of millions of dollars had not been diverted from the poor for whom it was intended to corporate coffers. Environmental issues also provide a promising basis for forging alliances. As we saw in chapter 1, black and brown communities are particularly subject to the health effects of environmental degradation. As in the case of organizing for economic justice, black, Latino, and other communities are allying in urban areas to fight for environmental justice. In the next sections, I conclude by discussing some of the other possible issues that have either generated or might generate new alliances.

COMBATING HATE CRIMES

On May 17, 2009, a demonstration took place in Virginia's rural Powhatan County in response to a grand jury decision regarding an incident in which one black youth was killed and another badly injured during an ambush by three white youths. The weapon involved was an AK-47 with an 83-shot drum clip. The white grand jury saw fit to reduce the charges from first-degree murder to involuntary manslaughter. During the same month, a white jury in Shenandoah, Pennsylvania, acquitted the young white thugs who killed Luis Ramírez, a Mexican immigrant, of murder and aggravated assault charges, convicting them only of simple assault—a misdemeanor. Ramírez's murderers shouted that the same would happen to other Latinos if they did not leave town. The four whites (only two of whom were brought to trial) were all local high school football players, and some of them star students as well. The foreman of the jury that acquitted the two youths on the serious charges called other jurors on the panel racist. He was also appalled at the behavior of the defendants. One defendant, he reported, wore a U.S. border patrol T-shirt to a Halloween party—after the murder had been committed. Another group of whites subsequently ended up in a fight with a mixed group of black and Latino teens in Shenandoah. Much as in the suburban parishes around New Orleans, local authorities in a nearby town had recently passed legislation intended to limit the Latino population by manipulating housing ordinances (struck down as unconstitutional by a federal judge). And as in Jena, Louisiana, the local non-white community also perceived collusion between white bullies and local school authorities when the latter claimed they could do nothing about a Latino child being bullied despite the family's pleas for help. When the father finally gave his son permission to defend himself, the Latino student ended up suspended. The similarities of the attacks, of both the legal and terrorist variety, against people of color in New Orleans, Virginia, and Pennsylvania should, one would hope, lead members of each group who see no community of interests among people of color to rethink their position.

Hate crimes against Latinos and immigrants are on the rise, according to the *New York Times*, having increased 40 percent between 2003 and 2007.[19] It is not just Latinos who are suffering from hate crimes. The *Los Angeles Times* reported the case of Ali Abdelhadi Mohd, who was killed by a suspicious explosion while cleaning up anti-Arab and white supremacist graffiti in an empty house he owned in Yermo, California.[20] Also in 2009, a black man was killed foiling an attack on the nation's Holocaust Museum in Washington, D.C. Police officers have been shot by perpetrators with sympathies at least for the fascist extreme of the right, as in Pittsburgh, for example, where police uncovered ties to Stormfront—a neo-Nazi website. While non-white groups are fighting each other over grievances, real and imagined, organizations devoted to killing all blacks, Jews, Latinos, Asian Americans, and Muslims are rapidly multiplying and increasing their membership. At the same time, the lunatic views of the far right seep increasingly into the public discourse of the more respectable parts of the conservative movement. Examples include the election of Audra Shay as head of the Young Republicans, discussed above, as well as Liz Cheney's comments in support of the Birther movement. We are seeing the evolution of a new phase in racism, in which the old-fashioned variety—the type that allowed political leaders like Shay to approve open talk about "coons" and violent racist attacks go relatively unpunished—is combined with a "blaming of the victim" motif disguised as a defense of conservative values. Combining the worst aspects of the hidden racism of the 1980s with the openly white supremacist racist politics of the first seven decades of the twentieth century, racism is emerging in a new virulent form. This is what was called by some social scientists in the 1980s and 1990s symbolic racism's true color: a hideous violent racism, as thinly cloaked as possible in the colors of "principled conservatism."

VOTING RIGHTS

Another issue around which all African Americans and people of color (immigrant as well as non-immigrant) should be able to unify is voting rights. Voting rights remains a critical issue, despite what we hear from many conservative commentators. If blacks, Asian Americans, and Latinos want to increase their political power and see their agendas implemented, they all have a pressing interest in increasing voter protections. The kinds of problems faced by each group in this domain do not overlap completely, which might make forging alliances more difficult. Yet each group needs the others, as well as the support of progressive whites, if their aspirations in regard to voting rights are to be achieved.

The relation between mass incarceration and felon disenfranchisement has become the subject of a growing literature, in particular as concerns black political power. As discussed in chapter 4, mass incarceration has a devastating effect on black society. It is also involved in the erosion of black political power. Table 15 displays felon disenfranchisement rates for the states of the four metropolitan areas that were analyzed earlier in the chapter.

While the overall felon disenfranchisement rates in 2004 were relatively low for all of the states except Florida, black disenfranchisement rates were significant in each, and in Florida they were astronomical. Since 2004 Florida has loosened restrictions on ex-felon voting. Nevertheless, it remains one of the nine states with at least a partial ban. Thirty-five states forbid the vote to people on parole, and thirty states disallow those on probation from voting. Even states that allow ex-felons and those on probation to vote—such as Illinois, California, and New York—still exhibit a significant attenuation of black voting power.[21] Not surprisingly, a very large majority of blacks, 72 percent, support voting rights for ex-felons (as seen in table 13). The same data also show, however, that feelings among Latinos, Asian Americans, and whites are much more ambivalent (with support in all three groups hovering around 50 percent). Blacks will have to work hard to find solid support among these groups for expanding democracy by providing voting rights for ex-felons.

Communities with large immigrant populations—particularly Latino and Asian American—have a strong interest in seeking out allies for expanding voting rights. Significant percentages of their communities are disenfranchised due to severe limits on non-citizen voting in most of the nation.[22] According to Ronald Hayduk, there are 12 million disenfranchised legal residents in the United States, even before we start considering undocumented workers.[23] In Los Angeles alone, nearly 25 percent of taxpaying residents are denied the vote. In New York, the equivalent statistic is nearly 20 percent; in Chicago, 13 percent; and for the Miami-Dade metropolitan area, 26 percent.[24] These numbers are generally greater than for felony disenfranchisement and should provide incentives for the most affected communities to seek allies in a broad movement to expand voting rights.

The disjuncture between substantial number of residents being required to pay taxes (and in some cases serve in the military) and not having the right to vote has the same neoliberal roots as many of the other anti-democratic phenomenon that have been discussed over the past several chapters. As

Table 15: Felon Disenfranchisement in Four States

	Total Disenfranchisement	Black Disenfranchisement
New York	1%	4%
California	1%	7.5%
Illinois	0.5%	3%
Florida	9%	19%

Hayduk argues, "The possibilities for exploiting displaced persons are too great if we make capital and labor mobile but political life immobile."[25] Non-citizen residents are stakeholders in the community. They pay taxes, participate in civic activities, and their children are often enrolled in public schools. In some communities, non-citizens are allowed to vote for local school boards; in a few places, they are also more generally able to vote in a broader set of local elections. Local voting by non-citizens was common both in this nation's past and in other contemporary polities including in the European Union. Support from non-immigrant progressive communities should not primarily depend on the fact that more often than not, when it comes to the issues, non-citizen voters have similar preferences on the issues as other communities of color, nor even on the need for different communities to unite so they can mutually support each others' claims for the expansion of voting rights. The main reason for expansion of non-citizen voting rights should be that it helps the process of building a more democratic America— the "more perfect union" toward which Americans should aspire.

Often the attacks we see with increasing frequency against immigrants are deeply imbued with racism in the public at large. Others invite comparison with practices normally found only in authoritarian states. A chilling example is the immigration raids that have unjustly and unconstitutionally targeted Latinos in the greater New York area. A report from the Immigration Justice Clinic at the Benjamin N. Cardozo School of Law has documented how homes were unconstitutionally entered without required consent.[26] Despite the tensions between African Americans, Latinos, and Asian American communities, or what are sometimes perceived as conflicts of interest between newcomers and those who were born here, there are strong reasons for all of these communities of color to unite around any number of pressing political issues. Those of us in this country and elsewhere who have belonged to groups that in the past have been persecuted for race, religion, or political ideas should remember that when authoritarian practices against an oft-vilified group become accepted, it is a very short step to see these practices eventually extended to other groups within the population.

As chilling have been the attacks of the Birther movement, who despite all evidence continue to claim that President Obama is not a citizen. This movement can no longer be considered a "fringe" movement due to the fact that elected officials, Lou Dobbs previously of CNN (even though his own network at the time thoroughly debunked Birther claims), and Republican notables such as Sarah Palin and Liz Cheney have all given credence to the movement and its claims. The fact that Obama's father was a black Kenyan Muslim and that the state of Hawaii (where every public official including the Republican governor has said the records prove the president was born in Honolulu) is the entity certifying his citizenship provide all the "evidence" the Birthers need to continue pressing their false claims. Even Fox News anchor Chris Wallace denounced the Birther movement by saying that the issue "isn't documentation, it's pigmentation." Certification from Hawaii is "suspect" because it is the first state to have a non-white majority and many Americans still consider it foreign. The problem with Obama's father, and more directly with the president himself, is simply that he is black, and for all too many Americans it is impossible to conceive of a black man being the legitimate commander in chief. If the president's "Americanness" can be so insanely but persistently challenged, African Americans should realize that they share more with non-white immigrants than many of us have realized. Despite our hundreds of years in North America, we are still considered not just the other, but "foreign" by too many of our fellow citizens. As mentioned in the prologue, the late Harvard Professor Samuel Huntington, when railing against continued immigration from Asia and Latin America—which he regarded as sources of immigrant populations incapable of assimilating into this nation—added that the only way blacks could become good Americans is by "becoming white." This is an unacceptable price for being accepted as full citizens. Building alliances between people of color is a necessary step if we wish to change the price of admission to American citizenship.

White men were 100% of the people that wrote the Constitution, 100% of the people that signed the Declaration of Independence, 100% of the people who died at Gettysburg and Vicksburg, probably close to 100% of the people who died at Normandy. This has been a country built basically by white folk.

Patrick Buchanan[27]

There are formidable obstacles to rebuilding the progressive coalitions of the 1960s and 1970s. There is also a wide range of issues—economic, political, and civic—that provide solid bases for building dynamic and powerful progressive coalitions. Adding disturbingly to these unifying interests is the specter of a violent and near fanatical right-wing movement that is not satisfied with just demonizing people of color and other groups they despise (such as gays, lesbians, Muslims, and Jews), but appears increasingly inclined to launch violent physical attacks against individuals and institutions based in these communities.

It is not only for reasons of self-defense and self-interest that these alliances must be built. There are multiple dimensions along which residents of this nation are denied full inclusion into the polity and civil society. Blacks, Latinos, and Asian Americans are excluded from full citizenship to varying degrees along each of these dimensions. The position of each of these groups represents states of what Elizabeth F. Cohen labels "semi-citizenship."[28] The struggle—as Malcolm X, in particular, emphasized a generation ago—is for human, not just civil, rights. Broad alliances are necessary to expand this nation's all too constrained democracy.

6 CONCLUSION: TOWARD NEW BLACK VISIONS

We are now faced with the fact that tomorrow is today. We are confronted with the fierce urgency of now. In this unfolding conundrum of life and history there is such a thing as being too late.
Martin Luther King Jr.[1]

In 1967 Martin Luther King asked all of us, "Where do we go from here?" There is more confusion about that question now than there was forty years ago. This is not to say that a generation ago there was black unity about future directions. There was not. There were clearly articulated black visions. During the last two years of his life, Dr. King provided in his writings, and displayed even more in his actions, a glittering, sharply edged vision of a robust, radical social democracy. In Oakland, California, the Black Panther Party demonstrated more in practice than theory their own vision of a street-inflected fusion of black nationalism and Third World Marxism. In Detroit the League of Revolutionary Black Workers, significantly guided by the theoretical work of James and Grace Lee Boggs, illuminated a vision of black Marxism incorporating nationalism in a way that differed from the Panthers. From Los Angeles to Newark, black nationalists offered their own alternative visions of black liberation.

During the twentieth century, poor and working-class African Americans often turned to leftist and nationalist movements inspired by indigenous black political theorists, such as Malcolm X, James Boggs, and the theoretically inclined leaders of the Black Panther Party. These theorists in turn were often heavily influenced by writings, many radical, from those viewed as leaders of the Third World, such as Amilcar Cabral, Kwame Nkrumah, Mao Zedong, George Padmore, Léopold Senghor, and C. L. R. James. Most influential among all classes of blacks was Martin Luther King Jr. His assassination cemented the radicalization of a generation of African Americans (at least for a decade), but his legacy has been both largely lost and fragmented to the degree it has survived. In particular, the democratic but radical path he was developing during the later years of his life has almost vanished from the popular imagination (although many conservatives remember it well).

The era of insurgency during which the visions of Malcolm X and Martin Luther King Jr. shone so brilliantly has given way to an era that Cornel West argues is characterized not by black visions, but by black nihilism. Black nihilism is a direct consequence of the hegemony of neoliberal ideology and policies and the unleashing of an even more voracious capitalism on state and society, to the great detriment of already-marginalized populations. Insurgent populations have been demobilized, and political discourse severely constrained. The major black visions of a generation ago are now seen as unacceptable even for discussion. The new ideologues of U.S. corporate interests, neoliberal and neoconservative alike, spread a sham democracy abroad while simultaneously decrying the democratic domestic insurgencies of the last generation and their weak reflections in this period.

Jacques Rancière's description of republican discourse in France during the 1990s is also an apt description of contemporary neoliberal hegemony in the United States and its attacks on domestic democratic movements:

> The government of science will always end up a government of "natural elites,"
> in which the social power of those with expert competences is combined with
> the power of wealth, at the cost once more of provoking a democratic dis-
> order. . . . [Neoliberal discourse has] served to support governmental decisions,
> even when they signaled effacing the political under the exigencies of the lim-
> itlessness of global Capital, and to stigmatize as "populist" backwardness any
> political struggle against that effacement. The only task outstanding was to
> attribute, ingenuously or cynically, the limitlessness of wealth to the voracious
> appetites of democratic individuals, and to make this voracious democracy the
> major catastrophe by which humanity shall destroy itself.[2]

The unholy alliance of experts and voracious capital has led to much misery—especially for those already disadvantaged. And it is also at the root of the financial collapse that plunged the globe into a deep economic crisis in 2008.

In the face of neoliberal hegemony, we once again need a politics that can generate what Rancière, following Arendt, labels "democratic disorder." The call for "democratic disorder" can be found in many left traditions. There was more than a hint of anarchy, ironically, in the Red Guards' infamous echo of Mao's injunction that "it's right to rebel." But the call for democratic disorder is not an invitation to anarchy. Like the slogan drawn from our own modern African American political tradition—"No justice, no peace!"—the promise is simply that there will be no business as usual as long as the injustice bred by the neoliberal regime remains the order of the day.

Black politics today, however, falls far short of having the ability to deliver on the promise of "no justice, no peace," and far short of being able to build a genuine movement for democracy and justice. The aftermath of Hurricane Katrina demonstrated the continuing weak condition of black politics, and while the election of Barack Obama may serve to counter somewhat the debilitating nihilism of recent decades, it has not in and of itself contributed to an increase in black political capacity. Again, this is not to say that no worthwhile political and civic work is being done, particularly at the local level. Much is. The local community residents who populate black civil society are building institutions to help children read and write, to combat the horrendous violence that is killing black children and youth, to support black families, and to come together in mutual aid for the families of the incarcerated. Harking back to a much earlier era, efforts to promote entrepreneurial activity among blacks and extended "buy black" campaigns can be found in virtually every black community—often with the support of organizations once associated with the Civil Rights Movement such as the Urban League. These are just a few of the examples of the often heroic work being done within black civil society, often with little or no aid from the state. Nevertheless, one of the critical lessons we relearned from Katrina is that civil society is not sufficient by itself to overcome the problems confronting black, poor, and other marginalized communities within this country. Dr. King spoke of the limitations of civil society and nationalist economics—criticizing what black radicals of an earlier generation also dismissed and described as bourgeois nationalism:

> However much we pool our resources and "buy black," this cannot create the multiplicity of new jobs and provide the number of low-cost houses that will lift the Negro out of the economic depression caused by centuries of deprivation. Neither can our resources supply quality integrated education. All of this requires billions of dollars which only an alliance of liberal-labor-civil-rights forces can stimulate. In short, the Negroes' problem cannot be solved unless the whole of American society takes a new turn toward greater economic justice.[3]

King made it abundantly clear that calling on "the whole of American society" involves making demands on the state. The goal must be full inclusion in the polity, with everything that entails. His early campaigns rested on the steadfast belief that race must no longer be a basis for exclusion from polity and society. His final, uncompleted campaigns were based on the equally deeply held premise that political and social exclusion were inseparable from practices that denied human rights in whatever form, reproduced the conditions of poverty, and promoted aggressive militarism. These hallmarks of exclusion, in King's view, were all antithetical to building a truly just democratic society.

The vision of the good life, the just society, that King embraced was one that many social democrats, and even a much earlier generation of American Democrats, could at least imagine. It included a decent education from kindergarten through college for any young person who desired an education and was willing to work, without respect to their economic background. It was a vision of a just society where jobs were available and in which during hard times work and relief were both provided by society and specifically the state. It was a vision that viewed health as it is defined in the preamble to the constitution of the World Health Organization, as "a state of complete physical, mental and social well-being and not merely the absence of disease or infirmity. . . . Governments have a responsibility for the health of their peoples which can be fulfilled only by the provision of adequate health and social measures." This definition of health and governmental responsibility is not reflected at all in the U.S. health-care debate being waged by politicians with financial obligations to health insurance, pharmaceutical, and other corporate interests. In short, beyond basic political rights, beyond the minimum standards of political emancipation, King was demanding full citizenship rights, which included egalitarian economic policies and human emancipation in its fullest sense.

While these goals were embedded in the political programs of last century's West European social democrats, and if not in the program at least in the imaginations of some New Deal and Great Society–era Democrats in the United States, neoliberal dominance of political, economic, and social discourse makes these goals not only exceedingly difficult to win, but even hard to discuss without being demonized. King's real program of economic and political emancipation, for which he was fighting as he died, flies in the face of contemporary neoliberal and neoconservative orthodoxy. Even within black political discourse, neoliberal discourse, particularly among black elites, makes it increasingly difficult to engage in the type of critiques that could get to the real modern roots of systemic disadvantage and injustice.

In the decades following King's death, there have been many setbacks in building a truly just democratic society. Recently, there have also been some sporadic political victories. Often they were the result of local, regional, and national black communities rallying against injustice, as in the case of the Jena Six. Certainly the African American community mobilized in support of Barack Obama at levels not seen in a very long time. In fact, the gap between black and white voting rates declined from 10 to 4 percent from 2004 to 2008. Blacks in the 18- to 44-year-old cohort actually voted at higher rates than any other racial or ethnic group. In 2008 there were two million more black voters, six hundred thousand more Asian American voters, and about the same number of Latino voters than in 2004, according to analysis reported in the *New York Times*. The result was that whites as a percentage of the electorate declined to 76 percent in 2008 from being nearly 80 percent in 2004.[4] As a Republican analyst pointed out, the change in the makeup of the electorate is even more startling if one takes a longer view. In 1976 whites made up 90 percent of the electorate. The steep decline of whites as a proportion of the electorate, along with non-whites voting in very large majorities for Obama, presents the Republican Party with a daunting electoral

calculus.[5] This electoral mobilization has not as of yet been effectively translated into substantial political gains for black and other marginalized communities. For that to occur, it will have to evolve beyond electoral politics
into a movement working to transform political and economic structures
responsible for disadvantaging African Americans as well as so many other
marginalized communities within the United States.

A new generation of young black activists is developing as a result in part
of both the Obama campaign and social movements emerging around issues such as the Jena Six and Hurricane Katrina. In response to Katrina,
young people of all races, but notably young blacks, gave up vacation breaks,
summers, and in not a few cases entire years to help in the physical and
civic rebuilding of the devastated Gulf Coast and especially New Orleans.
Young activists using a combination of new information technologies and
old-fashioned "get on the bus" methods fashioned a movement that led to
a march of thousands in Jena, Louisiana, and the mobilization of tens of
thousands to petition, make phone calls, and organize 150 events around
the country. These efforts were responsible in large part for a successful campaign to prevent the grave miscarriage of justice that threatened the Jena
Six. The organizing activities of this new generation can be found in many
local black communities, on college and high school campuses, and in many
and varied cultural activities, particularly in the "underground" music and
art scenes. Listening and working with this younger generation, one detects
a tendency on their part to romanticize the past, to glorify without critical analysis organizations ranging from the Panthers, to street gangs, to the
Nation of Islam. There is also a tendency to rely too much on civil society–
based, nationalist-tinged entrepreneurial activities. Yet there is also clearly
evident a passion for tackling the key social justice issues of our time.

An important question in this time of economic crisis and political tur-
moil is whether African Americans will differentiate by class and sector, en-
gaging with different legacies from the past or, either separately or together,
fruitfully explore new political directions. Some of the issues and directions
around which a new black politics must coalesce are obvious. Ongoing organizing for economic justice must continue, such as that found against the
predations of big box–based corporations in urban communities. Also obvious is that organizing must continue to defend black communities against

racist attacks. The rise in hate crimes and demonization of African Americans mean that it will continue to be necessary in this new century, as it was in Jena and elsewhere, to organize for self-defense. Similarly, ongoing organizing around public health issues in black communities is increasingly necessary as a different form of defense for black communities as state and local governments seek to "rationalize" health care, make it more "efficient," or simply close down facilities and services.

I use the rest of this concluding chapter to discuss two key topics for rebuilding black political movements. First is the need to rebuild black public spheres, as well as the black counterpublic—the black "public of publics." Second, I provide a thought experiment exploring how to develop democratic institutions as we rebuild civic capacity in urban areas. These topics are in no way meant to be exhaustive of the key theoretical and pragmatic questions that face us in revitalizing progressive black political movements. They are meant, rather, to be suggestive of the range of topics that those involved in rebuilding black political movements must consider. A central theme of the remainder of the chapter is that there is a dialectical link between rebuilding the black public sphere and black civil society, on the one hand, and building mass black political movements, on the other. The two processes must go hand in hand. Political debate within the black community is most robust when it has a solid institutional base and when it is conducted by publics actively engaged in the key political debates associated with flourishing political movements. Rebuilding the institutions of black civil society, particularly democratic political institutions, will necessitate building political movements capable of winning resources and making demands on the larger society and the state. These processes must be simultaneous and mutually constitutive. The three great periods of black political and social innovation—the Reconstruction era after the Civil War, the late nineteenth century and first quarter of the twentieth century, and the combined Civil Rights and Black Power era—were all marked by innovative initiatives within black civil society, a growing and robust black public sphere (counterpublic), and active and militant black political movements.

IF ROBUST BLACK POLITICAL MOVEMENTS ARE TO BE BUILT AND sustained, multiple institutional bases must be revitalized, including black civil society and the black public sphere. Black civil society provides the foundation for such movements, but equally important is a discursive space in which blacks can debate, argue, and analyze the theory, tactics, strategies, and policy proposals at the center of black politics. Thus a key goal must be to strengthen the black public sphere as a core component of black civil society. The black counterpublic provided the crucial discursive space through most of the twentieth century, where Ida B. Wells, W. E. B. Du Bois, Marcus Garvey, A. Philip Randolph, Malcolm X, Martin Luther King Jr., Angela Davis, and many others vigorously advanced their positions, proposed agendas, and debated both of these with an engaged public. This was likewise the site where institutions such as the Niagara Movement, Liberty League, African Blood Brotherhood, NAACP, Universal Negro Improvement Association (UNIA), various socialist organizations, Nation of Islam, Southern Christian Leadership Conference (SCLC), Student Nonviolent Coordinating Committee (SNCC), Black Panther Party, and Combahee River Collective debated, if sometimes not very productively, their alternative programs. Indeed, these organizations and others such as the black church provided the institutional linkage between black civil society and the black public sphere. One key lesson from the twentieth century is that each era develops its own set of critical organizations that shape that era's black public sphere. We need a new wave of democratic organizations if we are to rebuild black civil society and the black public sphere in a way that is conducive to political mobilization. By and large, the time of the organizations of the last century—the Black Panther Party, SCLC, SNCC, the League of Revolutionary Black Workers, and the myriad of other activist organizations—has passed.

I have made the contested claim that the black public sphere had undergone a dangerous decline in the last third of the twentieth century. The argument, in summary, holds multiple factors responsible for this decline, including the smashing of black radical movements and the erosion of the institutional base of the black public sphere due to changes in the American political economy. The combination of state repression and internal dissension destroyed or severely damaged many civil rights and Black Power organizations. The structural shift in the U.S. economy away from manufacturing and toward low-wage jobs in the service industry also contributed to the erosion of the institutional base of the black counterpublic and, in particular, its points of contact with other oppositional forces. The impoverishment of the black working class, a result of the disappearance of its base in manufacturing and public employment, sharpened class divisions among African Americans, subjecting many black communities to a state of near-permanent economic depression. This in turn harmed the organizational base of black politics, where organizations either shrank or disappeared as their financial resources dwindled and their programs came to seem less relevant to solving the problems of a devastated economy. At the same time, a new wave of black elected officials formed a buffer class between the black public and the centers of power, which helped delegitimate protest and worked to circumscribe what was regarded as "acceptable" political discourse within the black community. The disintegration of the institutional bases of the 1970s black counterpublic, combined with increasing skepticism among black activists in particular that there is in some meaningful sense a single "black agenda" derived from the bundle of issues and strategies relevant to black America, has led me to question the current viability of a black counterpublic. Do we have in this period a subaltern "public of publics" that successfully aggregates the concerns of multiple black publics—and if we do, just how "healthy" is it?

Melissa Harris-Lacewell and other astute critics have contested this claim about the degeneration of the black counterpublic. Conceding that some historical components of the black counterpublic have declined, these critics argue that key elements of a robust counterpublic remain firmly in place, including the black church, which continues to be a central institution, in both a secular and sacred sense, in most black communities, as well as sites of black political discourse such as families, barbershops, and hair salons.[6] Equally important, according to Harris-Lacewell and others, the black public sphere has migrated, especially for younger blacks, into new realms, such as black-oriented broadcast outlets and cyberspace—often enabled by new information technologies.

Even these critics agree, however, that for black politics to be rebuilt, the black public sphere must be strengthened. How successful we are in this endeavor can be measured according to three criteria. First, the black public sphere must be robustly grounded in black communities and must play the central role of aggregating various black publics, while providing a critique of racialized America and injustice more generally. Second—and to me this is the more problematic proposition—the black public sphere must be shown to have the ability to project the key themes, areas of consensus, and controversies found in the black public sphere into mainstream American political discourse. Relatedly, black publics also have to be in discourse with the multiple publics of other people of color. Third, and also critical, the black counterpublic must be further democratized, as Gwendolyn Pough has argued.[7] The black counterpublic must once again become a transformative space where black women and all African Americans feel empowered and safe to voice their concerns, critiques, and demands for respect, equality, and power within black communities and movements.

To accomplish these goals, we need to better grasp the relationships among public spheres, new information technologies, and corporate influence. Many theorists have sketched aspects of these relationships, much of it focused on individual and community innovation. But there remains a paucity of work that then theorizes these findings in relation to publics, counterpublics, and public spheres. Conceptualizing how race fits into this theory adds another layer of complexity. Also in need of analysis are the effects of the combination of racialized events—both more and less traumatic (such as the O.J. Simpson trial, the aftermath to Hurricane Katrina, or the Obama campaign)—and the media and its powerful framing effects on subverting or reinforcing racial boundaries and identities within and across publics. A well-functioning black public sphere would defend the legitimacy of black identities, while simultaneously developing, questioning, and probing their content and boundaries.

Rebuilding the black public sphere also presupposes answers to a number of empirical questions. For example, what are the makeup and contours of current black publics? What is their institutional base, and to what degree do they overlap each other? How do historically important venues such as the black church extend their discourses online? To what degree does the church interact with new publics such as those influenced by hip-hop and environmental justice and anti-globalization movements? What role do visible black media figures—ranging from those who are extremely visible and influential, such as Oprah Winfrey, to those known for their political activism, such as Tavis Smiley—play in the shaping of black politics? How do public intellectuals, academics, and the black intelligentsia more broadly shape publics through media appearances and websites such as TheRoot .com? Do black-oriented progressive Websites such as Colorlines.com, BlackAgendaReporter.com, and BlackCommentator.com have much influence in shaping black opinion? We know that on occasion they can prove instrumental in mobilizing efforts due to their role in providing information to and coordinating the activities of activists. To what degree can public intellectuals and other active participants in black publics be held accountable for the views they advance? With the diminished institutional basis of the black public sphere that we see today, the mechanisms of accountability have also been weakened. Online activists are able now to shape discourse without being publicly accountable to any specific organization, institution, or constituency.

Another key political task is to assess the degree to which black-oriented publics overlap and interact with publics centered on other predominantly non-white publics, as well as with mainstream, predominantly white publics. To what degree do black-dominated publics influence publics associated with electoral politics, the mainstream left, right, and center of American political discourse, and transnational political movements, such as those discourse communities that TransAfrica works within? There is some basis for pessimism on this score. We have already seen how black publics were ineffective in both inserting their views and winning over predominantly white publics to their point of view during the aftermath to Katrina. There is some preliminary research that details the isolation of black publics by examining how much coverage the 2006 Weblog Awards candidates devoted to the Jena Six controversy. It is not surprising to see many of the top black blogs spending considerable time on the Jena Six. It is probably not surprising either that in most cases the top-ranked conservative blogs provided significantly less coverage. Yet predominantly white liberal blogs, as well as the online outlets of mainstream news sources such as the *New York Times*, likewise had relatively little coverage. Some key progressive websites and blogs paid extremely little or no attention to the Jena Six issue. This preliminary research suggests that the central political concerns of some black publics are not being reflected in predominantly white online spaces. A related set of questions here concerns how successful black publics have been in making themselves heard, whether using new media or older technologies. How effective have they been in influencing political campaigns, whether electoral or non-electoral, and in mobilizing for them both within and outside of black communities?

There is of course skepticism about whether the online world—cyberspace—has any potential whatsoever for progressive organizing and politics. The Retort collective provides a relatively typical example of this strand of criticism. They argue:

> For two decades the dream of the digital went largely unchallenged. Who would have predicted, even five years ago, the swiftness and completeness with which the dreaming became a thing of the past? . . . No wonder the actual *subjects* of the information world regard the hustlers and hucksters of cyberspace—the fifty-year-olds who go on believing the hype—in much the same way as Reaganite children once did their "sixties" parents puffing a joint and telling their Woodstock stories again.[8]

The problem with this line of argument is that it overlooks the numerous counterexamples of new technologies being used to challenge oppressive state power, including the effective use of cyberspace, also by the black counterpublic, for purposes of mobilization and democratic debate and critique. The first half of 2009 saw opposition movements in both Iran and China using new information technologies (satellite links, Twitter, and cell phone–based video footage, most of it funneled to the Internet, often to YouTube) in movements of mass mobilization and resistance. Over the past several decades, new information technologies, especially mobile technologies, have been used by pro-democracy forces in the Philippines and other parts of the developing world. In the United States, supporters of both the Jena Six and immigration reform have successfully used online venues and the new technologies. In a more quotidian fashion, progressive and conservative websites receive extremely heavy traffic as activists and the grassroots citizens search for alternative new sources of information and analysis, and to engage in debate. The Gore campaign and, even more spectacularly, the Obama campaign effectively used the new information tools for fundraising first of all, but eventually for massive, bottom-up mass mobilization.

In much of the world, these technologies play an integral role in building discursive publics and movements, particularly movements opposing forms of state authority, ranging from the theocrats of Iran to the state apparatus of the People's Republic of China. Part of what Retort misses is the large number of young people around the world, including in the United States, who are highly wired and who use their ubiquitous cell phones, laptops, netbooks, and other technologies to access sources of information and as ways to organize their own lives and that of their social network.

Of course, there remain dangers and complications that must be taken into account if black publics and the black public sphere are to be rebuilt in the digital era. One widespread concern is what some have called cyberbalkanization. Research does suggest a tendency for individuals to seek out opinions and discussions conforming to their preexisting political dispositions and ideology. The result is often that discursive communities that may already be insular become more extreme and isolated. This proposition has not yet been conclusively demonstrated empirically, but it must be kept in mind as a potential problem.

Also to be considered is a generational rift as regards to cyberspace access in general, specifically among African Americans. Older activist organizations often face difficulties integrating modern and vital information technologies, which cause them to be slow in responding to new opportunities. Across classes, the young are generally more fluent in information technologies than their elders. There is also a deep digital divide in the United States and internationally. Some new technologies are extremely common across strata—cell phones, for example, are increasingly replacing more traditional landlines both in the United States and abroad due to cost considerations. But there remains a class-based divide in access and expertise in regard to the Internet specifically, so that some popular sites, such as Facebook, that are used for political and social organizing are not readily available among several critical populations. All of this is to say, as we rebuild the black public sphere, that we must do so in a way that is as inclusive as possible—making effective use of old and new venues as opportunities present themselves.

Reinvigorating black politics will strengthen black publics and the black counterpublic. Political, social, and civic movements bring people into multiple discourses. They serve an educational function as well, often consciously, as they attempt to win community residents to their understanding of the world, focusing their attention on the questions of where we go from here and what is to be done. The information networks of black public spheres are reactivated, spread, and become more robust to disruption as political institutions strengthen and build their own communication and information apparatuses. Political movements enable black discourse to be interjected into mainstream white political discourse and have also facilitated discourse between black and other non-white public spheres. Just as rebuilding black public spheres and the black counterpublic is necessary for reinvigorated black political movements, healthy black political initiatives, organizing, and institutions are necessary for strengthening black publics.

IF WE ARE TO REBUILD BLACK PUBLICS AND THE BLACK PUBLIC sphere, black civil society must also be revitalized as an institutional and democratic foundation.[9] Here I provide a thought experiment on how black communities can make use of outside funds—from the stimulus package, reparations, or other sources—to improve material conditions for African Americans while simultaneously creating and strengthening local democratic processes and institutions. This proposal and any similar effort to win state resources to build local democratic organizations necessitate an accompanying political movement. Rebuilding the institutions and foundations of black civil society requires rebuilding the political institutions capable of winning resources for and defending black civil society.

Building black political movements also requires resources for invigorating civic and political organizations in ways that inspire popular engagement and cultivate progressive values. As some democratic theorists have argued, the nation should seriously consider modest government aid as a way to strengthen American civic life. Both Cornel West and Michael Walzer (West focused particularly on the black community) see the rebuilding of civil society in terms of a political challenge to strengthen democratic institutions. William Julius Wilson argues that Americans are more likely to be receptive to programs dedicated to this purpose if they are framed in racially neutral terms, and Lawrence Bobo and James Kluegel provide some empirical support for this proposition.[10] I would add that such initiatives should also be relatively cheap. A community capital fund is an example of a program that would meet these requirements. It would provide modest funds (allocated perhaps by congressional district) to elected community boards that would in turn make small grants to community organizations as seed money for specific community-improvement projects. Church groups, parent-teacher organizations, art groups, political organizations, small businesses, corporations—anyone would be eligible to apply for such a grant as long they were based in the community and the money was to be devoted to a community-approved project.

Engagement could be encouraged by requiring public debate over each proposal, extensive publicity for board elections, and minimum standards of electoral participation before funds would be released. Technical expertise could be provided by using tax incentives to encourage accountants and other professionals to donate expertise to the board and proposal writers. Reciprocity could be encouraged by making grant winners from one year ineligible for grants the following year and requiring them to aid the following year's applicants.

The purpose here would be not only to provide modest funds and encourage creative efforts toward community improvement, but also to strengthen community organization, civic engagement, and norms of citizenship participation and obligation. While Will Kymlicka rightly stresses that citizenship must be tied to obligations and duties,[11] additional considerations come into play concerning our most devastated neighborhoods, where the polity is not meeting its obligation to some of the nation's most vulnerable citizens. This thought experiment is an attempt to examine how institutional structures could be used to strengthen both sides of the bond between citizens and the state, while emphasizing the need to rebuild the very institutions and networks that are often the most effective at community improvement and mobilization.

Implementing a proposal such as this would have its messy side. Like the Community Action Programs of the Great Society, some of these programs would be used to mobilize political action—causing a measure of discomfort and anger among elected officials. Safeguards would have to be devised to minimize the risk of corruption and discourage patronage politics, even as the modest amounts involved in individual grants would likely attenuate such problems. Undoubtedly, a board from the affluent northern suburbs of

Chicago would have a different funding profile than one in a predominantly black South Side congressional district. But that is the point. The aim of such a proposal would be to encourage discussion of community priorities and to strengthen community institutions, which would provide benefits far in excess of the dollar amounts spent or even the immediate payoff of the programs initially funded.

Seriously advancing such a proposal—or anything like it, including initiatives proposed by Queen Mother Moore and other activists—will inspire opposition. The fundamental truth remains, as David Harvey states clearly, "Neoliberal theorists are . . . profoundly suspicious of democracy."[12] This is another reason such proposals are worthy of consideration. A fight to establish local democratic institutions could very well help expose the real enemies of democracy. These institutions would facilitate building social movements that would take on the job that Phil Thompson describes as "rebuilding the nation's social and physical infrastructure, and strengthening our democracy to empower our citizens to make economic institutions accountable."[13] Thompson also argues that such a progressive movement is necessary not only to rebuild the infrastructure, but also to shift the economy to one that is environmentally sustainable. To do so requires an alliance of progressive forces including those such as labor and black communities that are both fighting to rebuild movements capable of once again winning just social change and political power.

As we know from previous waves of black political and social innovation, such movements require dedication and steadfastness. The right-wing onslaught launched during the 2008 presidential campaign has only gained fury and has already begin to seriously erode the wave of black optimism that was generated by the Obama phenomenon. In just the last six months of 2010, black pessimism grew by nearly 10 percent, and Latino pessimism grew even more rapidly. This growing pessimism could serve to sap the dedication and steadfastness necessary to building grassroots movements. Such movements will demand the willingness to keep going, as well as fidelity to the democratic aims of disadvantaged communities. What these times once again demand of us is the type of determination and commitment to democratic and egalitarian principles that were so strongly evident in the movement that Dr. King helped to build and lead.

WHEN MARTIN LUTHER KING JR. WENT TO MEMPHIS IN MID-
March 1968 to support black municipal sanitation workers, in what proved
to be his final protest campaign, he was engaged in cutting through the
American spectacle by exposing the dark side of American politics, society,
and capitalism. Following in Dr. King's footsteps requires not forgetting,
not living with a comfortable amnesia about both the past and the present. It
requires recognizing, despite the progress some have made, that rampant injustice remains a normal quotidian fact of American life. I am arguing here,
as Michael Rogin did in another context, that the most scandalous failures
of the American democracy "owe their invisibility not to secrecy but to political amnesia."[14] Among the invisible scandals Rogin was calling to mind
were the covert actions of imperialism. But just as memory loss sustains the
imperial spectacle, it also sustains domestic spectacles, especially in the domain of race in the United States. American political amnesia, Rogin argues,
is rooted specifically in the domain of race and racial subordination. In matters of race in particular, "the concept of political amnesia points to a cultural
structure of motivated disavowal."[15]

A key aspect of how spectacle works is that it "attaches ordinary, intimate
existence to public displays of the private lives of political and other enter-
tainers."[16] We've seen plenty of this in the seemingly endless Republican and
celebrity sexual follies. There is a real danger of the Obama era being transformed to one in which spectacle is dominant. The hint of a cult of personal-
ity growing around the president as well as the media emphasis on Michelle
Obama's fashion sense, instead of her astute political understanding of this
country or her policy initiatives, are also worrying signs.

Spectacle, by promoting political amnesia, helps the nation forget the real
divisions, the real clashes of interests, that threaten to further polarize the
nation along partisan, class, and racial lines. Due in large part to the Obama
phenomenon, we have on more than one occasion of late seen sensibilities
being ruffled, to put it mildly, by intimations of the racial order that dominates the American polity. To be blunt, even the hint that President Obama
has views about racial incidents at variance with that of many whites, that he
is willing to voice an opinion about a racial controversy, is sufficient to provoke white racial resentment at such a level that causes not only his approval
rating among whites to plunge, but jeopardizes his political agenda. A battle

is under way about what may legitimately be said in our racial discourse. The real danger in even the discussion of reparations, say, or of the affairs involving Reverend Wright is that the real America still has at its core racial disunity and ugliness that the glorious racial narrative of the Obama campaign and presidency have not, should not, and cannot fully erase. Rogin made this argument about race and spectacle over two decades ago:

> American imperial spectacles display and forget four enabling myths that the culture can no longer unproblematically embrace. The first is the historical organization of American politics around racial domination. . . . The second is redemption through violence, intensified in the mass technologies of entertainment and war. The third is the belief in individual agency, the need to forget both the web of social ties that enmesh us all and the wish for an individual power so disjunctive with everyday existence. And the fourth is identification with the state, to which is transferred the freedom to act without being held to account that in part compensates for individual helplessness but in part reflects state weakness as well.[17]

Katrina was the "anti-spectacle" precisely due to the fact that for a period it ripped away the mask of American unity and progress, as well as the myth of the efficacy of individualist, privatized solutions to the nation's infrastructural and social problems that had been the hallmark of the American spectacle. Due to Katrina, racial reality was once again in one's living room, as it was during the Birmingham marches featuring Bull Conner, as it was during the mid-1960s, and in a very different way on account of Vietnam later in the decade. President Obama's inauguration did not completely erase the memory of Katrina, but for some segments of the population, it was extremely effective in moderating discomfiting memories of the very recent past.

As Rogin argues, Reagan restored this modern version of the American spectacle with more support at the polls from white men than any presidential candidate since the administrations of the founders. This is what has so unsettled the right, that the racial equation has been reversed—white men can no longer count on electing "their" candidate. This is why Fox News host Glenn Beck calls Obama a racist. This is why the late Harvard professor Samuel Huntington shortly before his death railed against the influx of Asians and Latinos into the United States, while demanding that blacks "act white." This is why Pat Buchanan rants desperately about how it was exclusively white men who built this country. The country, at least symbolically, is no longer fully "theirs." In this sense, Obama's election was to some extent subversive, and it raises the question of whether American national identity can be reinscribed so that it has a new more inclusive racial component, albeit one still compatible with corporate capitalism and an imperialist agenda. The jury is out. This disjuncture that has so unsettled the right provides a space for new opportunities. But as King said in the quote that opens this chapter, tomorrow is now. We cannot afford to wait for another generation to rebuild sustainable black and other progressive movements.

Dr. King—whose life was dedicated to unburying the past, speaking truth to power, and building a unity to rip away the charade of American race relations—would have been aghast at the spectacle of today's American politics. He would have demanded that once again we focus not only on racial injustice, but also the injustice caused by poverty and by an aggressive and militaristic foreign policy. During the last weeks of his life, Dr. King argued:

> Poverty is a glaring, notorious reality. . . . It is poverty amid plenty. It is poverty in the midst of an affluent society, and I think this is what makes for great frustration and great despair in the black community and the poor community of our nation generally. . . . I think it is absolutely necessary now to deal massively and militantly with the economic problem.

King linked the fight against poverty to the fight against U.S. militarism. It is true today as well that a key aspect of building democracy at home requires demanding a democratic foreign policy. This had been a central component of black politics since the early twentieth century. It has not been as key a part of black politics the last few decades, and it also needs to be revitalized. Dr. King explained why:

> We feel that there must be some structural changes now, there must be a radical re-ordering of priorities, there must be a de-escalation and a final stopping

of the war in Vietnam and an escalation of the war against poverty and racism here at home. . . . One of the great tragedies of the war in Vietnam is that it has strengthened the military-industrial complex.[18]

Why should we work toward this kind of change? Because it is the right thing to do. Dr. King explained his support of the Memphis strikers as his moral duty:

> If I do not stop to help the sanitation workers, what will happen to them? That's the question. . . . Let us rise up tonight with a greater readiness. Let us stand with a greater determination. And let us move on in these powerful days, these days of challenge to make America what it ought to be. We have the opportunity to make America a better nation.[19]

The series of events, the sacrifice, the struggle that we once labeled during the combined Civil Rights and Black Power era, the black liberation struggle, have been betrayed. I am using the precise definition of betrayal formulated by the French philosopher Alain Badiou, who writes that betrayal is "to give up on a truth in the name of one's interest."[20] Badiou further argues, echoing a claim often heard in black political thought, that emancipatory politics are always conflictual and unsettling; it names its enemies and, in a word, is militant. As King and Malcolm X lamented decades before Badiou, it is all too easy to succumb to corruption by simply ceasing to try—either because of one's self-interest or simply because one becomes tired. Fidelity to the cause of human emancipation is tiring, but emancipatory politics demands nothing less—nor anything more than that one keeps trying. The enemies of black emancipation, and by extension human emancipation, remain white supremacy and the renegade capitalism that dominates this neoliberal era.

For the claims of a group to be truly emancipatory, to transcend the narrow self-interest of the group, to demand that others take up the group's causes, they must serve the universal cause of human emancipation.[21] Black politics must return to its roots and once again be dedicated to overturning white supremacy, not only state-sanctioned white supremacy, but also that found permeating civil society in the United States. To win a better life for the black poor, but also humanity more generally, black politics must also rededicate itself to fighting the rogue capitalism that today dominates all aspects of our lives. Then, once again, black politics will regain its emancipatory nature. Once again the demands raised through the political struggles that comprise black politics will entail nothing less than the thorough transformation of American civil society, economy, and state. Once again black politics will be the site of demands that compel the support of progressives who desire the emancipation of humanity. At that point, as Cornelius Castoriadis argues, blackness becomes politically once again "a positive condition, for it is our own particularity which allows us access to the universal."[22]

It is our generation's task to continue to fight for justice, democracy, and an America that one day may live up to its promise.

EPILOGUE: TAKING THE COUNTRY BACK

ONE STEP FORWARD, TWO STEPS BACK

During the same week that former President George W. Bush whined that the Kanye West affair during the Katrina disaster was the low point of his presidency, that West's comments disgusted him, his even more conservative colleagues were crowing about "taking the country back." George Bush's continued bafflement, like that of white America at the time of Katrina, at the extremely deep black anger aimed at him is indicative of the power and bankruptcy of the myth of a post-racial America. This myth was further exposed, if not finally demolished, during the 2010 midterm elections as the Tea Party–fueled Republican Party stormed back to power on the twin motors of justifiably deep voter anger about the continuing devastating economic crisis, and white racial resentment that was particularly strong among older voters. This white resentment was manipulated, mobilized, and stoked by the Tea Party and their fellow travelers (the rest of the Republican Party) under the slogan of "taking our country back." The racism of this slogan is revealed when the meaning who is included in "our country" and the meaning of "back from whom" is analyzed.

According to a 2010 NAACP report, "The Tea Party movement has unleashed a still inchoate political movement who are in their numerical majority, angry middle-class white people who believe their country, their nation has been taken from them."[1] All but one of the key Tea Party networks, according to the organization's report, have raised bogus Birther challenges to President Obama's birth certificate.[2] The movement was funded by Wall Street corporations that resented the weak controls that were imposed to check their rapacity, and right-wing funders who cynically wanted to use the national disaster that their policies created to return to power. This task was accomplished by mobilizing older white voters who comprised a much larger percentage of the voting electorate in 2010 than they did in 2008.

In the meantime, Tea Party activists and their fellow travelers in the congressional leadership continue to stoke religious and racial hatred. Judson Phillips, founder of one of the three largest Tea Party groups, called on the movement to defeat Minnesota member of Congress African American Keith Ellison, at least in part because he is Muslim. Judson stood firm about his stance toward Ellison when sharply questioned about it, stating, "I, personally have a real problem with Islam."[3] Old-fashioned racism reared its head as Republican operatives in Delaware, Wisconsin, Illinois, Texas, California, and elsewhere attempted to suppress and intimidate the black and Latino vote. Tea Party activists were directly involved in attempting to prevent black South Carolina college students from voting.

The Tea Party and the Republicans more generally scoff at the charges of racism, when they are not bristling, pointing to the election of a few non-white conservatives as proof of their lack of racism. One of the two new black members of Congress, Allen West, is so far out of the black (and for that matter Latino and Asian American) mainstream that he not only relishes attacking Obama's manhood; he also has pronounced "institutional racism is dead."[4] Yet despite the exclamations of racial innocence on the part of Bush and his Tea Party successors, we see South Carolina state senator and gubernatorial candidate Jake Knotts attack fellow conservative South Asian Nikki Haley by saying calling her a "fucking raghead . . . [we] got a raghead in Washington: we don't need one in South Carolina."[5] Like the racist attack on Ellison, the new racism combines old-fashioned anti–people of color racism with in this case false allusions to their purported Muslimness. With Knotts we get a two-for-one racist attack as he goes after both the South Asian conservative Haley as well as black Obama. Along with Muslims, Latinos also received special attention for racial vilification and hatred from coast-to-coast. In California and elsewhere, we saw campaign ad after campaign ad proclaim that Latino citizens and immigrants represented a criminal danger to "real" Americans. If one analyzes the racial subtext of the campaign, we can only conclude that "our country" seems not to include blacks, Latinos, and particularly Muslims.

That a frightening proportion of white Americans has a false image of world where people of color are the undeserving beneficiaries of state- and private-sector discrimination was demonstrated in a public opinion study conducted in late 2010. A large majority of white Tea Party adherents, only slightly fewer white Republican identifiers, and half of white independents believe "today discrimination against whites has become as big a problem as discrimination against blacks and other minorities."[6] In one real sense, as Du Bois recognized a century ago, when it comes to race, facts still do not matter. The systematic advantage that whites as a group continue to enjoy when compared with people of color is not only unrecognized by the majority of white Americans, but indeed those who remain on top now see themselves as the victims.

In one sense, the majority of whites are victims—victims of the same rapacious economic system that has ravaged particularly black and Latino communities for well over a decade. Instead, as would be rational, turning on an economic system that has abandoned them, many have taken the historic easy way out and have directed their anger at communities of color, including Muslim communities, and the state that is allegedly the ally of the colored undeserving. The economic crisis has produced feelings of fear, anger, displacement, and of no longer being in control, particularly among the white middle classes and the more advantaged sectors of the white working class. These feelings when combined with Tea Party sentiments of xenophobia, religious hatred, uncritical nationalism, and racism have produced a populist hysteria, a moral panic, that is the stuff out of which fascist movements have been built in the past, and out of which fascism could be built again.

The populist hysteria and moral panic generated by the incessant religious and racial hate that has been a feature of the political terrain since the 2008 campaign as well as the ongoing economic crisis have created a political climate in the capital and states that enables a right-wing policy backlash. A Tea Party Congress will seek repeal of health-care reform, as modest as it was. There will be efforts, quite possibly successful, to extend massive tax cuts for the super rich costing billions, while in the name of austerity the extension of unemployment benefits are derailed. Sane energy policy, reproductive rights, forward-looking science policy, the labor movement, quality public education at all levels, and indeed all the social innovations from the New Deal on that have enriched the United States and substantial segments of its population, including social security itself, are threatened by the new corporate-backed majority. No longer content to try and roll back the Civil Rights Movement and the Great Society, the new conservatives want to return to the out-of-control era of the robber barons of a century ago. This time the looting of a nation will be managed using the best modern corporate strategies that neoliberal technicians can craft. What is particularly new is the marriage of neoliberal corporate capitalism with a fundamentalist religious movement that has an incoming energy-committee chair arguing that we need not worry about climate change since God's covenant with Noah precludes a new flood—forgetting that the same texts also tell us that God helps those who help themselves. Some fundamentalists are using the pulpit to generate a movement to once again give corporate capitalism an unfettered hand. Bringing down Obama and his program is considered a necessary first step to achieve both the corporate and fundamentalist components of the Tea Party movement's aims.

The irony, of course, is that Obama's arguably so far successful mission was to save capitalism. As a fervently pro-capitalist *New York Times* commentator observed:

> For no matter your view of President Obama, he effectively saved capitalism. And for that, he paid a terrible political price. Suppose you had $100,000 to invest the day Barack Obama was inaugurated. Why bet on a liberal Democrat? Here's why: The presidency of George W. Bush produced the worst stock market decline of any president in history. The net worth of American households collapsed as Bush slipped away. And if you needed a loan to buy a house or stay in business, private sector borrowing was dead when he handed over power. As of election day, Nov. 2, 2010, your $100,000 was worth about $177,000 if invested strictly in the NASDAQ average for the entirety of the Obama administration.[7]

Obama's program has been unrelentedly pro-capitalist, moderate, and consensus seeking to the extent that numerous segments of his base—including African Americans, Latinos, LGBT communities, the labor movement, and

progressives—have been sorely disappointed in both the lack of strong policy initiatives and the administration's seeming reluctance to take the fight
to those that oppose even the moderate program of the administration and
congressional Democrats.

In the meantime, some aspects of racial order that severely disadvantage
particularly poor blacks and Latinos continue unchecked—for example, two
black women, Gladys and Jamie Scott, who since 1993 have been serving
double life sentences in Mississippi for allegedly participating in an armed
robbery that netted $11 and in which no one was harmed. Contrast this
"justice" with the case of Oscar Grant. In late 2010 the police officer who
was convicted of killing Oakland resident Oscar Grant received only a two-
year sentence. Judge Perry rejected the jury's finding that would have been
grounds for a much longer sentence. The value of some black life continues
to be severely discounted when compared to most property crime or the degree to which a rogue police officer should be punished for unjustly taking a
life. The level of violence in communities of color such as South Los Angeles
has grown to the point that a Rand survey found that rates of post-traumatic
stress syndrome among children is a more serious problem among children
in South Los Angeles than among children in Baghdad. It will take an independent political movement to address the economic and physical violence
that is all too common in the country's urban communities. It will take such
a movement to answer those who wish to take "their" country back. Our
answer to those striving to take their country back? No.

ACKNOWLEDGMENTS

Book manuscripts and research projects tend to have a mind of their own once under way. The research project that spawned this book was one focused on analyzing the change in black public opinion during the early twenty-first century in the context of a continuing racial divide. The project was supposed to lead to one fairly academic book. Instead, this project has generated three books all coming out within a short period of time. This is the first of those books and is not the traditional academic book (which is still coming). This book is aimed at a more general audience, and its explicit political point of view is due to the person who provided the impetus and the opportunity that allowed me to write a book that comes from research and pointed political analysis. Henry Louis Gates Jr.—the fabled director of Harvard's W. E. B. Du Bois Institute—strongly urged me to write a book on black politics that would be *political*. I am thankful for both his prodding and encouragement, and I hope the final project meets his expectations.

The book is founded on years of boisterous yet serious conversations about black politics with a truly amazing group of scholars who are as dedicated to having their scholarship aid the cause of justice while also meeting the most rigorous intellectual standards. Conversations and often arguments with Melissa Harris-Perry, Robert Gooding-Williams, Phil Thompson, Larry Bobo, Lani Guinier, Bill Wilson, Tommie Shelby, Cathy Cohen, and Michael Hanchard took place during hours spent breaking bread, sharing beverages, and heatedly trying to understand the future of black politics and the pathologies of the politics of race in the United States.

A group of former students who have gone on to distinguished careers has cheerfully taken revenge for what one of them described in print as the boot camp that masquerades as the University of Chicago Department of Political Science doctoral program. Mark Sawyer, Chris Parker, and Taeku Lee all pushed me to make my work better, to read the extra book, to try the additional estimation, and to generally attempt (not necessarily always successfully) to make my work live up to my own standards. Their continued and generous feedback has improved every chapter of this manuscript. Thanks, guys.

Marcus Board, Alexandra Moffett- Bateau, and Abimbola Oladokun provided expert, timely, and indispensable aid as research assistants. Rohit Goel went far beyond his duties and provided critical insights that greatly strengthened this and the project's other manuscripts. Julie Lee Merseth completed herculean tasks managing the data and conducting analyses. It is only just that her role has evolved from valued research assistant to even more valued collaborator.

Several groups of scholars have allowed me to try out my ideas on them as I developed my argument. The Departments of African American Studies and Ethnic Studies at my alma mater, Berkeley, invited me for a talk at an important juncture, and Taeku Lee afterward invited me to a lively session of his graduate seminar. I received extremely good feedback from colleagues and friends at a presentation at Northwestern University. Several collectivities at the University of Chicago provided the intense and inspired feedback that the university is known for. I am thankful to the political communications, political theory workshops, as well as the reading group on neoliberalism led by my colleagues Robert Gooding-Williams and Bernard Harcourt.

This project is based on ten years of collecting public opinion data, and none of the manuscripts would have been possible without that data. I was blessed with three extraordinary collaborators and leaders from whom I learned much. Larry Bobo, Cathy Cohen, and Melissa Harris-Perry are formidable giants in the field of public opinion research, and each has reshaped the study of race as well as the study of black politics. Generous institutional support for these studies was received from the Ford and Rockefeller Foundations, and generous funds were also provided from both the University of Chicago and Harvard University. Institutional support of another kind was provided by African American–centered political, cultural and social website TheRoot.com. During the 2008 presidential campaign, they gave me the opportunity to express many of my early ideas, which are now part of chapter 3.

Providing constant guidance, criticism, and support was a group of friends in the Chicago area, each deeply involved in their own critical intellectual projects, who made time to read multiple drafts, listened to mock talks, organized sessions around various aspects of the projects, and provided spiritual and material sustenance as needed. My very deep thanks go out to Lauren Berlant, Traci Burch, Cathy Cohen, Don Reneau, Lisa Wedeen, Linda Zerilli, and Alice Furumoto.

I am sure that John Tryneski hoped that he would not have to once again read a line in the acknowledgments thanking him for his patience. Sadly, I must once again thank the editor supreme at the University of Chicago Press for his patience. Much more important, however, is that John had a faith in this book that ensured its survival. He recognized and supported my need to maintain core sections of the argument and believed that the argument could be preserved and still made accessible to a general audience. He literally rescued the book at a time that I thought the project was dead. For that, I owe him a great debt and hope that he finds the final product at least somewhat worthy of his faith. As always the team at the University of Chicago Press has been outstanding, and in particular I have been awed by the ability of Erin DeWitt to turn my mangled prose into something readable.

My family has sustained and lovingly supported me through trying times and many physical and a few spiritual challenges. No part of this project was not improved without the touch of my lifelong partner, Alice Furumoto; no part of this project would have been completed without her aid. Her strength and cheer has illuminated many dark nights and this manuscript as well. This book is dedicated to the youth who throughout the world are once again trying to build a better world. May they reach the top of the mountaintop that Martin Luther King glimpsed in the spring of 1968 when a better world seemed achievable in our lifetimes.

NOTES

PROLOGUE

1. Huntington 2004.

2. King 1967, 36.

3. Rogin 1990, 99–123; Debord (1967) 1995, 12. But also see *Afflicted Powers* (Retort 2005) for another useful application of the concept of spectacle to modern American politics.

4. Wedeen 1999, 156.

5. I thank Don Reneau for the concept of thinking about the aftermath to Katrina in terms of "anti-spectacle."

6. Malcolm X quoted in Scott Simon 1998.

7. King 1967, 188–89; emphasis in original.

CHAPTER 1

1. For detailed information on the survey studies reported in this table and elsewhere in the book, see the author's website at www.michaeldawson.net.

2. Subsequently with little discussion, an apology was passed in Congress.

3. Habermas (1983) 1990, 135; emphasis added.

4. C. Cohen 1999.

5. Rogin 1990.

6. Dawson forthcoming.

7. Bobo et al. 1995. Bobo was able to make a stronger causal argument than normal using survey research. Half of his data was collected before the verdict was issued, half afterward. Thus, he was able to demonstrate a very large shift in affluent black's opinion with the clear single causal factor responsible for the shift being the verdict and its aftermath.

8. Unless otherwise stated, statistics are from the "Racial Equity Status Report" (Reece 2008).

9. U.S. Department of Labor, Bureau of Labor Statistics 2009.

10. Western and Pettit 2005.

11. Unless otherwise stated, from Warren 2008 and/or Liptak 2008.

12. Mays, Cochran, and Barnes 2007.

13. Smedley et al. 2003.

14. Franks et al. 2006.

15. Ash et al. 2009.

16. Ash and Fetter 2004.

17. All statistics from August 2008 CDC HIV/AIDS Fact Sheet "HIV/AIDS among African Americans."

18. For a particularly egregious example of the left's "forgetfulness" when it came to race, see Afflicted Powers: Capital and Spectacle in a New Age of War (Retort 2005).

CHAPTER 2

1. The World Saxophone Quartet 2006. "The Political Blues" song lyrics from CD of the same name.

2. Giroux 2006b.

3. Tisserand 2006.

4. The data are from the "2005 Racial Attitudes and the Katrina Disaster Study," principal investigators: Michael C. Dawson, Melissa V. Harris-Lacewell, and Cathy J. Cohen (see Dawson, Harris-Lacewell, and Cohen 2006). The study was in the field—October 28–November 17, 2005. The total sample includes 1,252 respondents: 703 whites, 487 blacks, 10 classified as "other," and 52 Latinos. The Pew questions were taken from their report about their polling on Katrina (Pew Research Center 2005).

5. From data compile by author.

6. Louisiana Recovery Authority Support Foundation (LSRAF) 2006, 12. A number of agencies, including the Louisiana Department of Health and Hospitals and the Centers for Disease Control and Prevention, undertook a careful population survey of Orleans Parish in October 2006, under the auspices of the LRASF. Their 2006 survey sampled randomly from area residents as well as collected interviews among the Diaspora.

7. See Dawson 2009.

8. LSRAF 2006, 13.

9. Quoted in Dawson, Harris-Lacewell, and Cohen 2006.

10. These figures represent aggregate response. For any of the reported percentages, simply subtracting the reported number from 100 will give the reverse portrayal. So, in this case, 91% of blacks believed that West's remarks were justified.

11. The World Saxophone Quartet, "Spy on Me Blues," song lyrics from Political Blues CD (2006).

12. Public Enemy, Rebirth of a Nation CD (2006).

13. Data such as these became readily available from a variety of sources following the storm, and many excellent narrative accounts of the disaster and its aftermath appeared.

One particularly rich source is Dyson 2006, from which much of the abbreviated narrative offered here has been drawn. Except where explicitly noted, the following statistics are from Dyson 2006.

14. Bustillo 2006.

15. Wilson and Stein 2006. The desperate plight of many of the evacuees was documented by Wilson and Stein, who interviewed evacuees in Houston shelters in September 2005 and then again in November of the same year and July 2006. The last two waves of interviews occurred mainly in apartment complexes, as those who had been in the shelters found more permanent housing. The sample was 98 percent African American.

16. Dyson 2006, 5.

17. Quoted in Wilson and Stein 2006, 19.

18. Berggren and Curiel 2006, 1549–52.

19. Sharkey 2006.

20. Biguenet 2006.

21. Hill 2006.

22. Dyson 2006.

23. Bustillo 2006.

24. Bustillo 2006.

25. Giroux 2006a.

26. It should be noted that these figures include applications from the victims of Hurricane Rita, so the Texas numbers are inflated with respect specifically to Katrina.

27. Logan 2006; see also Clark-Flory 2006.

28. Bustillo 2006.

29. Wilson and Stein 2006.

30. Lee 2006; Bustillo 2006.

31. Lil Wayne, "Georgia . . . Bush," *Dedication 2: Gangsta Grillz* CD (2006).

32. Oxfam America 2006, 12, 2.

33. Simmons 2006.

34. Cooper 2005.

35. Nossiter 2006.

36. Burdeau 2007.

37. Cass and Whoriskey 2006.

38. Quoted in Kusmer 2006.

39. See Habermas (1992) 1996 for one influential example.

40. Quoted in Simmons 2006.

41. Simmons 2006.

42. Simmons 2006.

43. Venkatesh 2006; see also Cohen and Dawson 1993.

44. Brown 2006; Konigsmark 2006; White 2006.

45. Quoted in Brown 2006.

46. Quoted in Konigsmark 2006.

47. Hill 2006; Lee 2006.

48. Associated Press 2007.

49. See Holden 2006 and Goldstein 2006, as two examples of reviews of Lee's *When the Levees Broke*.

50. See Biguenet 2006; Sharkey 2006; Taranto 2006.

51. Murray 2005.

52. Media Matters 2007.

53. Hill 2006.

54. I thank Don Reneau for pointing out this parallel.

55. "The 2004 Racial Attitudes Survey," Michael C. Dawson, principal investigator. This study is part of the series of studies described earlier in this essay from which the Katrina attitudinal data was drawn.

56. C. Cohen 1999, 274.

57. This analysis was also conducted with the addition of the respondent's self-reported partisanship. The results remained the same. Race overwhelmed all other characteristics, including the respondent's party identification. See author's website, http://www.michaeldawson.net, for full details on the estimation.

58. See chapter 1 of my book Black Visions (2001) for a more developed exposition of the concept of a black counterpublic.

59. J. Cohen 1999.

60. J. Cohen 1999, 74.

61. When I refer to the black counterpublic, I am talking about a "public of publics" such as the one described by Jean Cohen in "American Civil Society Talk" (1999). Just as she discusses the mainstream of society as being comprised of multiple publics, so too are there multiple publics within black civil society.

62. Warner 2002, 122; see also Fraser 1989.

63. Habermas (1992) 1996, 359; emphasis in the original.

64. Rogin 1987, 193.

65. Ferme 1999, 163.

66. Jefferson (1785) 1999, 145.

67. Rogin 1987, 195.

68. Dawson 2004.

69. Dawson 2001.

70. Rogin 1987, 62.

71. See my forthcoming *Blacks In and Out of the Left: Past, Present, and Future* (Harvard University Press).

72. I thank Linda Zerilli for pushing me to develop this point and suggesting lines along which the argument could be developed.

73. Rogin 1987, 63.

74. See Mills's *Racial Contract* (1997) for one key examination of this phenomenon.

75. I thank Don Reneau for making this observation.

76. Reed 2005.

77. See Kelley 2002 and Dawson 2001 (especially the chapters on black feminism, black Marxism, and black nationalism), for two different, but complementary studies on the black radical movements of the twentieth century.

78. We will have to see the degree to which these racial differences persist in the Obama era.

79. See Sharkey 2006; Taranto 2006.

80. Sewell 1996.

81. I thank Chris Parker for pushing me on whether Katrina represented a critical event.

82. Data compiled by author from previously cited 2004 racial attitudes study. This question was asked in both the 2000 and 2004 studies, and the percentages were consistent for both blacks and whites. For reference, the black percentage in the same categories for whites cited above was 13 percent.

83. I wish to thank Mark Sawyer for suggesting this line of argument.

84. Quoted in Dawson 2001, 259.

CHAPTER 3

1. Most of the material from this and the next section is adapted from the essays I wrote during the 2008 presidential campaign for TheRoot.com. Links can be found at my website.

2. Baldwin 1984, 36.

3. See http://www.michaeldawson.net for further description of the studies that produced the data.

4. See my 2001 book, Black Visions, for statistical details and the question wording for these three separate questions.

5. See Dawson 2001 for a full discussion of modern black ideologies.

6. There are other positions on the black movement and the demands it produced that can be found in the history of the American left, including ones that recognize African Americans' just demands up to and including the right for blacks to self-determination. But the cited positions were the ones that were often used to justify ignoring or attacking the demands made by black activists.

7. Wilentz 2008.

8. Ewers 2009. john a. powell uses lowercase letter in his name.

9. Associated Press 2008.

10. CBS 2 Chicago 2008.

11. Blitt 2008.

12. All quotes from Beck's February 23, 2009, War Room program are from a transcript downloaded from FOXNews.com.

13. Salon.com, May 11, 2009.

14. Quoted from Salon.com, May 11, 2009; emphasis added.

15. New York Times, April 17, 2009.

16. Washington Times 2009.

17. Zernike and Thee-Brenan 2010; emphasis added.

18. Blow 2010b.

19. D'Souza 2009.

20. Details of the statistical estimations that follow can be found on the author's website, www.michaeldawson.net. In all cases when changes in probabilities are reported, a number of other variables are controlled for, including age, family income, education, gender, whether one resides in the South, and, where appropriate, other attitudinal measures.

21. Age in years of the respondent, on the other hand, had no effect on white warmth toward Obama.

CHAPTER 4

1. Richard Baker, Louisiana 6th District, *Hannity and Colmes*, Fox News, September 30, 2005.

2. Of course, patronage remains alive and well in Chicago. What the dismantling of the party-based patronage machine meant, however, was that patronage jobs began to be more oriented toward middle-class and business interests and less oriented toward the working and lower-middle classes.

3. Wall 2009, 35.

4. Wall 2009, 38.

5. By "translocal" I mean movements in which the organizing and conflict occurs at the local level, while there is often sharing of information, tactics, and some coordination between localities. These movements in the local areas often include activists with strong local roots as well as activists tied to national organizations who may move from locality to locality. Sometimes the local activists belong to a national organization that has a federal structure.

6. Sites 2007, 2642.

7. Parks and Warren 2009; Sites 2007.

8. Parks and Warren 2009; Sites 2007.

9. Featherstone 2005.

10. Featherstone 2005.

11. Cummings 2007.

12. Cummings 2007, 1961.

13. Cummings 2007.

14. Parks and Warren 2009.

15. Sites 2007, 2632.

16. Harvey 2009 has an excellent and thorough analysis of how spatial analysis can aid in tracing the political, economic, and social consequences of neoliberal processes.

17. Molnar 2004. Table adapted from presentation of Project on Human Development in Chicago Neighborhoods demographics data.

18. Parks and Warren 2009, 2.

19. Featherstone 2005.

20. Featherstone 2005.

21. Cummings 2007; Featherstone 2005.

22. Cummings 2007.

23. Parks and Warren 2009.

24. Parks and Warren 2009.

25. Sites 2007, 2644.

26. Dawson 2001; Du Bois (1935) 1979.

27. Cummings 2007.

28. While I independently developed the language of "neoliberal Kool-Aid," Reverend Jackson publicly used similar and more pointed language (Kool-Aid and cyanide) much earlier, directly in his criticism of apologists for Walmart inside and outside the black community.

29. Lucia Blacksher, quoted in Ratner 2008.

30. FRELIMO slogan from the national liberation forces in Mozambique and adopted by black activists throughout the African diaspora.

31. Ratner 2008.

32. Ratner 2008.

33. *Hannity and Colmes*, Fox News, September 30, 2005.

34. All statistics from Eaton 2007.

35. Preceding material and stats drawn from a report from Quigley 2008.

36. Carr 2009.

37. Quoted in Faussett 2009.

38. Faussett 2009

39. Faussett 2009.

40. Quoted in Finch 2009.

41. Thompson 2008, 3.

42. Parks 2008; Thompson 2008.

43. Thompson 2008.

44. Oxfam America 2008, 4.

45. Oxfam America 2008.

46. Klein 2007, 6.

47. Thompson 2008.

48. Oxfam America 2008, 11.

49. Oxfam America 2008, 12.

50. Oxfam America 2008, 12.

51. Oxfam America 2008, 15; emphasis added.

52. Oxfam America 2009.

53. Oxfam America 2008, 1.

54. Oxfam America 2009, 2.

55. Oxfam America 2009, 3. See Wilson and Taub 2006 for similar asymmetries between black and Latino opinion in Chicago.

56. Oxfam American 2009, 5.

57. D. Roberts 2009.

58. D. Roberts 2009.

59. For much fuller presentations of my summaries of this history, see chapter 2 of Behind the Mule and chapter 1 of Black Visions.

60. Wacquant 2008, 29.

61. Pager 2007.

62. Dawson 1994, 33.

63. Allegreto, Amerikaner, and Pitts 2010.

64. Bertrand and Mullainathan 2003.

65. Pager 2007, 98.

66. Western 2006, 78.

67. Western and Pettit 2005.

68. Raphael and Ronconi 2007.

69. Grodsky and Pager 2001.

70. I have the data for the intervening years, and the income divisions have remained relatively the same across the twenty-plus years of data.

71. Western 2006.

72. I thank Linda Zerilli for suggesting this line of argument. Robert Gooding-Williams 2009 makes an extended argument along these lines about the need to constitute black movements through contested politics.

73. Polanyi 1944.

74. Wacquant 2008.

75. Wedeen 2008, 187.

76. Wedeen 2008, 187.

77. Wedeen 2008, 193.

78. Wedeen 2008, 196.

79. Harvey 2005, 7.

80. In noting others, I have in mind primarily William Connolly 2008 in his otherwise excellent book on the twin rise of the right-wing and evangelical movements in

the United States, two movements that in tandem were responsible for the triumphant instantiation of the neoliberal state in the United States.

81. Harvey 2005, 50.

82. Lester Spence has written an important paper on this subject, "The Neoliberal Turn in Black Politics" (2009).

83. Sites 2007; Katznelson 1981.

84. Sites 2007.

85. Harvey 2005, 16.

86. Wacquant 2008, 7.

87. Wacquant 2008.

88. Harvey 2009, 118.

89. The statistics in the above section are drawn from Oliver, Johnson, and Farrell 1993, 117–41.

90. Friedman 2007, 537.

91. Cohen and Dawson 1993.

92. 215

93. Herrnstein and Murray 1996, 533–34.

94. Herrnstein and Murray 1996.

CHAPTER 5

1. One example should suffice to demonstrate the perils of equating correlation with causation. Health data from the 1940s shows that there was a strong correlation between race and cancer rates. Blacks had much lower cancer rates than whites. Did some aspect of being black cause a greater resistance to cancer? No. Blacks on average died at such early ages that by and large cancers had less time to develop.

2. For a brief review of the racism faced by black workers, see Dawson 2001. For a fuller account, see Arnesen 1994. For a review of some of radical alliances between people of color, see Kelley 2002 as well as Perry 2009. See also Dawson, Blacks In and Out of the Left: Past, Present, and Future (forthcoming).

3. Kelley 2002; Dawson 2001.

4. Kelley 2002; Dawson 2001; Kim 2000.

5. See Hamilton 1979.

6. I argue that although immigration reform occurred in the United States in 1965, the effects on political movements were not felt until the mid-1970s and beyond.

7. Kim 2000, 16.

8. I am using the terms "terrain" and "space" semi-interchangeably. Both "terrain" and "space" are three-dimensional constructs. The concept of terrain speaks to more of a Gramscian (1971) political configuration through which political forces must maneuver. I use "space" more when I am discussing the political, ideological, and in this case status locations of groups or individuals relative to one another.

9. Shklar 1991; Du Bois (1903) 1996.

10. Arnesen 1994; Shklar 1991; Dawson 2001.

11. Huntington 2004.

12. I would like to thank Alice Furumoto-Dawson for suggesting this line of argument about the relationship of achieving democracy in the United States to eliminating racialization.

13. Some Marxists often forget that Marx himself had a broad view of what human emancipation necessitated. Marx's "On the Jewish Question" is one classic statement.

14. Gawker 2009.

15. Unfortunately, in the 2008 study, we did not have survey questions that allowed us to probe whether the ordering along the economic status dimension is reflected in public opinion. The prediction, however, is clear. Along this axis, opinion should still be anchored either by blacks and whites on opposite ends of the spectrum, or by blacks and Latinos jointly anchoring the more progressive end of the distribution with whites remaining the most conservative group.

16. The correlations referred to in this paragraph can be found in table 14.

17. Data compiled by the Pew Hispanic Center 2008 from tabulations of the 2006 American Community Survey.

18. U.S. Census Bureau, 2006 American Community Survey.

19. Urbina 2009.

20. Kelly 2009.

21. Statistics from the Sentencing Project 2008: "Felony Disenfranchisement Laws in the United States." Unfortunately, according to the Sentencing Project, statistics for Hispanics are not separately provided by the Bureau of Justice Statistics (the original source for their data). A scholar of Latino politics with whom I have spoken strongly suggested, however, that this is also a large problem for Latino communities.

22. It is likely that Latino communities suffer a double bind—disenfranchisement both from restrictions on ex-felon and non-citizen voting. As explained earlier, statistics are not available from the Bureau of Justice Statistics to calculate ex-felon disenfranchisement, although it is likely to be substantial in states such as Florida and California.

23. Hayduk 2004, 499.

24. U.S. Census Bureau, 2006 American Community Survey.

25. Hayduk 2004, 503.

26. Hajela 2009.

27. Patrick Buchanan, *The Rachel Maddow Show*, July 16, 2009.

28. Cohen 2009 identifies other dimensions of exclusion, affecting members of the LGBT community, for example, including some whites. My discussion here is focused on three highly racialized dimensions of exclusion and is not meant to suggest that exclusion and marginalization does not exist in other significant forms.

CHAPTER 6

1. King 1967, 191; emphasis in the original.
2. Rancière 2006, 69–70.
3. King 1967, 50.
4. New York Times 2009.
5. Greener 2009.
6. Harris-Lacewell 2004.
7. Pough 2004.
8. Retort 2005, 188; emphasis in the original.
9. See chapter 2 for a more extended discussion of this point.
10. Bobo and Kluegel 1993.
11. Kymlicka 1995.
12. Harvey 2005, 66.
13. Thompson 2010, 18.
14. Rogin 1990, 106.
15. Rogin 1990, 105.
16. Rogin 1990, 106.
17. Rogin 1990, 107.
18. King (1968) 1986, 675.
19. King (1968) 1986, 285.
20. Badiou 2000, 91.
21. Badiou 2000; Zerilli 2005.
22. Quoted in Zerilli 2009, 310.

EPILOGUE

1. Zernike 2010.
2. Zernike 2010.
3. Elliot 2010.
4. Jefferson 2010.
5. Sen 2010.
6. Blow 2010a.
7. Egan 2010.

REFERENCES

Allegreto, Sylvia, Ary Amerikaner, and Steven Pitts. 2010. "Data Brief: Black Employment and Unemployment in November 2010." University of California, Berkeley Center for Labor Research and Education. December 6.

Appiah, Kwame Anthony, ed. 2005. *The Ethics of Identity*. Princeton, NJ: Princeton University Press.

Arnesen, Eric. 1994. "'Like Banquo's Ghost, I Will Not Down': The Race Question and the American Railroad Brotherhoods, 1889–1920." *American Historical Review* 99: 1601–33.

Ash, Michael, James K. Boyce, Grace Chang, Manuel Pastor, Justin Scoggins, and Jennifer Tran. 2009. "Justice in the Air: Tracking Toxic Pollution from America's Industries and Companies to Our States, Cities, and Neighborhoods." Amherst, MA: Political Economy Research Institute. April.

Ash, Michael and T. Robert Fetter. 2004. "Who Lives on the Wrong Side of the Environmental Tracks?: Evidence from the EPA's Risk Screening Environmental Indicators Model." *Social Science Quarterly* 85 (2): 441–62.

Associated Press. 2007. "Houston Mayor: Evacuees Increased Murders." *Salon*, January 1.

———. 2008. "Obama Rally in St. Louis Draws 100,000." *Huffington Post*, October 18.

Badiou, Alain. 2000. *Ethics: An Essay on the Understanding of Evil*. Translated by Peter Hallward. New York: Verso, 2000.

Baldwin, James. 1984. *Notes of a Native Son*. Boston: Beacon Press.

Berggren, Ruth E., and Tyler J. Curiel. 2006. "After the Storm—Health Care Infrastructure in Post–Katrina New Orleans." *New England Journal of Medicine* 354 (15): 1549–52.

Bertrand, Marianne, and Sendhil Mullainathan. 2003. "Are Emily and Greg More Employable Than Lakisha and Jamal?: A Field Experiment on Labor Market Discrimination." National Bureau of Economic Research Working Paper Series No. 9873.

Biguenet, John. 2006. "You're Probably Wrong." *Return to New Orleans* blog, *New York Times*.

Blitt, Barry. 2008. "The Politics of Fear." *New Yorker*, July 21.

Blow, Charles M. 2008. *New York Times*, October 17.

———. 2009. "The Enemies Within." *New York Times*, April 17.

———. 2010a. "Let's Rescue the Race Debate." *New York Times*, November 19.

———. 2010b. "A Mighty Pale Tea." *New York Times*. April 16. http://www.nytimes .com/2010/04/17/opinion/17blow.html?th&emc=th.

Bobo, Lawrence, and James R. Kluegel. 1993. "Opposition to Race-Targeting: Self-Interest, Stratification Ideology, or Racial Attitudes?" *American Sociological Review* 58 (4): 443–64.

Bobo, Lawrence D., Camille L. Zubrinsky, James H. Johnson, and Melvin L. Oliver. 1995. "Public Opinion Before and After a Spring Discontent." In *The Los Angeles Riots: Lessons for the Urban Future*, edited by M. Baldasare. Boulder, CO: Westview Press.

Brady, Henry, and Paul Sniderman. 1985. "Attitude Attribution: A Group Basis for Political Reasoning." *American Political Science Review* 79: 1061–78.

Brown, Sasha. 2006. "MIT Assists $1.2 Billion New Orleans Project." *MIT News*, June 14.

Brubaker, Rogers, and Frederick Cooper. 2000. "Beyond 'Identity.'" *Theory and Society* 29: 1–47.

Burdeau, Cain. 2007. "Ninth Ward Fairly Sound, Study Says." *Washington Post*, January 8.

Burmon, Andrew. 2008. "Where the GOP Could Get Dirty." *Salon*, October 22.

Bustillo, Miguel. 2006. "Houston Grumbles as Evacuees Stay Put." *Los Angeles Times*, August 21.

Carr, Sarah. 2009. "Orleans Parish School Board Fighting for Relevance in Charter-Dominated System." *New Orleans Times-Picayune Online*, March 17.

Cass, Julia, and Peter Whoriskey. 2006. "New Orleans to Raze Public Housing." *Washington Post*, December 8.

Cavell, Stanley. 1981. *Pursuits of Happiness: The Hollywood Comedy of Remarriage*. Harvard Film Studies. Cambridge, MA: Harvard University Press.

CBS 2 Chicago. 2008. "Illinois. Man Declares 'No Brozos' with Anti-Obama Sign." October 17.

Centers for Disease Control and Prevention. 2008. "HIV/AIDS among African Americans." CDC HIV/AIDS Fact Sheet. Revised August 2008. http://www.cdc.gov/hiv.

Clark-Flory, Tracy. 2006. "Whitewashing the New Orleans Vote?" *Salon*, April 15.

Cohen, Cathy J. 1999. *The Boundaries of Blackness: AIDS and the Breakdown of Black Politics*. Chicago: University of Chicago Press.

———. 2001. "Social Capital, Intervening Institutions, and Political Power." In *Social Capital and Poor Communities*, edited by S. Saegert, J. P. Thompson and M. R. Warren. New York: Russell Sage Foundation.

Cohen, Cathy J., and Michael C. Dawson. 1993. "Neighborhood Poverty and African American Politics." *American Political Science Review* 87 (2): 286–302.

Cohen, Elizabeth F. 2009. *Semi-Citizenship in Democratic Politics*. New York: Cambridge University Press.

Cohen, Jean L. 1999. "American Civil Society Talk." In *Civil Society, Democracy, and Civic Renewal*, edited by R. K. Fullinwider. Lanham, MD: Rowman & Littlefield.

Connolly, William E. 2008. *Capitalism and Christianity, American Style*. Durham, NC: Duke University Press.

Cooper, Christopher. 2005. "Old-Line Families Escape Worst of Flood and Plot the Future." *Wall Street Journal*, September 8.

Cummings, Scott L. 2007. "Law in the Labor Movement's Challenge to Wal-Mart: A Case Study of the Inglewood Site Fight." California Law Review 95. SSRN: http://ssrn.com/abstract=998056.

Dawson, Michael C. 1994. *Behind the Mule: Race and Class in African-American Politics*. Princeton, NJ: Princeton University Press.

———. 2001. *Black Visions: The Roots of Contemporary African-American Political Ideologies*. Chicago: University of Chicago Press.

———. 2009. "Black and Blue: Black Identity in an Era of Conservative Triumph." In *Measuring Identity: A Guide for Social Sciences*, edited by R. Abdelal, Yoshiko Herrera, Iain Johnston, and Rose McDermott. New York: Cambridge University Press.

———. Forthcoming. *Blacks In and Out of the Left: Past, Present and Future*. Cambridge, MA: Harvard University Press.

Dawson, Michael C., and Ronald Brown. 1993–94. National Black Politics Study.

Dawson, Michael C., Melissa Harris Lacewell, and Cathy J. Cohen. 2006. "2005 Racial Attitudes and the Katrina Disaster Study." Center for the Study of Race, Politics, and Culture, University of Chicago.

Debord, Guy. (1967) 1995. *The Society of the Spectacle*. New York: Zone Books.

D'Souza, Dinesh. 1995. *The End of Racism: Principles for a Multiracial Society*. New York: Free Press.

———. 2009. "Obama and Post-Racist America." *Townhall*, January 28. http://townhall.com/.

Du Bois, W. E. B. (1903) 1996. *The Souls of Black Folks*. Modern Library Edition. New York: Modern Library.

———. (1935) 1979. *Black Reconstruction in America, 1860–1880*. New York: Atheneum.

Dyson, Michael Eric. 2006. *Come Hell or High Water: Hurricane Katrina and the Color of Disaster*. New York: Basic Civitas.

Eaton, Leslie. 2007. "In New Orleans, Plan to Raze Low-Income Housing Draws Protest." *New York Times*, December 14.

Egan, Timothy. 2010. "How Obama Saved Capitalism and Lost the Midterms." *New York Times*, November 2.

Elliot, Justin. 2010. "Tea Party Founder: I Have a Real Problem with Islam." *Salon*, October 27.

Ewers, Justin. 2009. "Obama and Race Relations: Civil Rights Leaders Aren't Satisfied." *U.S. News and World Report*, April 30.

Fausset, Richard. 2009. "New Orleans Rebuilds, but Along the Same Lines?" *Los Angeles Times*, May 31.

Featherstone, Liza. 2005. "Race to the Bottom." *Nation*, March 9. http://www.thenation .com/article/race-bottom.

Ferme, Mariane. 1999. "Stating Politisi: The Dialogues of Publicity and Secrecy in Sierra Leone." In *Civil Society and the Political Imagination in Africa*, edited by J. L. Comaroff and J. Comaroff. Chicago: University of Chicago Press.

Finch, Susan. 2009. "Morial Says Mistrust Remains in N.O.: Ex-Mayor Blames Idea to Shrink City." *New Orleans Times-Picayune*, April 1.

Franks, Peter, Peter Muennig, Erica Lubetkin, and Haomiao Jia. 2006. "The Burden of Disease Associated with Being African-American in the United States and the Contribution of Socio-Economic Status." *Social Science & Medicine* 62 (10): 2469–78.

Fraser, Nancy. 1989. *Unruly Practices: Power, Discourse, and Gender in Contemporary Social Theory*. Minneapolis: University of Minnesota Press.

Friedman, Thomas L. 2007. *The World Is Flat: A Brief History of the Twenty-First Century, Further Updated and Expanded*. New York: Farrar, Straus and Giroux.

Gawker. 2009. "Young Republican Leader Audra Shay Is Crazy, Illiterate, Racist." July 10. http://gawker.com/#!5311792/young-republican-leader-audra-shay-is-crazy-illiterate-racist.

Giroux, Henry A. 2006a. "The Politics of Disposability." *Dissident Voice*, September 1.

———. 2006b. "Reading Hurricane Katrina: Race, Class, and the Biopolitics of Disposability." *College Literature* 33 (3): 171–96.

Goldstein, Patrick. 2006. "Eye of Hurricane Spike." *Los Angeles Times*, August 21.

Gooding-Williams, Robert. 2009. *In the Shadow of Du Bois: Afro-Modern Political Thought in America*. Cambridge, MA: Harvard University Press.

Gramsci, Antonio. 1971. *Selection from the Prison Notebooks of Antonio Gramsci*. Translated by Q. Hoare. New York: International Publishers.

Greener, Bill. 2009. "My GOP: Too Old, Too White to Win." *Salon*, July 20.

Griffith, D. W. 1915. *The Birth of a Nation*. Film, USA: D. W. Griffith.

Grodsky, Eric, and Devah Pager. 2001. "The Structure of Disadvantage: Individual and Occupational Determinants of the Black-White Wage Gap." *American Sociological Review* 66 (4): 542–67.

Habermas, Jürgen. (1983) 1990. *Moral Consciousness and Communicative Action, Studies in Contemporary German Social Thought*. Cambridge, MA: MIT Press.

———. (1992) 1996. *Between Facts and Norms: Contributions to a Discourse Theory of Law and Democracy*. Translated by W. Rehg. Cambridge, MA: MIT Press.

Hajela, Deepti. 2009. "Report: NY, NJ Immigration Raids Violated Rights." Associated Press, July 21.

Hamilton, Charles. 1979. "The Patron-Recipient Relationship and Minority Politics in New York City." *Political Science Quarterly* 94 (2): 211–27.

Harris-Lacewell, Melissa. 2004. *Barbershops, Bibles and Bet: Everyday Talk and Black Political Thought*. Princeton, NJ: Princeton University Press.

Harvey, David. 2005. *A Brief History of Neoliberalism*. New York: Oxford University Press.

———. 2009. *Cosmopolitanism and the Geographies of Freedom, Wellek Library Lectures in Critical Theory*. New York: Columbia University Press.

Hayduk, Ronald. 2004. "Democracy for All: Restoring Immigrant Voting Rights in the US." *New Political Science* 26 (4): 499–523.

Herrnstein, Richard J., and Charles Murray. 1996. *The Bell Curve: Intelligence and Class Structure in American Life*. New York: Simon and Schuster.

Hill, Lance. 2006. "The New Orleans Convention Center Disaster: Incompetence or Racism." *Commentaries by Lance Hill* blog. Southern Institute for Education and Research.

Holden, Stephen. 2006. "'When the Levees Broke': Spike Lee's Tales from a Broken City." *New York Times*, August 21.

Huntington, Samuel P. 2004. *Who Are We?: Challenges to American National Identity*. New York: Simon and Schuster.

Jefferson, Cord. 2010. "They're Both Black, Republican and Tea Party Approved." *The Root*. November 11. http://www.theroot.com/views/scott-and-west-2-very-different-trailblazers.

Jefferson, Thomas (1785) 1999. *Notes on the State of Virginia*. Edited by Frank Shuffelton. New York: Penguin.

Katznelson, Ira. 1981. *City Trenches: Urban Politics and the Patterning of Class in the United States*. 1st ed. New York: Pantheon.

Kelley, Robin D. G. 1994. *Race Rebels: Culture, Politics, and the Black Working Class*. New York: Free Press.

———. 2002. *Freedom Dreams: The Black Radical Imagination*. Boston: Beacon Press.

Kelly, David. 2009. "FBI Investigating Fatal Blast at a San Bernardino County Home as a Hate Crime." *Los Angeles Times*, July 10.

Kim, Claire. 2000. *Bitter Fruit: The Politics of Black-Korean Conflict in New York City*. New Haven, CT: Yale University Press.

King, Martin Luther, Jr. 1967. *Where Do We Go from Here: Chaos or Community?* 1st ed. New York: Harper & Row.

———. (1967) 1986. "I See the Promise Land." In *A Testament of Hope: The Essential Writings of Martin Luther King, Jr.* Edited by James M. Washington. San Francisco: Harper & Row.

———. (1968) 1986. "Conversation with Martin Luther King." In *A Testament of Hope: The Essential Writings of Martin Luther King, Jr.* Edited by James M. Washington. San Francisco: Harper & Row.

Klein, Naomi. 2007. *The Shock Doctrine: The Rise of Disaster Capitalism*. New York: Henry Holt.

Konigsmark, Anne Rochell. 2006. "AFL-CIO Plans New Orleans Boom." *USA Today*, June 13.

Kusmer, Ken. 2006. "Nagin Blames Delays on Racism, Red Tape." Associated Press, August 18.

Kymlicka, Will. 1995. *Multicultural Citizenship: A Liberal Theory of Minority Rights*. Oxford Political Theory. New York: Clarendon Press.

Lee, Spike. 2006. *When the Levees Broke: A Requiem in Four Acts*. Film, USA: HBO.

Lil Wayne. 2006. *Dedication 2: Gangsta Grillz*. Audio CD.

Liptak, Adam. 2008. "1 in 100 U.S. Adults Behind Bars, New Study Says." *New York Times*. February 28. http://www.nytimes.com/2008/02/28/us/28cnd-prison.html.

Logan, John R. 2006. "The Impact of Katrina: Race and Class in Storm-Damaged Neighborhoods." In *Katrina and the Built Environment: Spatial and Social Impacts*. Brown University.

Louisiana Recovery Authority Support Foundation (LRASF). 2006. "2006 Recovery Survey: Citizen and Civic Leader Findings." http://katrinaresearchhub.ssrc.org/2006-south-louisiana-recovery-survey-citizen-and-civic-leader-research-summary-of-findings/resource__view.

Mays, Vickie M., Susan D. Cochran, and Namdi W. Barnes. 2007. "Race, Race-Based Discrimination, and Health Outcomes among African Americans." *Annual Review of Psychology* 58 (1): 201–25.

Media Matters. 2005. "Glenn Beck Called Hurricane Survivors in New Orleans 'Scumbags,' Said He 'Hates' 9-11 Families." September 9. http://mediamatters.org/mmtv/200509090003.

Mills, Charles W. 1997. *The Racial Contract*. Ithaca, NY: Cornell University Press.

Molnar, Beth E. 2004. "Strengthening Our Future: Developing Healthy Children and Youth, Strong Families, and Safe Communities." Presentation at the 2004 National Conference of the National Center for Mental Health Promotion and Youth Violence Prevention.

Murray, Charles. 2005. "The Hallmark of the Underclass." *Wall Street Journal*, October 2.

National Advisory Commission on Civil Disorders [Kerner Commission]. 1968. "Report of the National Advisory Commission on Civil Disorders [Kerner Report]." Washington, DC.

New York Times. 2009. "2008 Surge in Black Voters Nearly Erased Racial Gap." New York Times Online, July 21.

Nossiter, Adam. 2006. "Outlines Emerge for a Shaken New Orleans." *New York Times*, August 27.

Oliver, Melvin L., Jr., James H. Johnson, and Walter C. Farrell Jr. 1993. "Anatomy of a

Rebellion: Apolitical-Economic Analysis." In *Reading Rodney King: Reading Urban Uprising*, edited by R. Gooding-Williams. New York: Routledge.

Oxfam America. 2006. *Forgotten Communities, Unmet Promises: An Unfolding Tragedy on the Gulf Coast*. Research report, August 21. http://www.oxfamamerica.org/publications/forgotten-communities-unmet-promises/.

Oxfam America. 2008. *Mirror on America: How the State of Gulf Coast Recovery Reflects on Us All*. Research report, August 22. http://www.oxfamamerica.org/publications/mirror-on-america.

———. 2009. *Building Common Ground: How Shared Attitudes and Concerns Can Create Alliances between African-Americans and Latinos in post-Katrina New Orleans*. Research report, June 16. http://www.oxfamamerica.org/publications/building-common-ground.

Pager, Devah. 2007. *Marked: Race, Crime, and Finding Work in an Era of Mass Incarceration*. Chicago: University of Chicago Press.

Parks, James. 2008. "Three Years after Hurricane Katrina, New Orleans Still Reeling." *AFL-CIO Now* blog, August, 28. http://blog.afl-co.org.

Parks, Virginia, and Dorian Warren. 2009. "Investment or Invasion?: Community Responses to Big-Box Commercial Development in Chicago." Paper prepared for the Social Services Centennial: The City Revisited: Community and Community Action in the 21st Century, University of Chicago, May 8, 2009.

Perry, Jeffrey Babcock. 2009. *Hubert Harrison: The Voice of Harlem Radicalism, 1883–1918*. New York: Columbia University Press.

Peterson, Paul E. 1981. *City Limits*. Chicago: University of Chicago Press.

Pew Hispanic Center. 2008. "Statistical Portrait of Hispanics in the United States, 2006." January 23. http://pewhispanic.org/factsheets/factsheet.php?FactsheetID=35.

Polanyi, Karl. 1944. *The Great Transformation*. New York: Farrar & Rinehart.

Pough, Gwendolyn D. 2004. *Check It While I Wreck It: Black Womanhood, Hip-Hop Culture, and the Public Sphere*. Boston: Northeastern University Press.

Public Enemy. 2006. *Rebirth of a Nation*. Audio CD.

Quigley, Bill. 2008. "Half New Orleans Poor Permanently Displaced: Failure or Success?" *Facing South*, March 3. Institute of Southern Studies, www.southernstudies.org.

Rancière, Jacques. 2006. *Hatred of Democracy*. Translated by Steve Corcoran. London: Verso.

Raphael, Steven, and Lucas Ronconi. 2007. "The Effects of Labor Market Competition with Immigrants on the Wages and Employment of Natives: What Does Existing Research Tell Us?" *Du Bois Review* 4: 413–32.

Ratner, Lizzy. 2008. "New Orleans Redraws Its Color Line." *Nation*, August 27. http://www.thenation.com/article/new-orleans-redraws-its-color-line.

Reece, Jason. 2008. "Racial Equity Status Report." Kirwan Institute for the Study of Race and Ethnicity, the Ohio State University. http://4909e99d35cada63e7f757471b7243

be73e53e14.gripelements.com/publications/Final__Draft__Kirwan__Racial__
Equity__Status__Report__September__2008.pdf.

Reed, Adolph, Jr. 2005. "Class-ifying the Hurricane." *Nation*, October 3.

Retort. 2005. *Afflicted Powers: Capital and Spectacle in a New Age of War*. London: Verso.

Roberts, Deon. 2009. "Talking Black." *City Business*, June 8.

Roberts, Sam. 2009. "Surge in Black Voters Nearly Erased Racial Gap." *New York Times*, July 21.

Rogin, Michael Paul. 1987. *Ronald Reagan, the Movie: And Other Episodes in Political Demonology*. Berkeley: University of California Press.

———. 1990. "'Make My Day!': Spectacle as Amnesia in Imperial Politics." *Representations* 29: 99–123.

Rorty, Richard. 1998. *Achieving Our Country: Leftist Thought in Twentieth-Century America*. The William E. Massey Sr. Lectures in the History of American Civilization, 1997. Cambridge, MA: Harvard University Press.

Sen, Riku. 2010. "The Most Racist Campaign in Decades, and What It Demands of Us." *ColorLines*, October 28. http://colorlines.com/archives/2010/10/the__most__racist__campaign__in__decades__and__what__it__demands__of__us.html.

Sentencing Project. 2008. "Felony Disenfranchisement Laws in the United States." http://www.sentencingproject.org.

Sewell, William H., Jr. 1996. "Historical Events as Transformations of Structures: Inventing Revolution at the Bastille." *Theory and Society* 25 (6): 841–81.

Sharkey, Pat. 2006. "Were Whites Really More Likely than Blacks to Die in Katrina?: A Re-Analysis of Data on Race and the Casualties of Katrina." Cambridge, MA: New Vision.

Shklar, Judith N. 1991. *American Citizenship: The Quest for Inclusion*. Tanner Lectures on Human Values. Cambridge, MA: Harvard University Press.

Simmons, Ann M. 2006. "Racial Current Runs through This Campaign." *Los Angeles Times*, April 17.

Simon, Scott. 1998. Radio interview with Taylor Branch. National Public Radio transcript, *Saturday Weekend Edition*, April 4.

Sites, W. 2007. "Beyond Trenches and Grassroots?: Reflections on Urban Mobilization, Fragmentation, and the Anti-Wal-Mart Campaign in Chicago." *Environment and Planning A* 39 (11): 2632–51.

Smedley, Brian D., Adrienne Y. Stith, and Alan R. Nelson, eds. Committee on Understanding and Eliminating Racial and Ethnic Disparities in Health Care, Board on Health Sciences Policy, Institute of Medicine. 2003. *Unequal Treatment: Confronting Racial and Ethnic Disparities in Health Care*. Washington, DC: National Academies Press.

Spence, Lester. 2009. "The Neoliberal Turn in Black Politics." Paper presented at the annual meeting of the Western Political Science Association, Vancouver, British Columbia, March 18–21.

Taranto, James. 2006. "Nothing to Fear but Victory Itself." *Wall Street Journal*, January 6.

Thompson, J. Phillip. 2008. "Race in New Orleans since Katrina." Unpublished ms., Massachusetts Institute of Technology, August 27.

———. 2010. "The Meaning of the Mid-Term Election." Unpublished ms., Massachusetts Institute of Technology, November 11.

Tisserand, Michael. 2006. "The Katrina Factor." *Nation*, January 1.

Urbina, Ian. 2009. "After Pennsylvania Trial, Tensions Simmer over Race." *New York Times* Online, May 17.

U.S. Census Bureau. American Community Surveys. http://www.census.gov/acs/www/.

U.S. Department of Labor, Bureau of Labor Statistics. 2009. "Economic News Release: Employment Situation Summary, March 2009." http://www.bls.gov/data/.

Venkatesh, Sudhir Alladi. 2006. *Off the Books: The Underground Economy of the Urban Poor.* Cambridge, MA: Harvard University Press.

Virno, Paolo. 2005. *A Grammar of the Multitude: For an Analysis of Contemporary Forms of Life.* Translated by I. Bertoletti, James Cascaito, and Andrea Casson. *Semiotext[e]* Foreign Agents series. Los Angeles: Semiotext[e].

Wacquant, Loïc J. D. 2008. *Urban Outcasts: A Comparative Sociology of Advanced Marginality.* Cambridge, MA: Polity.

Wall, Amanda J. 2009. "The 2008 Democratic Primary in the 26th State Representative District of Illinois: A Case Study on Race and Candidate Self-Presentation." BA thesis, University of Chicago.

Wallace, Deborah, and Rodrick Wallace. 1997. *A Plague on Your Houses: How New York Was Burned Down and National Public Health Crumbled.* London: Verso.

Walsh, Joan. 2009. "That's Mighty White of You, Liz Cheney!" *Salon*, July 23.

Warner, Michael. 2002. *Publics and Counterpublics.* New York: Zone Books.

Warren, Jenifer. 2008. "One in 100: Behind Bars in America." Pew Center on the States. http://www.pewcenteronthestates.org/uploadedFiles/One%20in%20100.pdf.

Washington Times. 2009. "Yes, Ty'Sheoma, There Is a Santa Claus." *Washington Times*, February 26.

Wedeen, Lisa. 1999. *Ambiguities of Domination: Politics, Rhetoric, and Symbols in Contemporary Syria.* Chicago: University of Chicago Press.

———. 2008. *Peripheral Visions: Publics, Power, and Performance in Yemen.* Chicago: University of Chicago Press.

West, Cornel. 1993. *Race Matters.* Boston: Beacon Press.

Western, Bruce. 2006. *Punishment and Inequality in America.* New York: Russell Sage.

Western, Bruce, and Becky Pettit. "2005. Black—White Wage Inequality, Employment Rates, and Incarceration." *American Journal of Sociology* 111 (2): 553–78.

White, Jaquetta. 2006. "AFL-CIO to Invest $700 Million to Revive Region." *New Orleans Times-Picayune*, June 14.

Wilentz, Sean. 2008. "Race Man." *New Republic*, February 27.

Wilson, Rick K., and Robert M. Stein. 2006. "Katrina Evacuees in Houston: One-Year Out." Report supported by *SGER: Cooperation among Evacuees in the Aftermath of Hurricane Katrina*, edited by the National Science Foundation.

Wilson, William J., and Richard P. Taub. 2006. *There Goes the Neighborhood: Racial, Ethnic, and Class Tensions in Four Chicago Neighborhoods and Their Meaning for America*. New York: Knopf.

Winant, Gabriel. 2009. "The Young Republicans Elect a Real Joker." *Salon*, July 13.

World Saxophone Quartet. 2006. *Political Blues*. Audio CD.

Zerilli, Linda M. G. 2005. *Feminism and the Abyss of Freedom*. Chicago: University of Chicago Press.

———. 2009. "Toward a Feminist Theory of Judgment." *Signs: Journal of Women in Culture and Society* 34 (2): 295–317.

Zernike, Kate. 2010. "N.A.A.C.P. Report Raises Concerns about Racism within Tea Party Groups." *New York Times*, October 20.

Zernike, Kate, and Megan Thee-Brenan. 2010. "Poll Finds Tea Party Backers Wealthier and More Educated." *New York Times*, April 14. http://www.nytimes.com/2010/04/15/us/politics/15poll.html?th&emc=th. Last visited 4/16/2010.

INDEX

ACORN (Association of Community Organizations for Reform Now), 42
AFL-CIO (American Federation of Labor and Congress of Industrial Organizations), 43, 109–10
American Federation of Labor and Congress of Industrial Organizations (AFL-CIO), 43, 109–10
amnesia, 176; concept of, 6; effect on black public opinion, 101; neoliberalism's effect on, 101
Arendt, Hannah, 162
Arnesen, Eric, 143
Association of Community Organizations for Reform Now (ACORN), 42

Badiou, Alain, 179
Baker, Richard, 92, 107
Baldwin, James, 65–66
Barbour, Haley, 110
Beck, Glenn, 46, 80, 85, 177
Bethea, Ty'Sheoma, 85
Biguenet, John, 30, 45
Bin Laden, Osama, 78
Birth of a Nation, 53
Black Panthers, 80, 160, 167
black political economy: class division within, 124–25; Hurricane Katrina's effect on, 3, 21, 24–25, 28–52, 55–57, 59, 105–14, 133, 153, 165; neoliberalism's effect on, 92–93,

98–101, 106, 125–26, 129–35, 162, 179–80; relative to whites, 92, 116–25, 143, 145; social and political disadvantage of, 9–10, 17–19
black politics: Black Panthers, 80, 160, 167; black power, xi–xii, 15, 51, 62, 76, 128, 139, 145, 179; civil rights movement, 15, 47, 51, 61–62, 112, 128, 139; civil society/counter-public/public sphere, viii–xi, 1, 21, 36, 39, 41, 44, 47–51, 59–62, 162, 166–75, 194; class divide in, x, xv, 13, 20, 93–94, 97; definition of, ix; deinstitutionalization of, 7–9, 42–44; demobilization of, 8, 42–43, 60–61, 95; failures of, ix–x, 3, 7–8, 13–14, 21–22, 42–44, 51, 59–60, 90, 101, 104, 162, 167; and Hurricane Katrina, 3, 8–9, 19–20, 24, 36, 39, 40–45, 48, 50–52, 55–58, 61, 104, 135, 162 ; intersection of race and class in, 2, 94–97, 100; liberalism in, 67–68; nationalism in, 67–70, 76; neoliberalism's effect on, 93, 94–95, 101, 104, 115, 129–31, 135, 156, 162; 9/11's effect on, 19; and Obama election, 12, 19–20, 91, 164–65, 171–72; progressive features of, x; white America's demonization/exclusion of, 4–5, 7, 9, 21, 26, 32, 40, 44–48, 51–53, 55–56, 58, 60, 62, 71, 74–75, 79, 90, 106, 113, 131, 134–35, 155, 157
black public opinion, x, xiv, 4, 5, 7, 11–12, 19, 22–24, 65; amnesia's effect on, 101; divide

black public opinion (*continued*)
from white/others' public opinion, xv, 2, 7, 12–13, 22–24, 27, 63–66, 86–90, 148–52; in fall 2005, 3–5, 7, 65; and Latino public opinion 113–14; media shaping of, 90; optimism of, 1, 10, 10–14, 63, 66–67, 86, 90, 92, 146, 148–49, 162; pessimism of, viii, 1, 7, 10–14, 24, 66, 86, 90, 92, 148–49, 161, 175

black public sphere, viii, xi, 1, 21, 36; as counterpublic, x, xi, 21, 39, 41, 44, 47–51, 59–62, 166–75

Blacksher, Lucia, 105

Blow, Charles M., 77, 82

Bobo, Lawrence, 11, 70, 173, 191

Boggs, Grace Lee, 160

Boggs, James, 160

Booker, Cory, 14, 40

Brazile, Donna, 72

Brown, Ronald, 11

Brubaker, Rogers, 54

Buchanan, Patrick, xii, 158–59, 178

Burns, William, 94–96

Bush, George H. W.: administration of, 53

Bush, George W.: administration of, 2, 4, 9, 11, 12, 14, 19, 25, 31–32, 49, 65, 68, 73, 83, 110–12, 181–82

Cabral, Amilcar, xii, 161

Carr, Sarah, 108

Castoriadis, Cornelius, 180

Chadha, Paul, 97

Cheney, Liz, 155, 158

civil rights movement, 15, 61–62, 112, 128, 139

civil society/black civil society, x, 162; deinstitutionalization of, 7–9, 42–44

Civil War and Reconstruction, 25, 51, 54, 81, 103, 127, 166

Clinton, Bill, 11, 19, 65, 72, 84

Clinton, Hillary, 64, 68–69, 71–73

Clyburn, James, 72

Cohen, Cathy J., 5, 22, 48

Cohen, Elizabeth F., 159, 200

Cohen, Jean, 26, 50, 61, 194

Cone, James, 66

Conner, Bull, 177

Connolly, William, 126, 129, 198–99

Cooper, Frederick, 54

Daley, Richard M., 102–3

Davis, Angela, 167

Dawson, Michael C., x, xiii, 11, 22, 116, 131, 194–96, 198–99

Debord, Guy, xiv

DeMint, Jim, 79

Democratic Leadership Council (DLC), 15

Deneen, Bob, 97

Denton, Nancy, 116

de Tocqueville, Alexis, 55

Dixon, Thomas, 53

DLC (Democratic Leadership Council), 15

Dobbs, Lou, 158

Douglass, Frederick, 62, 67

D'Souza, Dinesh, 86–87, 89

Du Bois, W. E. B., 67, 71, 104, 115, 142, 145, 167, 183

Duke, David, 31, 106

Dyson, Michael Eric, 31, 193

Edsall, Mary, 54

Edsall, Tom, 54

Edwards, John, 68

Ellison, Keith, 182

Farrakhan, Louis, 67, 76

Ferme, Mariane, 52, 55

Ford, Harold, Jr., 14, 40

Fraser, Nancy, 50

Friedman, Thomas, 132

Furumoto-Dawson, Alice, 200

Garvey, Marcus, 76, 167

Giroux, Henry, 21, 32

Gitlin, Todd, 54

Goldstein, Patrick, 194

Gompers, Sam, 138

Gooding-Williams, Robert, 198

Gore, Al, 73, 171

Gramsci, Antonio, 199
Grant, Oscar, 9, 185
Grodsky, Eric, 121–22

Habermas, Jürgen, 5, 51, 54, 61, 193
Haley, Nikki, 182
Halliburton, xii
Hamilton, Charles, 199
Harris-Lacewell, Melissa, 22, 45, 168
Harrison, Hubert, 138
Harvey, David, 126, 128–30, 197
Hayduk, Ronald, 156–57
Herrnstein, Richard, 134
Hill, Lance, 30
Holden, Stephen, 194
Holder, Eric, 74
Horton, Willie, 53
Howell, Susan, 42
Huckabee, Mike, 79
Huntington, Samuel, vii, 144, 158, 178
Hurricane Katrina, ix, x, 4, 14, 71, 74; and
    American race relations, xv, 89, 114, 169;
    as anti-spectacle, xiv, 177; black public
    opinion on, 1, 2, 3, 7, 11, 12, 24, 90; divide
    in white/black public opinion on 2, 12, 22–
    24, 26–27, 45–47, 49–50, 53–54, 58–59,
    65, 86, 114, 170, 181; effect on American
    civil society, 27; effect on black politics, 3,
    8–9, 19–20, 24, 36, 39–45, 48, 50–52,
    55–58, 61, 104, 135, 162; government
    response to, 24, 37–45, 47, 51, 53, 107–13,
    115, 135, 153; media coverage of, 114; neo-
    liberal response to, 39–41, 62, 93, 105–13,
    115, 127–28, 153; resonance in black art,
    25; socioeconomic effects on New Orleans'
    black population, 3, 21, 24–52, 55–57, 59,
    105–14, 133, 153, 165

Ice Cube, 25
immigration, effect on American racial order,
    xv, 3, 41

Jackson, Jesse, 16, 68, 72, 94, 95–96, 104, 197
Jackson, Jesse, Jr., 96

Jackson, Phillip, 96–97
James, C. L. R., 161
Jefferson, Thomas, 52–53
Jeffries, Elga, 97
Jim Crow, 7, 47–48, 54, 106, 115, 128, 152
Jindal, Bobby, 147
Johnson, Bob, 69
Johnson, Kenny, Jr., 94–96

Kabacoff, Pres, 44
Katznelson, Ira, 129, 145
Keating, Frank, 79
Kelley, Robin D. G., 195, 199
Kennedy, Ted, 70
Kerner Commission (National Advisory Com-
    mission on Civil Disorders), xi, 27
Kerrey, Bob, 72
Keynesian economics, 127
Kim, Claire, 141–42, 144
King, Martin Luther, Jr., viii, xi, xv, 4, 55,
    66–67, 71, 104, 145, 160–61, 162–64, 167,
    175–76, 178–79; pragmatic utopianism of,
    xii–xiii, xvi, 146
King, Rodney, 11
KKK (Ku Klux Klan), 47, 106
Klein, Naomi, 110
Kluegel, James, 173
Knotts, Jake, 182
Ku Klux Klan (KKK), 47, 106
Kymlicka, William, 174

Lee, Spike, 25, 32, 45
Lieberman, Joseph, 15; lifeworld/worldview
    concept, 5; mainstream American white,
    6, 21
Lil Wayne, 25, 37
Limbaugh, Rush, 81
Logan, John, 33, 42
Lopez, Fred, 29
Ludacris, 78

Malcolm X, viii, xv–xvi, 55, 70, 77, 83, 104,
    118, 145, 159, 160–61, 167, 179
Marx, Karl, 200

Massey, Douglas, 116
McCain, John, 73, 77–79
McClurkin, Donnie, 69
McRoberts, Omar, 116
Mills, Charles W., 195
Mohd, Ali Abdelhadi, 154
Mondale, Walter, 69
Moore, Queen Mother, 175
Morial, Marc, 109
MoveOn, 58–59
Murray, Charles, 46, 134–35

NAACP (National Association for the Advancement of Colored People), 42, 62, 99, 104, 167, 181
Nagin, Ray, 38, 40–43, 110
National Advisory Commission on Civil Disorders (Kerner Commission), xi, 27
National Association for the Advancement of Colored People (NAACP), 42, 62, 99, 104, 167, 181
Nation of Islam, 79, 167
neoliberalism, x, xiv, 2, 162, 164, 184; black politics' complicity in, 7–8, 41, 55, 60–61, 95, 146, 161; definition of, 126–28; effect on black politics, 93, 104, 115, 129–31, 156, 162; the left's complicity in, 6–7; as race-inflected, 92–93, 98–101, 106, 126, 129–35, 162, 179–80; response to Katrina, 39–41, 62, 93, 105–13, 115, 127–28, 153; of the Tea Party, 85, 139, 181–84; Walmart/big boxes, 98–105, 128, 197
Nixon, Richard: administration of, 11
Nkrumah, Kwame, 161

Obama, Barack, 9, 19, 23, 136; association with white politics/center-left politics/ "new black realism," 14–15, 40–41, 68, 70, 73–74, 76, 90, 93–94, 96, 101, 147, 184–85; black political criticisms of, 12; effect on black optimism, 1, 10–14, 63, 90, 92, 146, 162; effect on black politics, 19–20, 91, 164–65, 171–72; effect on white/black divide in public opinion, 12–13, 64–65,

86–88; effect on white/black racial divide, 15, 64–66; election as spectacle, ix–x, 91, 176–77; and post-racial America, ix, xv, 16, 63–67, 86–91; racist/distorted attacks against, xii, 12, 64, 69, 71–74, 77–85, 89, 147, 158, 169, 175, 177–78, 181–82; racial politics of, 74–76
Obama, Michelle, 80, 176

Padmore, George, 161
Pager, Devah, 116, 119–22, 131
Palin, Sarah, 77–78, 158
Paris (rap performer), 25
Parker, Chris, 195
Parks, Rosa, 61
Parks, Virginia, 99, 100, 102–3
Pastorek, Paul, 108
Perry, Jeffrey B., 199
Perry, Robert J., 185
Peterson, Paul, 133–34
Phillips, Judson, 182
Polanyi, Karl, 125
post-racial America, as spectacle, ix–x, xiv, 86–91, 181
Pough, Gwendolyn, 169
Powell, Colin, 16, 77
powell, john a., 74
Public Enemy, 25, 28
public sphere, xv, 6–7, 26–27, 41

racial/ethnic alliance building, 113–14, 130, 132, 135, 137–41, 151–54, 156–59; challenges in, 136–38, 140, 151–53, 159
racial order, x–xi, 1, 5–6, 21, 28, 41, 45–46, 48–49, 56, 58, 79, 100–102, 109–12, 115–16, 125, 139, 141–49, 152, 169, 185; immigration's effect on, xv, 3, 41
racism, in America: anti-black pogroms, 7; black incarceration, 8–9, 16–18, 120–21, 123, 136, 155–56; Erie, Pennsylvania, 9; hate crimes, 154–55; Jefferson Parish, 106; Jena Six, 8, 154, 164–65, 170–71; lynching, 71; minority voter suppression, 4–5, 79, 79, 155, 157; Obama election, xii,

12, 64, 69, 71–74, 77–85, 89, 147, 158,
169, 175, 177–78, 181–82; Philadelphia,
Pennsylvania, 9; Oscar Grant, 9; Southern
University, 43; stereotyping, x, 32, 53–54,
138–39, 145, 165–66; Tea Party, 85, 139,
181–84; Tenaha, Texas, 9
Rainbow Coalition, 16
Ramirez, Louis, 154
Rancière, Jacques, 161–62
Randolph, A. Philip, 101, 167
Ratner, Lizzy, 106
Rawls, John, 54
Reagan, Ronald: administration of, 3, 65, 68,
82–83, 127, 177
Reed, Adolph, 56–57
Reiss, James, 38
Reneau, Don, 191, 194–95
Retort collective, 171, 192
Rice, Condoleezza, 16
Richardson, Bill, 30
Rogin, Michael, xiv, 6, 26, 53, 55, 176–77
Roosevelt, Franklin D., 83, 85
Rorty, Richard, 6, 54
Rove, Karl, 77

Sawyer, Mark, 195
Scott, Gladys, 185
Scott, Jamie, 185
Senghor, Léopold, 161
Sessions, Pete, 81
Sewell, William H., Jr., 61–62
Sharkey, Pat, 195
Shay, Audra, 147, 155
Shelby, Richard, 83
Shelby, Tommie, 69–70
Shklar, Judith, 59, 142–43
Simpson, O.J., 169
Sites, William, 98, 103, 129
Small, Mario, 116
Smiley, Tavis, 169
spectacle: concept of, xiv, 176–77, 191; of
Obama election ix–x, 91, 176–77; of post-
racial America, ix–x, xiv, 86–91, 181
Spence, Lester, 199

Steele, Michael, 14
Stein, Robert M., 193

Taranto, James, 46, 60, 195
Tea Party, 85, 139, 181–84
Thatcher, Margaret, 83
Thomas, Clarence, 16, 69
Thompson, J. Phillip, 43, 109, 175
Tisserand, Michael, 21
Todd, Ashley, 79

Venkatesh, Sudhir, 42

Wacquant, Loïc, 116, 126, 130–31
Wall, Amanda, 96
Wallace, Chris, 158
Walzer, Michael, 173
Warner, Michael, 50
Warren, Dorian, 99–103
Washington, Harold, 95
Wedeen, Lisa, xiv, 126–28
Wells, Ida B., 67, 167
West, Allen, 182
West, Cornel, viii, 115, 161, 173
West, Kanye, 25–27, 49, 181
Western, Bruce, 120, 131
White, Bill, 45
White, Theodore, 54
Wilentz, Sean, 71–72, 74
Wilson, William J., 116, 173, 193
Wilson, Woodrow, 52–53
Winfrey, Oprah, 169
World Saxophone Quartet, 21, 25, 28
Wright, Jeremiah, 64, 66–67, 71, 75–76, 79,
90, 177
Wright, Richard, 65–66

Young, Andrew, 69, 72, 104
Young, Cathy, 45, 60
Young, Iris Marion, 48

Zedong, Mao, 161–62
Zerilli, Linda, 55, 194, 198